WILDERNESS FOR SALE

BOOKS BY WALTER HAVIGHURST

FICTION

PIER 17

THE QUIET SHORE

THE WINDS OF SPRING

NO HOMEWARD COURSE

SIGNATURE OF TIME

GENERAL

WILDERNESS FOR SALE
The Story of the First Western Land Rush

UPPER MISSISSIPPI
(Rivers of America Series)

THE LONG SHIPS PASSING

LAND OF PROMISE

GEORGE ROGERS CLARK

ANNIE OAKLEY OF THE WILD WEST

AMERICAN PROCESSION SERIES

HENRY G. ALSBERG
GENERAL EDITOR

Wilderness for Sale

THE STORY OF THE FIRST WESTERN LAND RUSH

BY

WALTER HAVIGHURST

HASTINGS HOUSE, PUBLISHERS, NEW YORK

Published simultaneously in Canada
by S. J. Reginald Saunders, Publishers,
Toronto 1

Library of Congress Catalog Card Number: 56–8123

Printed in the United States of America

ACKNOWLEDGMENTS

In attempting to picture the first huge western frontier in America, and the process of its acquisition from the Indians, its survey, sale, settlement, and the beginnings of its culture and economy, I have put myself in debt to many previous writers, some of whose works are listed in my bibliography.

For help in acquiring information and materials I am grateful to Mr. E. W. King and Mr. L. S. Dutton of the Miami University Library, Mr. James H. Rodabaugh of the Ohio Historical Society, Mr. Virginius Hall of the Historical and Philosophical Society of Ohio, Mr. George J. Blazier of the Marietta College Library, Mrs. Helen Jo Scott Mann of the Miami University Alumni Office, Miss Caroline Dunn of the Indiana Historical Society, and Mrs. Elleine H. Stones of the Burton Historical Collection of the Detroit Public Library.

To Mr. Henry G. Alsberg, editor of the American Procession Series, I am indebted for many suggestions about the scope and organization of this book.

WALTER HAVIGHURST

Shadowy Hills
Oxford, Ohio
January, 1956

CONTENTS

ix

CONTENTS

ILLUSTRATIONS

Fort Greene Ville, a conjectural drawing.
> Courtesy of Ohio Historical Society.

Gallipolis, as the French settlers found it in 1790.
> From Henry Howe's *Historical Collections of Ohio.*

Frontier Farm.

Anti-emigration cartoon.
> From Wilkey's *Western Emigration.*

Martin Chuzzlewit inspects drawing of the thriving City of Eden as it appeared on paper. Illustration by Phiz (Hablot K. Browne) in early edition of Charles Dickens' *Martin Chuzzlewit.*
> Courtesy New York Public Library.

The thriving City of Eden as it appeared in fact.
> Idem.

Railroad Lands in Illinois.
> *Illinois Central Railroad.*

Prairie scene, Indiana. Engraved especially for *Ladies Repository* (Sept., 1850, by E. Teel from painting by George Winter.)
> Courtesy Indiana Historical Society.

Detroit in 1820. Lithograph by Calvert Litho. Co. of Detroit, from painting by George Washington Whistler.
> Courtesy Burton Historical Collection, Detroit Public Library.

Hazen Grove, Fulton County, Illinois. Owned, settled and improved from wild prairie land.

xi

PART I

TWILIGHT OF THE TRIBES

CHAPTER ONE

THE TREATY MAKERS

I N ALL the wild Ohio country, stretching from Fort Pitt to the Illinois prairies and from the curving O-hy-o to the English Seas (today we call them the Great Lakes), there were not enough people to fill up the present town of Sandusky: some twenty thousand Indians of a dozen tribes, half as many whites—soldiers, hunters, squatters, settlers, not many of them yet with families at their sides. If the fifty million acres of the Ohio country had been divided among them equally, each person, red and white, old and young, male and female, would have had seventeen hundred acres. Some wanted more than that; most of them got considerably less. In the end the Indians, whose country it had been for time uncounted, had none at all. Their Good Ohio Land—*Wesheasiski* in the musical Shawnee tongue—soon was plotted into ranges, townships, and sections in the American land offices.

In the peaceful summer of 1795, after four long years of forest warfare, the most populous place in the western country was a log fort, far out in wilderness. Three roads led into Fort Greene Ville, from the south, the north, and the northeast—the wagon traces that General Wayne had slashed from the Ohio River to the mouth of the Maumee. Look closely and see the older paths of that country, the narrow track of deer and panther, the shadowed trails of the hunting tribes. Over the raw new roads had come the soldiers, some two thousand lean and weathered men, the Legion of the United States. By forest paths, afoot and on horseback, came the chiefs and warriors of twelve tribes. A council fire was smoldering in the big log house at Fort Greene Ville and the great congress was assembling. A year before, Mad Anthony Wayne, *Kitcho Shemagana,* the Big Wind from the East, had crushed the tribes at Fallen Timbers; he had burned their towns and plundered their cornfields on the rivers of St. Joseph and St. Mary. Now the chiefs were gathering in the Big Wind's stronghold beside curving Greenville Creek. With Wayne and his captains they would smoke the ceremonial pipe and bid for peace.

Greenville would be a busy county seat in years to come, with a shopping street called Broadway and a stone statue of Justice crowning the stone courthouse. But in 1795 it was only a log stockade, closed with heavy gates and guarded by eight square blockhouses. Its rugged palisade, a mile and a quarter long, walled a tract of fifty acres. On the north it was bordered by Greenville and Mud Creeks; the southern and eastern blockhouses overlooked a wide cleared meadow where the garrison gardens striped the ground and waving stems of chicory and corn cockle softened the new stumpland. All around stretched the deep woods, old as time itself.

For hundreds of miles the forest rolled away, a green ocean with a few far "plains" making islands in the wild expanse. The Pickaway, Darby and Sandusky plains were Indian townsites, smoke rising from the cooking fires and cornfields spreading beside the creeks. From Fort Pitt a line of forts led westward—Fort McIntosh at the mouth of Beaver Creek, Fort Henry frowning over the Wheeling riverfront, Fort Harmar guarding the stockaded town of Marietta where the Muskingum joined the Ohio, Fort Washington on the steep bank of Cincinnati opposite the mouth of the Licking, Fort Nelson at the Falls of the Ohio where the settlers of Louisville were digging stumps out of Jefferson and Walnut streets, Fort Knox on the Wabash at Vincennes, Fort Massac on a rolling Illinois plain above the lower Ohio. These were dark little squares, with cannon bristling from their portholes, between the gloom of the woods and the gleam of the water. Another, newer line of forts ran north from Cincinnati toward the Indian towns on the Maumee—Fort Hamilton, Fort St. Clair, Fort Jefferson, Fort Greene Ville, Fort Recovery, Fort Defiance, Fort Wayne. With this chain of stations in the forest, Wayne had beaten and subdued the northwestern tribes.

The Ordinance of 1785 had created the Northwest Territory of the huge mysterious land north and east of the Ohio and Mississippi rivers. But it was a land occupied for centuries by resolute Indians. Originally the French had claimed it by right of "discovery" and Indian treaty; in 1763 the British won it from the French; in the years of the Revolution, George Rogers Clark and his men in buckskin won it from the British; and still it was the Indians' country. Now the Americans would take it, step by step, tract by tract, from the unwilling tribes. The first step was the Treaty of Fort McIntosh in 1785 when a group of chiefs surrendered their claims to land on the upper Ohio. The final action came in Wisconsin in 1832, when Black Hawk and his beaten Sauks were driven across the Mississippi. A long stride was taken at Fort Greene Ville in the summer of 1795.

Fort Greene Ville, with it barracks, commissaries, magazine, storehouses, shops, and stables, was the strongest

station in the West. General Wayne's headquarters, near the
future site of Darke County's first courthouse, faced the
artillery park and the trampled parade. Ten rows of log
huts housed the troops, a regiment to a row, each hut quar-
tering six men. At the edge of the parade stood the council
house, a long log building empty except for a stone-lined
circle where the ceremonial fire smouldered through the
drowsy summer days. Here the chiefs and the Big Wind
made their deliberate speeches and puffed smoke from the
feathered calumet. In their words the future of the Ohio
country was being shaped.

There are places where the currents of history run
together, where past and future mingle like streams of water.
Picture the men at Fort Greene Ville in that summer of the
Treaty: General Anthony Wayne, friend of Washington, hero
of Brandywine, Monmouth, and Germantown, coming from
Philadelphia to the western wilderness with his gout and
rheumatism, his rigid bearing and his harsh commands;
beside him is his aide, young William Henry Harrison, lean
as a rail, a youth with a long-nosed, narrow face now marked
with the first lines of hardship and maturity. Here are two
young officers in the same division—Meriwether Lewis, just
turned twenty, and William Clark, twenty-four; they fought
together at Fallen Timbers, but their names would be linked
by another adventure, seven years later, in the snows of the
Rocky Mountains and the rain forests of Oregon. In the
council house on July 5th, Wayne's men and what Indians
cared to listen heard a sermon, "The Altar of Peace," by the
Reverend Morgan John Rhys, a restless Baptist clergyman
from Wales who was at Greene Ville for a fortnight's visit.
Beside him on the July Sunday in the council house was
Wayne's chaplain, the Reverend David Jones. Son of Welsh
settlers in Delaware, he had set himself a mission to the
western tribes in 1772-3, traveling down the Ohio with nineteen-year-old George Rogers Clark on his first journey to
the wilderness. Since then David Jones had served as chaplain under General Wayne from Ticonderoga to Monmouth,

rousing such revolutionary zeal, in and out of the ranks, that
the British offered a reward for his capture. Now he was on
leave from his Welsh Baptist Church in Chester County in
Pennsylvania, to campaign in the wilderness; he would sign
the Treaty as Chaplain of the U.S. Legion. Some swarthy men
in coonskin caps and buckskin shirts and leggings drew
rations with the troops. These were Wayne's scouts, spies,
rangers—William Wells, Isaac Zane, Henry Miller and his
brother Christopher, and others—all white men who had
lived among the Indians. Though serving under Wayne,
they had wives and children in the Wyandot and Miami
towns. They knew the languages of the tribes; during the
campaign they spied out Indian plans and movements; now
they were interpreters in the council house. It was a badly
mixed-up war.

All through June and July the tribesmen had come
in to Fort Greene Ville, some limping with the wounds of
Fort Recovery and Fallen Timbers. At last there were 1100
of them, camped on the cleared land outside the stockade
walls and under the blockhouse cannon. Here were the nations of the Northwest—dark-skinned Ottawas and Chippewas from the woods of Michigan, blanketed Wyandots from
Sandusky Bay, feathered Shawnees from the Scioto woods,
Delawares from the valleys of the Tuscarawas and the Muskingum, Miamis from the Wabash country, Weas and Piankeshaws from the creeks of Indiana, Potawatomis and Kickapoos
from great grasslands along the Illinois.

The Indians had a definition of a good time—fine
weather and plenty to eat. That summer Wayne's supply men
drove herds of cattle and hogs to Greene Ville, and forty
ox-teams plodded over the trace, bringing rice, cheese, barley,
coffee, rum, and whisky. The warriors feasted on the white
man's beef and pork, brown sugar and coffee; they gulped
his rations of whisky and puffed on his tobacco. The Indians
had a short memory; their victories over Harmar and St.
Clair and their defeat by Wayne faded in the excitement of
the great congress. They wandered around the fort, climbing

over the supply wagons, peering into the storehouses, watching the blacksmiths hammer white-hot iron on the noisy anvils. They raced their ponies in the pasture beyond the palisade; they tried tests of skill and strength with Wayne's soldiers. Most Indians could outrun a white man, but one of Wayne's scouts amazed the tribes with his athletic feats. Robert McClellan, from Cumberland County, Pennsylvania, was a man of average height and slight physique, but the pioneer biographer John McDonald called him "one of the most athletic and active men that has ever appeared on this globe." McClellan could leap over a standing horse or a yoke of oxen. On the parade ground, with a slight down-grade to help him, he cleared a canvas-arched wagon. The Indians could not catch him in a foot-race or match him in a broad jump.

At dusk fires twinkled over the big meadow, and after supper the tribesmen gambled for salt, sugar, candles, and tobacco, throwing colored plum stones on a blanket. They blew on bark whistles and cane flutes, they danced in the firelight till sweat varnished their naked bodies. Over Wayne's compound, in a slow smoke of oak and hickory, came the savage cries.

But the chiefs were silent. They knew that Wayne's couriers were hurrying from Philadelphia, bringing instructions from the War Secretary and the President. They remembered the treaties at Fort Stanwix, Fort McIntosh, Fort Finney, and Fort Harmar: at every one there had been feasting and the giving of gifts, and the Indians went home to shrunken hunting lands. Little Turtle, the great chief of the Miamis, remembered the exultation of victory when St. Clair's beaten men hurried back to Cincinnati, leaving their dead in the withered grass, their horses, wagons, tents, guns, and axes under the bare November trees; he also remembered the tribes' discord and defeat at Fallen Timbers and the ashes of the Miami towns beside the rivers. The Shawnee Blue Jacket, captain of the Indian forces at Fallen Timbers, could not forget the sting of that defeat, but now he had been bought by a promise of $300 a year; he wore a coat with gold epaulets and carried an ornate red-sealed scroll as an officer in Wayne's army. Another Shawnee, brooding old Black Hoof, remembered Braddock's defeat in Pennsylvania and the bloody battle at Point Pleasant when Cornstalk's men pushed their canoes into the Ohio and rifle shots sang after them in the October darkness. It was a seesaw struggle, but at the crucial times the white men won the battles. Leathery Buckongahelas, "Breaker in Pieces," war chief of the Delawares, could not forget the failure of the British to uphold the tribes at Fallen Timbers; now he felt more bitterness for them than for the Americans. He had a great delegation here, 381 Delaware warriors, but their lands were threatened. Tarhe, the Crane, bearing an arm wound from the Maumee battle, thought of his dwindling tribe and hoped for peace. He was the keeper of the Wyandot calumet and the only Wyandot war chief left alive after the years of forest warfare.

On July 20th the chiefs and captains stood in the long council house while the Great Soldier, in blue coat, cocked hat, crossed sword belt and silver-mounted sword, raked up the ashes of the smoldering fire. He puffed the calumet, the feathered ceremonial pipe, and sent it round the circle. He held up the great seal of the United States, the fierce eagle with a sheaf of arrows in one claw and an olive branch in the other —"Brothers, no longer shut your eyes to your true interests and happiness, nor your ears to this last overture of peace." They must make their choice, the arrows or the olive branch; the white men had come into the Ohio country to stay.

General Wayne had fought well and now around the ceremonial fire he was a shrewd and patient diplomat. He divided and confused the chiefs, pointing out their conflicting land claims, reminding them that they had previously sold lands to the French and the English, and to the Americans also. He recalled that the upper Ohio country had twice been paid for—at Fort McIntosh and Fort Harmar—but now the Fifteen Fires were ready to pay for it a third time, and they would slight no tribe or nation in the treaty.

For fifteen days the logs smoldered and the council went on. Repeatedly Little Turtle stepped forth, light glinting from his foot-long earrings and his silver necklace, head thrown back and eyes defiant. His tribe had never ratified the former treaties and cessions; his ancestors had possessed great hunting lands. With word and gesture he marked out a great square of wilderness, from Detroit to the headwaters or the Scioto, from the mouth of the Wabash to the shore of Lake Michigan. "I have now informed you of the boundaries of the Miami tribe, where the Great Spirit placed my forefather a long time ago and charged him not to sell or part with his lands, but to preserve them for his posterity."

It was a brave speech, and a nearly useless one. Wayne's dark eyes went slowly round the circle. "Brothers! All nations present, now listen to me! Having now explained these matters to you and informed you of all things I judged necessary for your information, we have nothing to do but bury the hatchet and draw a veil over past misfortunes. . . ."

At Wayne's side stood his aide-de-camp, William Henry Harrison, twenty-two years old, the son of a first family of Virginia, with memories of a mansion on the James River and of schooling in Prince Edward Country and Philadelphia. On his father's death he had joined the army. His guardian, William Morris, took a doubtful view—a youth reared in Virginia luxury heading for Indian wars in the Ohio wilderness. With a company of eighty recruits he marched over the mountains to Fort Pitt and took a flatboat down the Ohio. Arrived at lonely Cincinnati on a November day in 1791, they were greeted with the news of St. Clair's disaster in the Miami country. Thirty-seven officers and 593 men lay dead on the upper Wabash. Half that many got back to Fort Hamilton wounded; they got through because the Indians turned back to round up St. Clair's four hundred horses and plunder his abandoned camp. Harrison saw the limping remnants of that army and heard men muttering about their ambush. It was his introduction to the frontier.

Next spring Ensign Harrison, just turned nineteen, led a pack-horse train through disputed country to Fort Hamilton on the Great Miami. Back at Fort Washington, amid the log huts of Cincinnati, he helped to drill Wayne's recruits. In the fall of 1793 they moved north into Indian country, opening a wagon road through the October woods, throwing out scouts to protect their advance. Wayne's Trace led over low ridges and along Seven Mile Creek, splashing through streams and rocking over shelves of bluestone crusted with fossil shellfish from some ancient Ohio sea. At a meeting of two creeks they cleared the forest and built a big stockade for winter quarters. Wayne named Fort Greene Ville for his old comrade, Nathaniel Greene.

To keep his restless men busy Wayne marched a force twenty-five miles north to the scene of St. Clair's defeat. They arrived on Christmas day, and young Lieutenant Harrison had a somber Christmas. The bodies of St. Clair's men, hastily buried by Wilkinson's militia two years before, had been dug up by wolves and Indians. Wayne's troops had to scrape up bones before there was room to pitch their tents; in the next six days they gathered six hundred skulls. They hacked a deep grave in the frozen ground. Four of St. Clair's field pieces were found on the brushy creek bank; when Wayne read the burial service those cannon boomed in the bitter air. That winter the troops turned ax-men. They cleared the land for a thousand feet and raised a stockade in their clearing. With his sense of drama and history, Wayne named it Fort Recovery.

In the spring his scouts reported that the British were raising a fort at the Maumee Rapids and rallying the tribes. The clash was coming.

While the peace fire smoldered in the council house at Fort Greene Ville, Harrison listened to the speeches of the chiefs. He caught familiar words: *mauveghke,* the hills; *me,te quegh,ke,* the woods; *misheque,* the water; *tamashota,* prairie;

yung,ta,rah, the lakes; he heard familiar names: Pickawillany, Chillicothe, Sandusky, Olentangy, Wapatomika—and all that he had seen and heard of the Ohio country gathered in his mind. The meeting of the rivers at Fort Pitt, where army barges loaded men and wagons, horses, hogs, and cattle, tents and commissaries and cannon for the western posts. The old flint ridges above the forks of the Tuscarawas, with the Waldhoning flowing down from the deep woods of the north. The Indian town on the Pickaway Plains with trails fanning out to the Ohio and the great northern lake. The dense green spread of the Big Hocking forest, the great woods of White Woman Creek, the rocky gorges of the Cuyahoga and the wild ridges of the Olentangy. The buffalo swamp with ancient avenues tramped through the canebrake. The silent mounds above the rivers, platforms and cones, earthwork aisles and portals, at one point a huge earth serpent, 1300 feet long, writhing above a creek in the Scioto valley. The miles of moats and breastworks, above the deep gorge of the Little Miami, where an ancient people had built a strong place.

One August day in 1793 Harrison had accompanied General Wayne over the mounds at Cincinnati—long embankments, huge squares and circles. They climbed a fifty-foot cone and peered, as the vanished mound builders must have done, far down the curving valley of the Ohio. The western country had been fought for in forgotten times. Fallen Timbers was merely the latest battleground.

In his duffle Harrison had two books, Cicero's *Orations* and Blair's *Lectures,* but now he was reading the future of this wild land. It was federal domain, a part of the American nation—and who would possess it? Men like the restless soldiers passing outside the council house, stripped to the waist in the summer sun. They had land sense, these Pennsylvania, Maryland, Virginia, and Kentucky men. They looked over a new valley and saw the farms of the future. They stopped at a spring and pictured a cabin and cornfield and cattle and sheep in a rich pasture. They talked about slouglis, bogs, bottoms, about clay, loam, marl, and deep black earth. They kept judging soil even in deep woods: walnut, hickory, cherry, white ash, sugar maple indicate good earth; but don't blaze your corners on locust, swamp oak, or sycamore. Men like these would clear the forest and open the earth to the sun— if the land speculators did not get there first.

Lieutenant Harrison knew how the land had gone in Kentucky. In the spring of 1795 he had spent a leave in Lexington where he met a dark-eyed girl who before the year was over would become his wife. She was the daughter of John Cleves Symmes, a New Jersey man who had contracted with Congress for a million Ohio acres between the Great and Little Miami rivers. That contract was in the Kentucky manner, for the state of Virginia had granted whole provinces of western tcrritory to planters and promoters in the Old Dominion. Before Kentucky's statehood the choice lands were gone. Two hundred and fifty men had grants ranging from 10,000 to 90,000 acres; eight of them held a quarter million acres each. Some of the great holders had never seen Kentucky. Back in Tidewater mansions they kept records of their wilderness domain, while men who had defended Kentucky with their lives could not claim a forty-acre farm.

Now in the big council house Wayne was asking the Indians for a tract across the river from Louisville in the Ohio country, to make up bounty lands for the Kentuckians who had followed George Rogers Clark in his Vincennes campaign; there was no land left in Kentucky to reward them. The land policy shaped by Virginia planters took no heed of landless men. But the Ohio country was federal domain; it should become a country of small farms, not large plantations; it should be open to all. Harrison knew there must not be landless men in this wilderness, though he could not know the part he would have in its future.

Between the Indians and the Americans, above the seeping council fire, stood Captain William Wells, Wayne's chief interpreter. Day after day he translated the words of treaty-making. "It appears to me that if the Great Spirit, as you say, charged your forefathers to preserve your lands entire, for their posterity, they have paid very little regard to the sacred injunction." . . . Captain Wells knew both the savage and the civilized tongues, and he had led both lives. He was a white man who had been reared by Indians and who had fought on both sides. Now he stood between his military leader, Wayne, and his father-in-law, Little Turtle, transmitting their meaning. He had been captured by a band of Miamis in Kentucky at the age of twelve and carried across the Ohio. He became a hunter, woodsman, warrior. He married the chief's daughter, Manwangopath—"Sweet Breeze"—and had four black-eyed children. He had fought against the Americans under Harmar and St. Clair. At the St. Clair massacre he had been in charge of three hundred warriors who picked off the American artillerymen until their bodies were, as he remembered, "heaped up almost to the height of their field-pieces." Years later he told Colonel John Johnston, a supplier for Wayne and later Indian Agent at Piqua, that he tomahawked and scalped St. Clair's wounded until he could not raise his arm. But after that furious day his thoughts troubled him. Eventually, choosing to join the American side, Wells became the captain of Wayne's spies, scouting the Indian camps, bringing back word of the movements and councils of the tribes. Now he was chief translator at the treaty council.

Wells understood the difference between savage and civilized life—the inborn freedom of the Indian and the harrying ambition of the white man. He knew the wild country, the long lake trail through the forest of the Senecas and past the rivers where the fishing camps were pitched in spring, the frosty salt licks by the O-hy-o where the buffalo roads led in. He knew the Indian towns in the valleys with their dust and dogs, their trophies of hunting and warfare, the shaking of gourds around the council fires. He also knew the white man's barges on the river, loaded with muskets and cannon, and his forts where the bugle shrilled and flags flew in the wind.

He knew the Indian's contempt for the tamed life of the white man, a life as pale and bloodless as his skin. The whites were fearful, covering themselves with clothing, enclosing themselves in roofs and walls, locking their doors, reading from the Bible and quoting distant Presidents and Kings. They were afraid of hunger and solitude. They wanted possessions, cattle in their pastures, corn in their barns, fences around their fields. They were never silent and never at ease. A weak, degenerate, fearful people, they could not survive without their axes, guns, and horses. They were destroyers, leveling the forests, hacking out roads where the mossy deer trail ran, driving the game away. They were at war with the earth.

In the Ohio country were hundreds like William Wells, men and women both, who had been taken in childhood and reared among the tribes. Few of them ever chose to return to their blood people. The Indians were proud, improvident, and free; the Americans were shrewd and grasping, thinking of the future, meaning to change the wilderness beyond all recognition. Swarthy Captain Wells knew both sides in that struggle. The Indians were the better people, but the whites would win.

General Wayne stepped up to the charred circle. "—I now deliver to you the wide and straight path to the Fifteen Fires, to be used by you and your posterity forever. So long as you continue to follow this road, so long will you continue to be a happy people. You see it straight and wide, and they will be blind indeed who will deviate from it."

Captain Wells repeated this to the stern Miamis, White Loon and Little Turtle. Other translators relayed it to the Wyandots, old Tarhe and the Half King's Son; to Buckongahelas and Queshowsky of the Delawares; to the Shawnees, Blue Jacket, Black Hoof and Red Pole; to Little Beaver and Little Fox of the Weas and the Piankeshaws; to Chemung, Tapenebec, and Okea of the Potawatomis; to

La Malice, Augooshaway, and Secau of the Ottawas: to the Chippewas' Little Thunder, Mashipinashiwish, and Peshawkey. There was nothing for them to say.

The treaty terms were harsh. The Americans claimed all the country they had fought in, both the rich Miami valleys, all the broad Scioto valley, all the country up the Hockhocking and Muskingum and halfway up the Tuscarawas, all the land east of the Cuyahoga. They drew a line from abandoned Fort Laurens on the Tuscarawas to Fort Recovery, and from there south and a little west, to include the fertile valley of the Whitewater, to the Ohio opposite the mouth of the Kentucky. In addition to the land east and south of this treaty line, the Indians must cede two tracts in southern Indiana and a dozen scattered and strategic locations on the northern waterways.

So the United States came into possession of three-quarters of modern Ohio, the sites of Toledo, Detroit, Chicago, the turtle-shaped island of Michilimackinac, the headwaters of the Indiana rivers, and districts on the Wabash and the lower Ohio. Nearly twenty million acres were outlined in the treaty terms, which also gave the United States the right to negotiate for further Indian lands and promised the Indians protection from white intruders. For all this the tribes received $20,000 in trade goods, and a small annuity. In the future the United States would deliver annually a thousand dollars worth of horses and cattle, plows and harrows, axes and blankets to the Wyandots, Delawares, Shawnees, Miamis, Ottawas, Chippewas, and Potawatomis; the smaller tribes, Kickapoo, Ouitenon, Eel River, Piankeshaw, and Kaskaskia would receive annuities of $500. It came to one-tenth of a cent an acre, plus yearly payments of $9,500 to the tribes.

The three-thousand-word treaty covered two sheets of parchment twenty inches square; there was room for the signatures of ninety-two chiefs and twenty-seven white men. With the treaty signed and sealed, Wayne presented each of the chiefs with a six-inch bronze medal, shaped like a tear drop, showing on one side President Washington handing a long-

stemmed peace pipe to an Indian who had dropped his tomahawk, on the other, under a sunburst, the United States eagle
bearing a sheaf of arrows and a spray of olive leaves. The
Indians presented Wayne with an elaborately carved pipe, as
long as a rifle barrel. It was packed with pigtail tobacco,
lighted, and passed among the white and red signers. Then
Wayne ordered a double ration of whisky, a feast of pork and
beef, and gifts for all the tribesmen. It was August 3rd, 1795,
and the doors of the Ohio country stood open to the future.

In the shortening days of August, with hackberry
leaves turning brown and sycamore trunks scaling, the Indians tramped home with word of their shrunken hunting
grounds. Regiments marched out the timbered gate and back
to Cincinnati, leaving a remnant to guard the winter snows
on Greenville Creek and to feed the ragged and hungry Indians who wandered in from the woods. The great congress
was dispersed, chiefs and warriors, officers and men scattering
to the four winds and the changing future.

Sixteen months later General Wayne—"Old Horse,"
"Mars," the *Kitcho Shemagana* who slept with his eyes open
—was lying rigid with pain at Presque Isle, on his way back
to Philadelphia after directing the American occupation of
Detroit; he died at Presque Isle in a desolate blockhouse on
the shore of Lake Erie ten days before Christmas, 1796. The
Reverend David Jones was back in Chester County, preaching to his congregation and sleeping in a bed; but he would
go to war again, at seventy-six, serving as chaplain throughout the War of 1812. Lieutenant William Clark went to
Louisville and helped his lonely and bitter brother assign
lands in "Clark's Grant" to the veterans of his Illinois campaign; he kept up a correspondence with Meriwether Lewis
who had become President Jefferson's confidential secretary.
Old Chief Buckongahelas lived to sign two more land-cession
treaties—at Fort Wayne in 1803 and Vincennes in 1804.
Black Hoof went to live in the woods near Wapakoneta; for
forty years he saw the white man's settlements grow. He died

in the 1830's, an old man wrinkled as a walnut trunk; tradition says he was in his 111th year. Blue Jacket drew his private annuity and lived in peace until 1812; according to one report he was hanged by Tecumseh's followers at Prophet's-Town on the Wabash; another story tells of his death in Illinois. Tarhe, keeper of the Indian copy of the 1795 treaty, fought on the American side in the War of 1812, serving under William Henry Harrison, then a general. At the age of seventy the chief marched at the head of a file of Wyandot warriors in the invasion of Canada. Harrison called him "a venerable, intelligent, upright man," and at his death a mourning council was held by all the tribes in Ohio. He died near Upper Sandusky in 1818, the year when Illinois became a state and when the Treaty of St. Mary's was signed by Wyandot, Shawnee and Ottawa chiefs, surrendering the whole central portion of Indiana.

At the time of the St. Mary's Treaty a 672-acre tract, which included a village site of the Munsee tribe, was sold by a half-breed daughter of William Wells. A few years later it was platted as the town of Muncie, and in 1929 two American sociologists wrote it up as "Middletown," the typical American community.

From Fort Greene Ville the great chief Little Turtle went back to his two wives, one fifty and the other eighteen, on Eel River, living in a house that the United States built for him and telling his people to take up farming. In 1797 he journeyed with William Wells to Philadelphia, where George Washington presented him with a sword, Gilbert Stuart painted his portrait, the French philosopher Volney interviewed him, and he had a long talk with Thaddeus Kosciusko, the Polish general who had served with the American Revolutionary army. Kosciusko gave the chief a pair of silver-handled pistols, belatedly advising him to use them on the first man who came to subjugate him or despoil his country. The chief was inoculated for smallpox before his return to Indiana. From there, in 1802, he appealed to President Jefferson to curb liquor trading with the Indians, and five years later he made a journey to Washington to ask the President for a flour mill for his people. In 1812, suffering from gout and rheumatism and rejected by his tribe, he died at the home of his daughter, Mrs. William Wells, near Fort Wayne.

From the treaty council Captain Wells went back to the Miami country, settling on the banks of Spy Run, near the confluence of the St. Joseph and St. Mary rivers. He was appointed Indian Agent at Fort Wayne. In August, 1812, learning of orders for the evacuation of Fort Dearborn on Lake Michigan, he hurried to the defense of the Americans. He arrived at the mouth of the Chicago River on the fateful 15th of August, when five hundred Potawatomi warriors ambushed the sixty-nine fugitives from the fort. It was a hopeless battle, but William Wells rushed in. His body was found among the dead on the trampled lake front.

After the dispersal at Greene Ville Robert McClellan, the great jumper, made a long jump from the Ohio country. He went on to a new frontier, becoming a trader on the Missouri and a mountain man. On September 12, 1806, when Lewis and Clark were returning from Oregon, Captain Clark met McClellan in a keelboat with twelve men going up the Missouri to trade with the plains Indians. Clark spent the night with him, the two talking about what had happened to them since the treaty summer of 1795. Trader McClellan went on to the shining mountains. In 1807 with Ramsay Crooks he led an expedition to the upper Missouri. In 1810 he joined the Pacific Fur Company; after a grueling journey he reached Astoria, gaunt and ragged, in January, 1812. Six months later he made the long hard perilous return with Robert Stuart's party, through country never before seen by white men, arriving in St. Louis in the spring of 1813. Ill and penniless, he died near St. Louis in 1815 and was buried on the farm of William Clark, who had become governor of Missouri Territory. But he was not forgotten. Seventeen years after his wanderings had ended, McClellan lived again in the pages of Washington Irving's *Astoria*.

From Greene Ville William Henry Harrison went

back to Cincinnati. He would hold a succession of important offices in years to come—legislator, territorial governor, army general, statesman. But in the fall of 1795 he had less thought for the future of the Ohio country than for the small dark-eyed daughter of John Cleves Symmes in a house above the great curve of the Ohio at North Bend.

Eight months after the council fire burned out, Greene Ville was a deserted camp; its garrison was withdrawn in the spring of 1796. That fall settlers swarmed up the valley of the Great Miami. They burned the empty fort on Greenville Creek to get nails and iron hinges for their cabins. A few barracks huts escaped the flames and stood there, through winter snow and summer sun, in the charred square of the palisade. In 1808 Azor Scribner moved under one of those sagging roofs with a wagon load of blankets, knives and kettles. He traded with Tecumseh and his Shawnees, and with squatters who had hacked out clearings along the Stillwater, and eventually he opened the first tavern in the town of Greenville.

In the summer of 1811 his brother Abraham Scribner came to Greenville from the East, where he had run a coasting schooner between Cape Hatteras and Maine. Though just thirty, he was almost deaf from exposure in the wintry winds of the Atlantic. But he heard the voice of opportunity when settlers were creaking up Wayne's old wagon trace, when trees were crashing down to clear the streets of Hamilton, Middletown, Franklin, Waynesville, Dayton. In 1814 he married the daughter of John Devor who had laid out the town of Greenville a few years earlier. He paid the entrance fee of $80 on a quarter section of prairie beside Mud Creek and built a cabin there. Two years later he sold his quarter section to John Compton of Dayton for $1600. The wilderness had become real estate.

CHAPTER TWO

THE FALLING STAR

One of the principal topics of conversation in all places was the public lands—the price and the quality—the choice of location, tracts, quarter sections, entries, &c., &c.

—GORHAM A. WORTH: *Recollections of Cincinnati*

ONE SHAWNEE chief had not come to Fort Greene Ville at Wayne's bidding. Tecumseh, twenty-six years old, saw his warriors routed and one of his own brothers killed at Fallen Timbers, but he left the battle undefeated. While the great congress gathered for Wayne's council Tecumseh ranged over distant country, calling the tribes to a united resistance. After the Greene Ville Treaty Line was drawn he declared that the Ohio country was Indian land. Ten years later he came to Greenville, still unbeaten, and pitched a defiant camp where Wayne's council house had stood.

Western Ohio was Tecumseh's native country. He was born in the Shawnee village of Oldtown, near present Spring-

21

field, Ohio, on the Mad River which is usually a tranquil stream. At Tecumseh's birth the river was in flood, hurrying on to the Great Miami and the Ohio. One tradition says that he was the third of a set of triplet sons born to a Shawnee woman in March, 1768, and that at the hour of his birth a flaming meteor arced through the eastern sky; so he was named *Tikamthi*—Falling Star. Another tradition makes him the second of twin brothers. Whether she bore twins or triplets, that Shawnee woman changed the course of history on the frontier. Tecumseh and his twin brother, "the Prophet," organized the last great Indian resistance in the Ohio country.

The Shawnees were a small tribe—less than two hundred warriors in Tecumseh's time. But they were a bold, proud, restless people who kept in the center of frontier history. When Tecumseh was a six-year-old, playing with corncobs and bear claws at Oldtown, his father was killed at Point Pleasant where the Shawnee leader Cornstalk resisted the advance of Lord Dunmore's Virginians into the Ohio country. When Tecumseh was a weedy boy of ten, Daniel Boone was brought to Oldtown as a captive and was adopted into the Shawnee tribe. That same year rugged Simon Kenton, captured while stealing Shawnee horses, ran the gantlet at Oldtown and escaped with his stubborn life. When Tecumseh was twelve the village was burned by George Rogers Clark's raiding Kentuckians; after they were gone the boy stared at the charred ruins of the town and the trampled cornfields by the river. As a tall young warrior of nineteen Tecumseh began a roving life that took him beyond the Mississippi to the buffalo prairies of the Osages, to the valleys of Tennessee where the Cherokees were fighting back white settlers, through the autumn hills of Kentucky where he bested the Cherokee hunters by killing thirty-one buck deer in three days.

When he returned to the Ohio in 1790 Tecumseh was a mature warrior, and the old men listened when he spoke. During his three-year absence Congress had passed the Ordinance of 1787, which, among other things, provided for the eventual division of the vast Ohio region into states. The Yankee settlers had built their town of Marietta on the upper Ohio and John Cleves Symmes' party had begun settlement of the Miami country at Cincinnati and North Bend. Now, Tecumseh declared, the tribes must unite to drive the invaders from their land. During the next five years he fought the American advance above the Ohio. His scouting of St. Clair's army set up the ambush that destroyed that wretched expedition. At the head of raiding parties he ranged from the Miami valley to the Virginia mountains, stealing horses and cattle and burning settlers' cabins. In the struggle with Wayne he led a band of Shawnees and saw them riddled by the riflemen at Fallen Timbers in 1794. But he refused to join the council at Greene Ville and denounced the chiefs who ceded a rich hunting country, six days' horseback journey across, for a pile of trade goods and some kegs of whisky. After the treaty the defeated chiefs, Little Turtle, Tarhe, Buckongehelas, settled on restricted lands and told the tribes to live like white men. But young Tecumseh was still at war.

For ten years after 1795, while settlers swarmed up the valleys of the Muskingum, the Scioto, and the Miami, he roved the country as a hunter. But he was after more than venison and bear meat. From tribe to tribe he traveled, talking with the chiefs and sachems, sitting at council fires, drawing rough outlines with a charred stick on the ground. The tribes were weak when separated, but they could be strong if they stood together. The Americans had made a nation of their seventeen fires; the tribes were a hundred fires, scattered from the Great Lakes to the Gulf of Mexico, from the Allegheny forests to the plains of the Missouri. Tecumseh had a dream of a great Indian confederation that could resist the white man's armies and hold all the hunting lands in common. That bold picture of a sovereign Indian nation he carried to the scattered tribes.

While he traveled the long trade and hunting trails, urging a political alliance, his twin brother was on a religious mission through the Wabash country. Laulewasikau—"Loud

Voice"—had seen a vision and heard the voice of the Great
Spirit: the tribes should spurn the white man's trade, throw
away his firearms, pour his whisky on the ground. In 1805 an
old medicine man, Penagashega—"Change of Feathers"—
revered by the Ohio tribes as a prophet, died in his village
north of Greenville. Soon afterward, at a joint council of
Shawnees, Wyandots, Senecas and Ottawas on the Auglaize
River, Laulewasikau announced himself as the old sachem's
successor. He took a new name, Tenskawautawan—"Open
Door"—and began preaching with a new fervor. Going from
camp to camp where the tribes wore woolen clothing, cooked
their game in iron kettles, and traded peltry for whisky and
rum, he called for a return to native ways. Let the people wear
skins and furs, let them use stone knives and axes, let them
kindle their wood with the firestick and grind their corn
with stones. Let them spit out the white man's whisky. Let
them hold all their goods in common, as the Spirit of Life
intended.

   The Prophet was a striking figure, commanding his lis-
teners with outstretched hands and ringing voice. He wore the
old wild Indian dress—a Cherokee turban, jacket, leggings,
mantle of deerskin. Firelight played on his craggy face, on
his silver nose- and ear-rings. One eye-socket was empty, from
a hunting wound in his youth; the remaining eye was enlarged and hypnotic. As he described the future of the tribes
—strong and free on their own hunting lands, proud of their
own life and traditions—it seemed that the Great Spirit was
speaking through him.

   After a new vision he declared that Mishemenetoc, the
Spirit of Life, had directed him to establish a town at the
Big Ford. This was a dramatic revelation, for the ford was
on Greenville Creek, at the site of Fort Greene Ville, where
ten years earlier the tribes had surrendered their ancestral
lands.

   At Greenville Tecumseh joined his brother. The two
leaders, one political, the other religious, were upholding the
same dream, foretelling a new age of strength and integrity

for their people. The choice of Greenville as their headquarters was a defiant rejection of the humiliating past.

In 1805 the charred ruins of Fort Greene Ville stood in
a silent plain beside the curving creek. Some squatters had
come up the Stillwater and government surveyors were mapping the upper Miami valley, but there was no settlement
where Wayne had treated with the tribes. There Tecumseh
and the Prophet planted their village, on the white man's
side of the Treaty Line, building a timber council house and
a scattering of huts on the Mud Creek prairie. The town
grew, families arriving with their dogs and horses, their bales
and bundles, from the Wabash, the St. Joseph, the Maumee.
The two Shawnee brothers built a mud hut of their own a
mile away from the village, choosing a knoll at the mouth
of Mud Creek, just across from Wayne's vanished fort. The
knoll is still called Tecumseh's Point.

To the gathering tribesmen the Prophet poured out
his fervid gospel of Indian nationalism and the destruction
of the white invaders. Reports of his preaching went over distant trails. Men and families came from the shores of Lake
Superior and Lake Huron, from the dark forests of the Upper
Mississippi and the wide plains of the Missouri, to hear his
powerful prophecy. The village on Greenville Creek grew
into a restless town.

When Governor Kirker of Ohio heard that eight hundred savages, many of them armed with rifles, were established
on the American side of the Treaty Line, he called up the
state militia and sent two commissioners to the Indians. In
September, 1807, they rode over a hundred miles of leafy
trails from Chillicothe, the capital of Ohio since it had become a state in 1803, to Greenville. The commissioners were
Duncan McArthur, a burly surveyor and speculator who
held vast lands in the Scioto valley, and Thomas Worthington, just ending his term as Ohio's first Senator. Beside Greenville Creek they found the noisy Indian town—seven hundred
were gathered there, Miamis, Shawnees, Wyandots, Potawatomis, Chippewas—and were led to the outlying hut of the

two Shawnee brothers. The Prophet explained that his people had gathered for a religious council to seek the will and guidance of the Great Spirit. Tecumseh, with three other chiefs, consented to return with the commissioners to Chillicothe, to see the Ohio governor. So McArthur and Tecumseh, who would be rival generals in the War of 1812, rode together through the colored woods to the Ohio capital. Tecumseh had been there three years earlier, for a conference with Governor Tiffin. Chillicothe was a larger place now —fourteen stores, six hotels, two newspaper printing offices, a Methodist and a Presbyterian church, and some two hundred dwellings. In the new stone statehouse, under a peaked roof with a six-windowed cupola, Tecumseh spoke for three hours, his words interpreted by his old friend Stephen Ruddell, a white man who had grown up among the Shawnees. He recalled to the Ohio assembly the greedy advance of white men into Indian lands; he reviewed the treaties in which the tribes had been confused and separated; he described the wrongs endured by his people and the depravity that came with the white man's trade. Finally he declared that the tribes, though wanting peace, would yield no more land from their shrunken hunting grounds. After hearing this eloquent and high-minded speech, the governor ordered the militia disbanded.

Back at Greenville the Indian leaders resumed their mission—the Prophet stirring the tribesmen's superstitions, Tecumseh rousing their patriotism. The brothers rode off to villages on the Wabash and the Illinois, and returned with new followers. Day and night drums throbbed on Greenville prairie and chanting swelled as the Prophet passed from one tribal fire to another. Then came a rider from the West. He leaped off a lathered horse and delivered a message from William Henry Harrison, governor of Indiana Territory. In his message Harrison urged that the Indians leave Greenville.

As a Territorial delegate to Congress, Harrison had in 1800 secured passage of a bill which divided the Northwest

Territory. Ohio, with a population of 45,000 and aspiring to statehood, was split off from the rest of the western domain which became Indiana Territory and had a total white population of some 5,000. Indiana Territory comprised the present states of Indiana, Illinois, Michigan and Wisconsin—nearly all of it owned by the Indians. The sleepy little town of Vincennes on the Wabash became the capital of that huge territory. Harrison, already adept at political maneuvers, was appointed governor. In January, 1801, he arrived at Vincennes, a village of four hundred log and clapboard houses between the curving river and uplands of prairie and forest. This was an old French settlement, a year older than Philadelphia, where the Indians had brought peltry to French traders. The British had wrested it from the French, and then George Rogers Clark with a regiment of ragged men had taken it by surprise and daring from the British. On the river bank stood the log church of St. Francis Xavier and the ruins of old Fort Sackville where Clark had lowered the British flag and raised the Stars and Stripes on a chill February morning in 1779. In the twenty years since then American squatters had come up the Indiana rivers, hacking their tomahawk claims on Indian land; traders had brought flatboat loads of whisky to the Indian camps. The chiefs had seen their hunting grounds invaded, their game destroyed, their young men made drunk and cheated of their peltries. It was a losing traffic for the tribes. The Wea, Piankeshaw, and Eel River people were depleted and demoralized. After trading the winter catch of furs for a few gallons of whisky the redmen drew knives and axes on each other; one spring morning four Indians lay dead in the village street. In these lawless years the French villagers lived on in their whitewashed cottages, smoking on their galleries on summer afternoons, playing their fiddles by the chimney fire on winter nights. They wanted no more land than their orchards, gardens, and a tag of pasture; they had no interest in government or trade. Now in 1801 the old *habitants* watched a young American, lean as a roofpole, arrive in their little town that had become the capital of a territory as big as all of France. He would have his hands full—of violent and wheedling Indians, of heedless and headstrong squatters, of traders with their cargoes of rum and whisky.

Governor Harrison brought his family to the house of Colonel Francis Vigo, who had befriended the Americans in the years of the Revolution, and immediately made plans for a residence of his own. It was finished two years later, a mansion in a grove of walnut trees above the graceful Wabash, dominating the three hundred acres of his "Grouseland" estate. In the mansion's council room and under the trees outside, Harrison would meet the chiefs of all the western country.

Promptly in 1801 Harrison ordered trespassers off the Indian lands. Traders were forbidden to visit tribal hunting camps and were warned against exchanging liquor for the Indians' clothes and weapons. He reported to the Secretary of War that each year six thousand gallons of whisky went to the Wabash villages. He described the Wea, Piankeshaw, and Eel River tribes, nearest to Vincennes, as "a body of the most depraved wretches on the earth. They are . . . frequently intoxicated to the number of thirty or forty at once, when they commit the greatest disorders, drawing their knives and stabbing everybody they meet with, breaking open the houses of the citizens, killing their cattle and hogs, and breaking down their fences. But in all their frolics they generally suffer the most themselves. They kill each other without mercy."

Game was scarce, even though the tribes were shrunken. President Jefferson had pictured the Indian turning farmer, and Harrison relayed that proposition: "Your father, the President," he told a huddle of chiefs at Vincennes, "wishes you to assemble your scattered warriors and to form towns and villages, in situations best adapted to cultivation; he will cause you to be furnished with horses, cattle, hogs, and implements of husbandry, and will . . . instruct you in management."

Then Harrison raised another question close to the President's heart—the question of a land treaty. After a lengthy council the chiefs agreed to cede a tract of 1,600,000 acres extending across the Wabash River into Illinois. This was a start, and a start only. When Spain sold the huge territory of Louisiana to Napoleon, there was danger that a French army might ascend the Mississippi and the northern tribes would stiffen against the Americans. So Jefferson sent a confidential letter to the governor of Indiana Territory: ". . . Live in perpetual peace with the Indians. . . . The decrease of game rendering their subsistence by hunting insufficient we wish to draw them to agriculture, to spinning and weaving. . . . When they withdraw themselves to a small piece of land, they will perceive how useless to them are their extensive forests and will be willing to pare them off . . . in exchange for necessities. . . . We shall push our trading houses and be glad to see the good and influential individuals among them run into debt. . . . When these debts get beyond what the individuals can pay, they will be willing to lop them off . . . by a cession of lands."

Jefferson's aim, which became the undertaking of Harrison, was to secure cession of all the lands east of the Mississippi. When the United States purchased Louisiana from the French, there was no danger of an invasion up the Mississippi. But the Indian lands looked just as inviting to American settlement and expansion. Harrison still had his orders.

He did the job well—one treaty after another during the terms of his governorship—fifteen great land cessions in a space of twelve years. In 1803 he invited the Kaskaskias to Vincennes. Once a powerful confederacy of five Illinois tribes, they were now reduced by war, whisky and disease, to a handful of muttering men. Harrison bargained with them for the wide Illinois prairie that had been their ancestral land; he offered an annuity of four hundred dollars and an agreement to build a new house for Chief Ducoigne and a log church for the tribe and to fence a hundred acres of farming land. Just fifteen acres were fenced—"full as much as this tribe will cultivate," Harrison reported—and in return the United States acquired a sweep of land from the Ohio River to Lake Michigan, half the present state of Illinois.

In 1804 Harrison called the Delaware chiefs to council at Vincennes. From them and the Piankeshaws he bought a tract from the Falls of the Ohio (Louisville) to the mouth of the Wabash. For this important land, bordering the great waterway of the frontier, he promised annuities of three hundred dollars, plus work-horses, cattle, hogs, and eight hundred dollars' worth of trade goods. In October, 1804, with an escort of mounted troops, Harrison loped across the tawny prairie to St. Louis. There, at a council of chiefs from the Osage, Sac, and Fox tribes, he made a fantastic bargain. For annuities of a thousand dollars the chiefs, dressed up in white men's coats and military medals, signed over a vast country, all of the land between the Illinois, Wisconsin, and Mississippi rivers and several million acres in Missouri.

In 1805 came two purchases. In the drowsy heat of August a file of Indians arrived at Vincennes. They included some old friends of Harrison—Chief Little Turtle of the Miamis, Indian Agent William Wells, old Chief Buckongehelas of the Delawares, Chief Winamac of the Potawatomis. In the council room at Grouseland, surrounded by his Territorial officials, Harrison met the delegation. While the chiefs squatted in a circle, Harrison traced a map with a charred stick on the floor. The Indians wanted more annuities and Harrison wanted land—the land bordering the Ohio River between the Ohio boundary and the Falls (Louisville). The Treaty of Grouseland gave Harrison his wish, and the chiefs were awarded more than customary payments. For the last Indian lands on the Ohio, a tract totaling two million acres, Harrison provided four thousand dollars' worth of clothing, knives, traps and guns, and promised annual payment of sixteen hundred dollars for ten years. Special gifts were distributed—to one chief a castor hat and a silk shawl; to another a tent, a broadcloth suit, two scalping knives; to a third a fifteen-dollar saddle. The personal annuity of Little Turtle was increased from a hundred and fifty to two hundred dollars and he was given a Negro slave from Kentucky.

Later that year, after an autumn trip to St. Louis to quiet a quarrel between the Sacs and the Osages, Harrison returned to Vincennes to find a delegation from the dwindling Piankeshaws. From them he bought four million acres extending west from the lower Wabash.

At the end of his fifth year in office, Governor Harrison, thirty-two years old, had acquired from the divided and bewildered tribesmen without the firing of a single musket all the Illinois country, southern Wisconsin, southern Indiana. Vast new areas were now open to settlement, and after the War of 1812 further treaties would complete the cession of lands in Indiana. Soon the nation would have states extending to the Mississippi.

To remote Vincennes news came once a week, a post-rider from Lexington, Kentucky, jogging over the old buffalo trace through the forest. Other news came from traders poling up the Wabash, from Indians wandering in from the woods and prairies, from new settlers in the purchased lands along the Ohio. Occasional visitors came on official or unofficial errands to the executive chamber at Grouseland. One of Harrison's visitors was Aaron Burr. He came in the spring of 1806, talking vaguely about a colonizing project in the lands along the Washita and about the destiny of the Southwest. After he was gone Harrison heard increasing rumors of Burr's activities: he was building flatboats at the falls of the Ohio, recruiting an expedition, assembling arms and supplies. That winter came news of Burr's indictment, his flight and his capture and his dismissal after trial. Then Burr was a forgotten name on the frontier.

Meanwhile another rumor reverberated through the western country. From traders, hunters, and wandering Indians Harrison heard about two Shawnee brothers who were urging all tribesmen to unite against the Americans. In 1805 he heard that the Prophet had gathered a hundred followers on the white man's side of the Treaty Line at Greenville. The next year brought rumor of unrest among the Potawatomis, Chippewas, and Ottawas, and of their plot to destroy the garrisons at Fort Wayne, Detroit, Chicago, and Mackinac. In the summer of 1807 Indian Agent Wells reported a stream of warriors passing through Fort Wayne—fifteen hundred, he estimated, hurrying on to a great council at Greenville. That fall Harrison ordered Wells to send messengers to Greenville, urging the tribesmen to disperse. A few weeks later Wells reported to Harrison: ". . . The Indians have continued to flock to Greenville. . . . The Prophet tells them . . . the Great Spirit will in a few years destroy every white man in America. It is my opinion that the British are at the bottom of this business." That opinion was shared by others in the West. British officers had been seen on the Wabash and the Maumee; a British agent was reported to have visited the Prophet; a Shawnee party from Greenville visited the British post across the Detroit River and returned with clothing and supplies. Tension was growing in the frontier country.

Harrison's message, however, must have made some impression on the Shawnee brothers. A few months later, in the spring of 1808 they moved their following from Greenville to a site halfway up the Wabash, at the mouth of Tippecanoe Creek. The new settlement, in the heart of Indian country, became known as Prophet's Town.

Already that V of land between Tippecanoe Creek and the Wabash was a historic place. Originally the site of a Miami town, Tippecanoe was inhabited by the Shawnees until General Wilkinson burned it in his campaign of 1791. After the Treaty of Greenville the town was rebuilt by the Potawatomis. Here was an example to support Tecumseh's philosophy of land tenure. He had declared that the tribes had no fixed boundaries, that they shared all lands together, one tribe after another living on the same site, and that the American government could not validly purchase land except from all the tribes in common. At the Potawatomis' invitation the Prophet brought his restive following to Tippecanoe, and that village on the Wabash became the Indian capital in the Northwest. It was a strategic location—two hundred miles by water from Vincennes, somewhat nearer the British Fort Amherstburg on the Detroit River, within fifty miles of the chief Potawatomi, Miami, and Ottawa towns.

In August, 1808, a few months after the remove to Tippecanoe, Harrison invited the Prophet and a few followers to Vincennes. The Prophet came, with several hundred hungry warriors. They stayed for two weeks, camping in Harrison's walnut grove, while in daily conferences with the governor the Prophet explained that he was preaching peace and sobriety to the tribes. When the visitors declined an offer of whisky, Harrison was reassured. He fed the delegation, drawing on the granaries of neighboring farmers, and the Indians returned to Prophet's Town with full bellies and bags of seed corn. Meanwhile Tecumseh had been visiting the British at Fort Amherstburg. Along with feasts of beef and dumplings the British offered sympathy over the loss of Indian lands and urged the tribes to resist American expansion.

The next year, 1809, Harrison called a general council at Fort Wayne, ordering Colonel John Johnston, successor to Wells as Indian Agent, to summon the tribes. In September Harrison rode north and found a great encampment on the Fort Wayne prairie. He visited the various tribal camps, calling old acquaintances by name, smoking with the chiefs and their warriors. Fourteen hundred were assembled when he lighted the council fire; it was reminiscent of the Greene Ville Council, but now Harrison was the great white chief, talking and listening and talking again. When the council ended he had acquired three million acres, pushing the Indian border up the Wabash valley to the Ten O'clock Line —a boundary determined by the shadow cast by the sun at 10 A.M. on September 30th, when the treaty was signed. For ten thousand dollars and a small annuity half the country between Vincennes and Prophet's Town was ceded to the United States.

In high spirits Harrison returned to his family at Vincennes and to an appointment of a fourth term as Territorial Governor. He was winning what Tecumseh was determined not to lose. Soon the two leaders would meet.

That winter while a log fire glowed in his Grouseland study Harrison read ancient history and wrote long letters about the importance of a citizen militia; referring to ancient Carthage, Greece, and Rome, he found that "No instance can be produced of a free people preserving their liberties who suffered the military spirit to decline amongst them." Like an echo to his words came rumors from the north: the Tippecanoe warriors would strike at Vincennes; then they would attack Fort Wayne, Fort Dearborn, and St. Louis. The Prophet, according to a spying Piankeshaw, would enter Vincennes on a friendly mission, and at his signal his followers would begin the massacre. Amid growing tension Harrison sent a messenger to Prophet's Town. Tecumseh agreed to come to Vincennes, with thirty followers, to talk with the governor.

In the second week of August, 1810, Tecumseh came down the Wabash at the head of eighty canoes filled with painted warriors. On the afternoon of August 12th he was led to Grouseland where Harrison was reading and smoking on his front veranda. He stepped down to greet the Shawnee—Harrison in lounging clothing with a wing of coarse black hair falling down his forehead, Tecumseh dressed in buckskin and wearing in his belt a silver-mounted tomahawk and hunting knife, recent gifts from the British. Harrison offered the chief a bedroom at Grouseland, but Tecumseh preferred to make his camp beside the Wabash. Soon his party had supper fires twinkling in the walnut grove.

In that grove the council was held. A row of chairs facing the river held the Territorial officials. Tecumseh, spurning a chair, stretched out on the ground. For three days, while a company of militiamen lounged around the grounds eying Tecumseh's men, and Harrison's seven children peered from the porch and windows, they exchanged speeches, Harrison urging peace and patience and Tecumseh insisting that all the governor's treaties were invalid because Indian lands could not be sold without consent of all the tribes. Therefore, the chief declared, he could not honor the latest cessions at Fort Wayne. Harrison insisted that the government had acquired the territory by legal purchase and stated that surveyors would proceed to mark off the lands. On that cleavage the council ended and Tecumseh broke camp. His followers paddled back to Prophet's Town and Tecumseh went on a tour of tribes in Illinois and Michigan. That fall he was a guest at Malden across the Detroit River, where six thousand Indians had gathered to receive British gifts.

All winter disturbing reports came to Vincennes from the uneasy frontier. Settlers in Indiana were losing horses and cattle, a man was killed in his cornfield in Illinois, two Indians on the lower Missouri ambushed a hunting party of four white men. The next spring two surveyors in the newest purchase were captured and taken to Prophet's Town. From Missouri Harrison's old friend William Clark, now governor of Missouri Territory, reported that the Sacs were daubing themselves with war paint, and from the north came word that the Michigan tribes were dancing round the painted post of war.

A second meeting of Tecumseh and Harrison at Vincennes was an armed truce, with the governor's militia keeping a watch on two hundred armed warriors. This talk accomplished nothing. While tension grew, Harrison drilled his troops on the Big Prairie just north of Vincennes and paraded them through the town. In late October he marched north, building Fort Harrison on the Wabash at the site of present Terre Haute, hoping by that gesture to scatter the Indians from their fortified town at Tippecanoe.

The first battle of the War of 1812 was a needless blunder. On the afternoon of November 6, 1811, Harrison's troops drew near to Prophet's Town and were met by three mounted warriors waving a white cloth on a willow pole. Harrison rode forward on his gray mare. He assured them that his men would not attack if the Prophet met his demands; he asked for a campsite with wood and water. The Indians pointed north where a creek ran past their village. That night campfires flickered on a ten-acre prairie bounded by marsh and thickets. Harrison posted double sentries on the side facing Prophet's Town.

While Harrison's twelve hundred men slept lightly in a thin November rain, the Indians did not sleep at all. Tecumseh was away, having gone south to extend the confederacy, but the Prophet prepared his warriors. Stirring a kettle over a fitful fire he sprinkled a sacred mixture on their hunting shirts; now their clothing would turn away the white man's bullets. In the smoky light he made portentous movements with his hands and muttered a savage charm. Half the soldiers were now dead, he declared at the end of his incantation; the rest were under a spell. The warriors could surround and capture them like a herd of cattle. In the first rush they would slay the white chief from Vincennes; he could be known by his gray mare. Those who surrendered would be brought captive to the village. Every Indian woman, the Prophet promised, would have one of the white soldiers as a slave.

Two hours before daybreak the warriors went out. In the rainy blackness they slipped through the familiar cornfields, across the marshes, into the woods and brush around the ten-acre prairie.

In the first gray light Harrison pulled back his tent flap and looked at the camp. A few soldiers were poking at the fires, holding wet boots over the little blaze. With the help of his Negro boy George, Harrison got his boots laced. Suddenly a pair of sentries came running from the left flank.

A rifle banged, the sound magnified in the damp air. With a chorus of whoops and cries warriors swarmed out of the woods. Bullets tore into tents and sprayed sparks from the campfires. Shadowy figures grappled the bewildered troops. Harrison sent George to bring up his gray mare. In the uproar his mount had broken picket, and the boy brought a black horse instead. Harrison swung astride and called two companies of regulars to reinforce the breached left flank. A file of blackened faces rushed past him. *"Conee meshewa!"* a voice cried—"White horse!"—and Colonel Owen, riding behind his commander, fell from the saddle.

At signals from the chiefs the Indians rushed forward. They poured in rifle fire and dropped back to the thickets to reload. Harrison's black horse fell under him, a bullet through its neck. Another bullet punctured the governor's hat. As daylight grew the troops massed lines and sharpened their aim on shadowy targets. Harrison called the bugler and ordered a simultaneous attack on both flanks. In a final uproar the horsemen drove the warriors into the marshland. Dragging their dead and wounded, they went back to the log breastworks of their village, the troopers' bullets singing after them.

Then the troops thought about breakfast. Their hogs and cattle had stampeded, but scores of saddle animals lay dead on the trampled field. The men threw wood on the fires and began roasting horse meat while Harrison counted his casualties. Thirty-seven dead, a hundred and fifty wounded, two missing. That day they buried the dead and doctored the wounded, and discussed a rumor that Tecumseh was marching from the south with a fresh Indian army. But they could see the Indians moving out of Prophet's Town, splashing through the bottoms with bundles on their backs.

Next day the town was empty. Harrison's men filled their knapsacks with dried corn and beans and set fire to the village. The huts burned sullenly in the damp air, gray smoke drifting down the Wabash. When they marched next morning Tippecanoe was only a name, but thirty years later that name would carry Harrison to the White House.

When Tecumseh returned to a charred and empty town, his confederacy seemed a lost cause. But the British were waiting across the Detroit River. They controlled the lakes; their gunboats and cargo vessels could bring supplies for all the Indians who would take British orders. Tecumseh still hoped to drive Americans out of the Wabash country.

The news of Tippecanoe made Harrison a frontier hero. In that needless battle the West saw Indian aggression backed by the British. The British were entrenched across the border; the West wanted to attack. In Congress Henry Clay led the demand for war, voicing the anger and aspiration of the frontier. Britain's high-handed searches of American vessels on the high seas and impressment of American sailors had aroused great animosity in the East, which Clay, naturally, exploited to the limit. War was declared in June of 1812.

It was a disastrous summer for the West. Five garrisoned posts lay between the Ohio and Canada—Fort Harrison on the Wabash, Fort Wayne, Detroit, Fort Dearborn, and remote Fort Mackinac. The first hard blow fell at Fort Mackinac. Its garrison of sixty men did not know that war had begun when their island was invaded by six hundred stealthy Indians under British leaders. In the dark of night they hauled two cannon to a height above the fort. At daybreak the garrison surrendered without resistance. The next blow fell on the sandy shore of Lake Michigan where a growing band of Potawatomis camped around Fort Dearborn. Summer was radiant over the lake and the prairies, but there was gloom in the post. At news of the capture of Fort Mackinac, General Hull had sent a messenger from Detroit ordering the Dearborn garrison to retire to Fort Wayne. On the morning of August 15th Captain Heald dumped his spare ammunition into the Chicago River, loaded baggage

wagons, and marched out his sixty-four men, accompanied by
twenty-seven women and children. They started east, along
the murmuring shore. Then, over a ridge of sand-hills a row
of feathered heads thrust up and a storm of rifle fire pelted
the caravan. In twenty minutes fifty of Heald's company lay
quiet on the sand, the rest were captives. Next day the Indians plundered and burned the fort. There was nothing
but a smoking ruin beside the Chicago River. The third
blow fell at strategic Detroit. After the fall of Mackinac,
Hull feared the British would attack down Lake Huron.
While he waited, they moved troops from Niagara to Fort
Amherstburg at Malden. On August 15th, while the Potawatomis massacred the Dearborn garrison, the British began
shelling Detroit from across the river. That night several
hundred Indians led by Tecumseh in a British general's uniform crossed over and marched up the River Road toward
Fort Detroit. Confused by the threat and frightened because
his supplies had not come through from the south, Hull surrendered Detroit and all of Michigan Territory. With approval of the British, bands of Potawatomis, Shawnees and
Ottawas made camps along the river below Detroit. From
these bases they waged a war of attrition, running off American horses and cattle, rifling corn cribs and granaries, ran-
sacking farmhouses. A band of savages was reported surrounding the key post of Fort Wayne. The whole frontier
seemed lost.

After Hull's surrender William Henry Harrison was
given command of the Northwestern Army. Aiming to recap-
ture Detroit he assembled troops on the Ohio and marched
north to the Maumee. Near present Toledo he built Fort
Meigs in February, 1813, intending it as a base for an attack
on Detroit and Malden. But while he waited for new troops
the British came down the Maumee and besieged him at
Fort Meigs. British batteries were emplaced across the river,
a British gunboat trained its fire on the fort, and Tecumseh
at the head of eight hundred warriors called to Harrison to
come out and give battle. But Harrison was short of ammu-

nition. He offered a gill of whisky for every British cannon
ball that would fit the American swivels. Night after night
soldiers searched in the embankment and outside the walls;
before the siege was over they had claimed a thousand gills
of whisky. Meanwhile reinforcements were marching north
over every road and trail. When they arrived, Harrison was
strong enough to break the siege.

Impatient men wondered why Harrison did not proceed against Detroit. For that undertaking it was essential
that the United States control the Great Lakes, which were
patroled by British gunboats. Harrison's orders were to
await arrival of a fleet which Commodore Oliver Hazard
Perry, with a hundred Rhode Islanders, was building on the
forest shores at Erie, Pennsylvania. Perry had five ships in
the water by the end of May, but it was midsummer before
he got them rigged and armed and over the sand bar into
open water. Eluding the British patrol, he sailed west and
anchored his fleet in Sandusky Bay. There he sent word to
Harrison, camped with his army at Fort Seneca, thirty miles
inland.

On the rainy morning of August 19th Harrison rode
with two of his generals, Duncan McArthur and Lewis Cass,
to Sandusky harbor; with them went twenty friendly Wyandots under old Chief Tarhe, the Crane. Dinghies took them
out to Perry's flagship *Lawrence*. Tarhe and his warriors
clambered over the vessel, marveling at the ranked cannon,
the lofty masts, the massive bulkheads. From the raised bow
the commodore pointed out the other men-of-war in his fleet.
Tarhe, impressed with this demonstration, sent runners to
the Wyandot camp up the Detroit River, urging his people
not to support the British side.

All that cloudy afternoon and late that night Harrison talked with twenty-eight-year-old Commodore Perry. He
suggested Put-in-Bay, between South and Middle Bass Islands, as a protected anchorage, and he agreed to send Perry
some badly needed men. Back at Camp Seneca, Harrison
called for volunteer seamen. Some river boatmen stepped

forward, and a larger number of Kentucky sharpshooters who had never seen a mainsail or a capstan. A week later Perry received a hundred recruits. Then, from the anchorage at Put-in-Bay, he trained his glasses on the head of the lake, waiting for the British fleet to come out of the Detroit River.

Planning an invasion of Canada, Harrison contracted for 300,000 rations, to be delivered on the far side of the Detroit River. Hundreds of beef cattle were being driven toward Detroit by way of Fort Meigs. At noon on September 10th, under a serene blue sky, a rumble of thunder came to troops marching on the Lower Sandusky road. For two hours the thunder rolled and men looked toward Lake Erie with questioning eyes. While they looked the sky went silent. A great battle had begun and ended; the blue sky told them nothing more. Two days later a long-oared boat came splashing up the Sandusky River and a naval officer leaped ashore. He mounted a horse and raced to Fort Seneca. At headquarters he handed Harrison Perry's scribbled message: "We have met the enemy and they are ours—two ships, two brigs, one schooner, and one sloop."

With 4,500 men Harrison began his march toward Canada. General Proctor, the British commander, knowing that the lakes were in American hands, decided to abandon the Detroit River and retreat to York (Toronto). Tecumseh, with rank of brigadier-general and wearing a British medal around his neck, urged him to stand and fight. "When war was declared, our father stood up and gave us the tomahawk, and told us that he was then ready to strike the Americans; and that he would certainly get our lands back that the Americans had taken from us. . . . We therefore wish to remain and fight our enemy, should they make their appearance. . . . We now see our British father preparing to march out his garrison. Father! You have the arms and ammunition which our Great Father sent for his red children. If you intend to go away, give them to us, and you may go, and welcome so far as we are concerned. Our lives are in the

hands of the Master of Life. We are determined to defend
our lands, and if it be his will, we wish to leave our bones
upon them." After an evasive answer, in which General
Proctor declared that he too was ready to leave his bones
upon his land, Tecumseh said to the interpreter: "Tell the
dog that he has too much regard for his carcass to lay his
bones anywhere."

Hastily the British prepared to abandon. On Septem-
ber 20th they set fire to the public buildings at Detroit,
Malden, and Amherstburg, and under a rolling smoke the
British and Indians began their retreat northward to the
Thames River. Perry's men-of-war were now serving as
transports. They carried Harrison's army into the Detroit
River and landed them, with fife and drum corps playing
Yankee Doodle, at the smoking pile of Amherstburg. Plung-
ing after the enemy, Harrison overtook him on the brushy
banks of the Thames. In a frenzied twenty-minute battle the
Indians gave a stout resistance, with Tecumseh's voice ringing above the bang of rifle fire. But dismounted Kentuckians
broke the enemy lines in swamp and thicket, and other
troops pounded on horseback after the fleeing Indians. Most
of the tribesmen got away, but not their leader. Behind them
Tecumseh, the Falling Star, lay dead among the trampled
leaves.

In the quiet after battle American soldiers probed
among the slain redmen. Finding the famed chief's body—so
a stubborn tradition goes—they took gruesome trophies, cutting off the scalp and stripping long bands of skin from the
body. Years later in frontier taverns men told of old soldiers
under Harrison who came home with strips of dried brown
skin that they used for razor strops. Other traditions remember the Falling Star less violently. When he was safely dead,
when his confederacy was shattered and the tribes were
exiled beyond the Mississippi and the lands he fought for
were open to the inrush of a new civilization, Tecumseh became a folk hero, a part of the romantic story of the West.
Biographers told his life story, and artists painted him with

noble bearing and far-seeing eyes. A poetic drama, five acts in florid couplets, unfolded his doomed struggle:

> *Tecumseh has no grave, but eagles dipt*
> *Their rav'ning beaks, and drank his stout heart's tide,*
> *Leaving his bones to whiten where he died.*

It was remembered then that his enemy William Henry Harrison had said of him: "If it were not for the vicinity of the United States, he would, perhaps, be the founder of an Empire that would rival in glory Mexico or Peru."

His brother the Prophet survived the war, receiving a pension from the British government in Canada till 1826 when he went to live with the plains Indians beyond the Mississippi. In 1832 George Catlin, visiting the tribes in Kansas, found him there and painted his portrait—an old man, wrinkled as a pouch of leather, staring with one baleful eye at the white man's world.

After the victory on the Thames Harrison marched his troops back to Detroit and embarked them on Perry's ships, planning to sail north and retake distant Fort Mackinac. But the fleet grounded on shallows near Detroit and that expedition was abandoned. Instead, they sailed down Lake Erie to Niagara, where Harrison received word from the Secretary of War that he was at liberty to visit his family. Harrison had been at odds with his superior, and this was Secretary Armstrong's means of rebuking him. But the nation was on Harrison's side. News of the Battle of the Thames overshadowed all the previous defeats on the frontier. Newspapers throughout the East listed the fruits of that victory: "609 Regulars, 2 Colonels, 4 Majors, 17 Officers of the Line, 12 cannon, 6,000 stand of arms, and stores valued at a million dollars." In New York the city hall was hung with a huge picture of General Harrison surrounded by surrendering Indian chiefs.

On his way home to Cincinnati Harrison visited New

York, Philadelphia and Washington, and at each stop he had a hero's welcome. Then he took the Western Maryland stage for Pittsburgh, passing Christmas day, 1813, on the jouncing journey over the mountains. He reached Cincinnati by river early in January and had a heroic welcome there. But when he joined his family at North Bend he found a saddened household. His father-in-law, John Cleves Symmes, was dying of cancer.

Symmes had brought the first settlement to western Ohio and had watched Cincinnati grow into a prosperous and important place, while his own troubles multiplied. Because he could not meet his obligations to Congress, he could not give clear titles for the Miami lands; for years his settlers were harried by litigation and Symmes became the most hated man on the frontier. In 1811 enemies set fire to his house at North Bend. All his records were burned, and his collection of land payments ceased. He was an ill man then, and he grew worse. He died in February, 1814, poor, lonely, and embittered. But he had heard his son-in-law called "the Washington of the West."

War is followed by treaties. The Treaty of Ghent settled the war with England, and there was another treaty, less famous, on a famous treaty site. On a summer day in 1814 chiefs of the Wyandots, Delawares, Shawnees, Senecas, and Miamis gathered at Greene Ville to meet a treaty commission under William Henry Harrison and Lewis Cass. The tribes renounced their alliance with the British and pledged an end of resistance to the United States. Further treaties followed. In 1817 at the foot of the Maumee Rapids Governor Cass and General Duncan McArthur met chiefs of the Wyandots, Shawnees, and Delawares and bargained for the big area between the old Greene Ville Treaty Line and Michigan Territory. In 1818 came the huge New Purchase, all the heart of Indiana, ceded by the Miamis in return for a sawmill, a gristmill, fifteen thousand dollars in trade goods, and a yearly gift of a hundred and sixty bushels of salt. In

1819 the Kickapoos signed over their range in central Illinois. Now the West was open to the Mississippi, and a great land rush was pouring population in. Indiana became a state in 1817, Illinois in 1818. With Indian warfare at an end, settlement streamed over the Ohio and the Great Lakes. Twenty-six years after the second treaty of Greene Ville, on July 22nd, 1840, thousands crowded into Greenville for a great Treaty Celebration; they were addressed by William Henry Harrison, "Old Tippecanoe," candidate for the Presidency of the United States. Then the frontier had moved on across the Mississippi and the Ohio country tribes were gone from their ancestral lands.

There was to be one more Indian resistance east of the Mississippi. At Harrison's great purchase in St. Louis in 1801, when there were no settlers on the upper Mississippi, some undelegated chiefs had sold the land between the Illinois and Wisconsin rivers. For years that country remained as wild as in the centuries past. But in 1832 a party of Sacs, returning from their winter hunt, found their cornfields freshly plowed by American intruders. Chief Black Hawk appealed to the American officials, who advised him to take his people across the Mississippi. Black Hawk was not a figure like Tecumseh; he was a short, slight, quiet-spoken man of sixty. But he sounded like Tecumseh when he spoke of fighting for the homeland of his people. It was a brief and hopeless fight. The Wisconsin tribes did not rally, and the Sacs, men, women, and children, were cornered by United States troops at the mouth of Bad Ax Creek on the Mississippi. Some plunged into the mile-wide river, but only a few crawled up, exhausted, on the Iowa shore.

In that same summer of 1832 the last remnant of the proud Shawnees were moved from Ohio to new reservations beyond the Mississippi. With an escort of the U.S. Army they left their reservation on the Auglaize River and made a final camp at Tecumseh's Point on Greenville Creek. For two days they stayed there, recalling the promises of the

Prophet, twenty-five years before, remembering Tecumseh's dream of a sovereign Indian nation. They took a farewell of the Greenville graves, of the woods and prairies. Then they packed their wagons, shouldered their bundles, and filed away, leaving their land to the white man's future.

PART II

*TOMAHAWK RIGHTS
AND LAND WARRANTS*

CHAPTER THREE

VIEW FROM A BLOCKHOUSE

The fame of Ohio having gone into almost every nation upon earth . . .

—JOHN EYRE: *The Christian Spectator, being a Journey from England to Ohio, Two Years in that State.*

FOR TWENTY years Fort Washington stood above the huddled roofs on the river bank at Cincinnati. Somewhat larger than a city square, with twenty-foot blockhouses rising at the corners and rows of barracks within its rugged palisade, it was a stronghold in the western country. After the peace at Greene Ville there was no need for a fort on the Ohio. It would be razed in 1808, and twenty years later the old drill ground would be occupied by another famous building of the frontier; it became the site of Mrs. Trollope's fantastic hall with Turkish domes and spires rising above the roofs of Cincinnati. But in 1795 the log fort, on rising ground apart from the taverns, shops, and cabins along the river front, housed the military and civil authority of the Territory. It was the Pentagon, the Capitol, and the White House of the West.

On a raw January day in 1790 Governor Arthur St. Clair had arrived in Cincinnati—a tall, solid-striding man with a sternly handsome face and shadowed eyes. He carried his papers up the steep and frozen road that would become Broadway and took up quarters in a blockhouse of the fort. From there, in October, 1791, he led his regiments north into Indian country; six weeks later he brought the survivors back. Under the sloping roof with rows of portholes looking out at the cold river and the wintry hills, he wrote a bleak report to the Secretary of War: "Yesterday afternoon the remains of the army under my command got back to this place, and I now have the painful task to give you an account . . ."; and there he packed his records to face an inquiring committee of Congress. That was the beginning. For ten years he came and went between Fort Washington and Philadelphia, contending with political enemies in Congress, vetoing acts of the headstrong Territorial legislature, denouncing squatters who rushed into the western valleys. In that bare blockhouse room while a bugle shrilled in the compound and songs of flatboatmen drifted up from the river, he must sometimes have remembered his arduous and adventurous youth.

A native of the rocky coast of Scotland, descendant of an old and distinguished family, Arthur St. Clair left his medical studies in London to join the Duke of Cumberland's "Royal American Regiment" for service on the Canadian frontier. He fought under Lord Jeffrey Amherst at the siege of Louisburg and beside General Wolfe at the storming of Quebec. In 1767, at the age of thirty-three, he took command of the Pennsylvania station of Fort Ligonier, an outpost built by General Forbes on his road to Fort Pitt. On a grant of a thousand acres he built a gristmill and an iron furnace and put six hundred acres under cultivation. Life was secure at Ligonier, but in stormy 1775 he chose the hazardous American side and became a colonel in the Revolutionary army. His first assignment was to raise a regiment to serve in Canada; he arrived at Quebec, with his memories of triumph, barely in time to cover the American retreat. As brigadier general he served with Washington in New Jersey, shared the bleak winter at Valley Forge, and finally marched six regiments through seven hundred miles of hostile and desolate country to support General Greene (whose name would be given to Fort Greene Ville) in the Carolinas. After eight years in the Revolution he had lost much of his Pennsylvania property, but he was elected to the Continental Congress. As its president he led the Congressional session in 1787 which created the Northwest Territory. Appointed Territorial governor he came down the Ohio to Marietta in the summer of 1788. A year and a half later, to be nearer the center of the huge domain, he moved his headquarters to Fort Washington. It was his capital for twelve hard and lonely years.

Back and forth St. Clair journeyed over a territory five times as big as Scotland. Twice he made the long trip to Illinois to organize government in the old French settlements at Kaskaskia and Cahokia. Many times he traveled by river boat and horseback to Philadelphia, a hard month's journey, and back again to his blockhouse at Cincinnati. In that square bare room, with the sounds of a drill company coming up from the parade, he carefully kept his records and made his reports. Back in Pennsylvania his property was going to ruin, and his wife, troubled by a darkening melancholia, was cared for by his younger children. He saw other men grow rich on the frontier, while he became poor. St. Clair was a strict, straight man of strong ambition and deep disappointments. His career was his only comfort, and it ended in defeat.

From the narrow windows, three on each side of the low-roofed blockhouse, Governor St. Clair could see the curving Ohio with the Kentucky hills beyond, a huddle of buildings along the landing and dirt streets gashing the river bank,

and a system of burial and fortification mounds left by a vanished race on a plateau beneath the ring of inland hills. His
portholes looked at past, present, and future. For the past he
had only a passing wonder; the present he was troubled by;
the future he did not understand though he saw it coming.

When he first arrived at Fort Washington he changed
the name of the crude settlement from bizarre Losantiville
(*L* for Licking, *os* for mouth, *anti,* opposite—the town opposite the mouth of the Licking; it had been christened by a
wandering Pennsylvania schoolmaster) to plainer Cincinnati, in honor of the Society of Revolutionary Officers. He
saw it grow, season by season. Fourteen miles west lay the
settlement of North Bend, which John Cleves Symmes expected to make the metropolis of the Miami country. The
first troops sent to defend the Miami settlements had landed
at North Bend. But the commanding officer looked at the
black-eyed wife of a settler who soon moved to Losantiville.
He followed her there, and began the building of Fort Washington. So a roving-eyed woman made Cincinnati the military center of the region, and Symmes watched a city grow
over the hundred and twenty-five acres that he had sold to
Matthias Denman for a hundred and twenty-five dollars. It
was a boom town in 1795, flatboats lining the landing, warehouses sprawled on the bank, soldiers and settlers thronging
the taverns, newcomers asking the price of town lots and
Miami valley land.

By 1795 Governor St. Clair could look beyond the
curve of the river and the lift of the hills. He had traveled up
and down the great valley, rowing in an open boat over the
long Ohio, riding horseback over the rough trails. He knew
the dark interior where game trails led to the licking places
and Indian paths threaded the forest. From reports of scouts
and traders he knew the Indian towns, the salt licks trampled by bear, deer and panther, the portage paths between
the rivers. But it was a huge, wild, unmapped country,
and no man could grasp it all.

The Ohio country began in the diminishing ridges of the Alleghenies and went on vaguely to the back of beyond. There was no boundary between the Alleghenies and the Mississippi, though somewhere out there the Ohio country became the Wabash country and the Wabash country gave way to the prairie lands of the Illinois. The Ohio River bordered it all and Ohio was a far-extending name. It meant the first western wilderness, the wild new land beyond the mountains.

It was a silent, somber land, without history and without memory except for the tales of explorers and traders who had followed Indian trails to the scattered camps. All its traditions were yet to come. Wolves were howling in the woods where the Ohio capital would stand on the upper reaches of the Scioto. Indians were fishing in Sandusky Bay and pitching their camps on the Portage River. Beaver were gnawing trees on the Cuyahoga where Cleveland would grow above Lake Erie. Indian signs on slate-smooth beech trunks were the only writing in a country where Spencer would teach penmanship, McGuffey would compile his readers and Ray his arithmetic. Darkness hung over Milan Creek where a boy named Thomas Edison would watch the whale oil lights of wheat schooners, and passenger pigeons streamed over the forks of the Miami where the Wright brothers would experiment with flight.

The geography of North America is more orderly than that of any other continent, with coastal mountain ranges framing a vast interior basin. The Ohio valley, the most accessible part of the interior, soon became a tamed and prosperous region, but it was first known to the world as a remote wilderness. In London in 1813 when Lord Byron learned that his poems were in the Coonskin Library—five shelves of books purchased with coonskins—he wrote in his diary: "These are the first tidings that have sounded like fame to my ears—to be read on the banks of the Ohio." It was like a writer of today knowing that he is read on the Yukon.

Ohio was a name for danger and promise and the lure of far-off places.

The Ohio River began full-grown, where the muddy Monongahela joined the clear strong current of the Allegheny under the hills of Pittsburgh. It ended in the Mississippi, still a thousand miles from the sea. Like American destiny it flowed westward; more than any other feature of the continent it served the national destiny.

In 1795 just four settlements marked the long course of the Ohio. Marietta, built by New England adventurers in 1788, was a fortified town at the point where the Muskingum joins the Ohio two hundred miles from Pittsburgh. Another hundred miles downstream lay Gallipolis, a colony of French émigrés dancing minuets on a puncheon floor and trying to forget the wilderness around them; this huddle of barracks on the river bank was as unlikely a settlement as ever came to the American frontier. A hundred and fifty miles beyond the homesick Frenchmen stood Massie's Station, an alert and risky settlement of Kentucky woodsmen brought across the Ohio by shrewd Nathaniel Massie. At the mouth of the Little Miami were the neighboring villages of Columbia and Losantiville, later joined in Cincinnati, with Symmes' tiny colony of North Bend a few miles farther on. Four clusters of huts and cabins in four hundred miles of grand and silent river valley!

A hundred miles below Cincinnati the silent river grew loud, racing through a rocky, island-studded channel; only after the spring melting and the autumn rains would that swirling water carry heavy traffic. Here at the "Falls of the Ohio" the town of Louisville was spreading on the Kentucky shore, but the north bank was empty all the way to the Mississippi, save for the occasional shack of a squatter or a hunter's lean-to camp. Far in the west lay the old French settlements, left from the years of French trade and evangelism in that country. Vincennes on the Wabash, Kaskaskia and Cahokia near the Mississippi were outposts of the French dream of empire in America. Now they dozed on the prairie,

the half-breed farmers tending their ribbon fields and traders waiting for Indian peltry. Put all the settlements together in 1795, American and French, and they make a few
thousand people in a huge, wild land. You have to look close
to see them at all.

Forest and prairie paths linked the scattered Indian
towns—Pickawillany near the present Piqua on the Great
Miami, Old Chillicothe on the Little Miami near the site of
future Dayton, Sandusky on the big bay that breaks Lake
Erie's western shore, Tippecanoe on the upper Wabash,
Peoria on the Illinois. These were clusters of brush huts
with men lounging in the shade and women hacking at the
cornfields, children playing with broken arrows and dogs
sniffing at scraps of deerhide on the ground. The huts would
be burned and the tribesmen driven on, but the names have
stayed on the map of the country, smoldering like old campfires.

The forest was dark and endless in Ohio; it held
many openings in Indiana, giving way to grassland in the
country of the Illinois. The Great Prairie broke upon travelers like a rolling, windswept ocean. A hunter or trader, a
squatter or settler stood there at the edge of a new wilderness, his eyes forgetting the forest gloom in endless space
and light. The grass went on for two hundred and fifty
miles, a waving plain broken only by thickets of bottom
timber, to the Old Big Deep Strong River, the Mississippi.

In those years, with swamps feeding countless little
creeks and forest hemming the valleys, the side rivers were
navigable deep into the interior. Squatters and settlers poled
up the Muskingum, the Scioto, the Miami, the Whitewater,
the Wabash. Before 1820 hundreds of flatboats were built
in the river towns, loaded with corn, wheat, pork, whisky,
apples, and floated down to the Ohio and the Mississippi. In
the early years every land-seeker was a water-seeker too.
Squatter, settler, or town-site speculator, he looked for running water.

In 1780 it was all Indian country—Delawares living

in the woods and meadows of the Muskingum and the Tuscarawas, Shawnees roving the Scioto valley, Wyandots holding the Maumee and the Sandusky, Miamis ranging the
region of the Miami and the upper Wabash, Weas and Piankeshaws in the lower Wabash valley, Kickapoos, Potawatomis,
and Chippewas in the grasslands of the Illinois. But ambi-
tions which the Indians could not understand had come to
the interior of America. While seasons changed in the Ohio
woods, while December whitened the prairie and April
turned it green, their land had changed ownership three
times, from French to British to American, and still the
tribes were there like foxes in a forest that men buy and sell.
The Indians had no idea of private ownership of land; to
them the earth was like the air, necessary, plentiful and free.
Piece by piece they ceded it in "purchases" and treaties, not
knowing that the country would be fenced and bounded
and their ancestral hunting grounds would become the white
man's possession. They did not understand that land could be
bought and sold like a horse or a pile of peltry.

The kings of England knew next to nothing about the
geography of America. Though explorers had described far
journeys into the interior wilderness, the Tudor and Stuart
rulers still recalled Balboa's account of seeing both oceans
from the heights of Panama. In the king's grants to the colonies tracts of land fronting on the Atlantic were extended
across the continent. Six of the early colonies were given
"sea to sea" estates; Massachusetts, Connecticut, Virginia,
North Carolina, South Carolina and Georgia all had, by
charter, a coastline on the Pacific. In reality these colonies
had three fixed boundaries; the fourth was left for history to
decide. After the Revolution, when American territory extended to the Mississippi, Massachusetts, Connecticut, and
Virginia asserted ownership of lands in the Northwest, and
New York claimed all the country once dominated by the
Iroquois nations. But the small colonies without western
claims argued that the interior had been wrested from the

common enemy by the revolutionary struggle of all thirteen states; it should therefore be held as common property in a national domain. After long and strenuous debate the states agreed to cede western land claims for the common good. So the ousting of the Indians became a national action rather than an effort of the separate states, and the western territory was brought under a national land system.

The vaguest and vastest charter boundaries were those of Virginia—"from two hundred miles north to two hundred miles south of Old Point Comfort, up into the land, throughout from sea to sea west and northwest." The Old Dominion also had the strongest military claim to western land; Virginia colonists had settled Kentucky and George Rogers Clark had led Virginia troops against the British north of the Ohio. In yielding claim to all the Northwest, Virginia retained the tract between the Scioto and Little Miami rivers as a Military District to fulfill the bounties promised her soldiers. Connecticut, before forgetting western claims, withheld a Western Reserve of nearly four million acres along the shore of Lake Erie beginning at the Pennsylvania boundary. Some of this rich land went to sufferers from British raids in Connecticut during the Revolution; the rest produced a school fund for the state. Massachusetts ceded without reservation the lands claimed by charter beyond the western border of New York, and New York ceased all claim to territory beyond its own boundaries. North and South Carolina and Georgia, "for the benefit of all the states," gave up claim to lands extending to the Mississippi. To the federal government the states had yielded an area larger than all the thirteen colonies. The nation had room to grow in.

Of that vast domain the region north and west of the Ohio was nearest to eastern population and most tempting to settlers and promoters. In the Ordinances of 1784, 1785, and 1787 Congress provided for its survey, development and government, and for the eventual creation of western states. The land must be bought from the Indians and surveyed into uniform townships; then the doors would be open to settlement. Whether the wilderness would be used to pay the national debt or to provide opportunity for restless people, the future would determine.

St. Clair came with great expectations to the West, arriving on a high summer day in 1788 at Marietta, where forty-eight colonists from New England were building the first town north of the Ohio. In 1784 and 1785 the tribes had ceded land on the upper river, but they forgot the treaties when they saw settlers rushing in. St. Clair soon had the Indian Wars on his hands. As military commander he tried in 1791 to force the tribes north from the mid-Ohio valley. His defeat left the Indians dominant in the country, and for four years settlers hugged the few forts on the river. After his disaster St. Clair was exonerated by a committee of Congress, because of a failure of his quartermaster's and paymaster's departments—during a half year's service his sullen troops had but once signed the payroll for their three dollars a month. But General St. Clair then resigned from the army, relinquishing military authority and confining his duties to the civil office of Governor; he did not even attend the treaty council at Fort Greene Ville. An agent of Federalist policies, he was upheld by the influential Federalists in Congress.

For fourteen years he governed the Territory while the tribes were pushed out of their hunting valleys and settlers poured in. He knew the vastness of the West but he never grasped its destiny or understood its people. He objected to the creation of new counties, wanting to keep a tight hold on the Territorial government. When Ohio was approaching sufficient population for statehood, St. Clair put himself squarely in its way, proposing to splinter the territory into smaller units with too little populace for political status. In 1801 the Jeffersonians tried to oust him from office; with Federalist support he survived that threat. But not for long. At the Ohio Constitutional Convention of 1802 he questioned the validity of the Ohio Enabling Act of Congress. This was St. Clair's last stubborn stand. When his

speech was reported in Washington, President Jefferson removed him from the governorship. By that time he was as
beaten and bewildered as the Indians.

In a summary of his life St. Clair recalled his ambition as governor of the Territory. It was a colonial view; he
saw the West as a foreign country, remote from the nation
and subordinate to it, and he could not justify the willful-
ness of its settlers.

> From my long absence I lost all that influence at
> home [in Pennsylvania] which had once been very con-
> siderable, and was ruining myself in the public service
> abroad [in Ohio]. . . . When the migration from the
> United States to that country began . . . [my difficul-
> ties] were much increased; for the people being at liberty
> to settle where they pleased, their establishments were
> formed in every part from one end of it to the other, a
> distance of one thousand miles, in which there were
> neither roads nor intermediate places of accommodation;
> notwithstanding which I was under the necessity of visit-
> ing them all very frequently, first to put them in order
> and provide for the administration of justice among
> them, and afterwards to keep them in order, as from the
> influx of new settlers they were daily changing, and re-
> quired a great deal of attention to keep them in habits
> of obedience to the laws, and to prevent them from de-
> generating into savages. . . . To the establishment of
> that country which was by me led up from thirty men
> (the first American adventurers) to upwards of sixty
> thousand in about fourteen years, the government never
> contributed one cent, except the salary, which was not
> equal to my traveling expenses for a good many years.

St. Clair had not grabbed land, though land was all
around him; he was not a profiteer. Neither had he grasped
the headstrong independence of the first national frontier.
He was a man of order in a turbulent country. "Mine was a

laudable ambition; that of becoming the father of a country, and for laying the foundations for the happiness of millions then unborn." But the willful westerners did not want a father, and they sent the humiliated governor back to his ruined estate in Pennsylvania.

He had a long career in the New World: triumph with Wolfe at Quebec, darkness with Washington at Valley Forge and victory at Yorktown, honor and influence in the Continental Congress, authority over the huge western domain. But America had changed faster than he could change. Disowned by the region he had served with his best abilities, he went back to the old station of Ligonier on the busy Pennsylvania Road, an impoverished and broken man.

Debt and misfortune cornered him there. He had to sell his home, The Hermitage, his mill and iron furnace; even his personal possessions went to pay his creditors. At seventy-six, with an invalid wife and children and grandchildren under his care, he was penniless. "They left me a few books of my classical library and the bust of Paul Jones which he had sent me from Europe, for which I was very grateful." Four years later the federal government voted him a pension of sixty dollars a month, but a creditor intercepted it. Then Pennsylvania made him an annuity of three hundred dollars and the old man built a cabin on the rough slope of Chestnut Ridge on land belonging to the widow of his son. There he ran a tavern, selling corn meal and dried apples to travelers on the way to Pittsburgh. Old friends and old adversaries—William Henry Harrison, Lewis Cass, Henry Clay—pulled up their horses at his door. The old man, still tall and straight, his hair clubbed back with a piece of ribbon and his worn waistcoat brushed and clean, received them with a governor's dignity.

He lived till 1818—the year when the first steamboat stirred the bright waters of Lake Erie, when eight-year-old Abe Lincoln whittled pegs for his mother's coffin in the woods of Indiana, when lonely old George Rogers Clark died in his cabin across the Ohio from Louisville, when Illi-

nois became a state and settlers bought three million acres
in the western land offices. In January of that year Congressman William Henry Harrison proposed a federal pension of
a thousand dollars a year for Arthur St. Clair. The motion
was lost, though Congress finally renewed his allowance of
sixty dollars a month. The old Governor did not live to receive it. On a summer morning he started to town for supplies, driving a strong young horse not used to harness. The
horse ran away with him, as the Ohio frontiersmen had done
twenty years before. He was killed when his wagon crashed
over in the rutted road.

CHAPTER FOUR

WITNESS TREE

> In establishing the township and sectional corners, a post is
> first planted at the point of intersection; then on the tree
> nearest the post, and standing within the section intended
> to be designated, is numbered with the marking iron the
> range, township, and number of the section.
>
> —*The Ohio Gazetteer*

O N THE 22nd of September, 1785, a weather-lined man
of fifty-five stood on the far boundary of Pennsylvania
sighting to the west. Thomas Hutchins, Geographer of the
United States, was about to run the first section lines in
America. He was a far-ranging man. In his youth he had
gone West to the wars; he became an officer under General
Bouquet, laid out Fort Pitt at the forks of the Ohio, and
explored the western valleys of the Alleghenies. In 1766 he
began a mapping and exploring journey down the Ohio, not-
ing all its tributaries and the overland trails leading into the
interior. His map, estimating the length of the river at 1164
miles, and the accompanying description of the country gave

62

the first clear and accurate account of the great valley. In London ten years later, in the revolutionary weather of 1776, he resigned his British commission and was imprisoned. He escaped to America, by way of France, and in 1781 Congress appointed him Geographer of the national domain. When the Ordinance of 1785 called for a survey of the Northwest Territory, Hutchins assembled his deputy-surveyors, with their ax-men, chain-carriers, and pack horsemen, and began the task of mapping a wilderness so that every plot of ground could be measured, located, and identified.

Congress had ordered a survey of the public domain into townships six miles square, each township containing thirty-six sections of six hundred forty acres. Eventually most of the country between the Ohio and the Lakes would become public domain, but in 1785 only the land along the upper reaches of the Ohio had been ceded by the tribes. Here was the first tract to be surveyed, a district of seven ranges beginning at the intersection of the Ohio River with the Pennsylvania border. Townships were to be numbered from the river northward; a tier of townships comprised a range, and ranges were numbered westward from the boundary of Pennsylvania. After survey the land was to be sold at not less than a dollar an acre in minimum lots of one square mile.

Survey went slowly in that dense and broken country. Through tangled woods the ax-men chopped out a line for the surveyor's vision. The chain-men, scrambling across ravines and over blowdowns, splashing through bogs and wading rivers, measured the distance and noted the location of streams, lakes, swamps and Indians trails. The surveyor entered the tallies in his notebook, along with details of soil, timber, running water, signs of coal, iron, or salt, and all plants or roots which might offer nourishment or healing. At sundown, stung by insects and raked by briars, the men came ravenous to camp. Another day, another dollar for the surveyor, and some new witness trees to mark tomorrow.

With mosquitoes swarming from the swamps and

thickets bristling on the hillsides it was a hard country. It was
also hostile. When the Indians attacked—seeming unaware
of the Treaty of Fort McIntosh—Hutchins got his crews together and fell back to the Ohio. But he had run his "Geographer's Line" forty-two miles into the Ohio woods, and he
had enough knowledge of the country to send Congress a report on the public domain. ". . . For the distance of Forty
six Chains and Eighty six links . . . the land is remarkably
rich, with a deep black Mould, free from Stone. . . . The
whole of the above described Land is too rich to produce
Wheat, the aforementioned rising ground being excepted,
but it is well adapted for Indian Corn, Tobacco, Hemp,
Flax, Oats, &c and every species of Garden Vegetables, it
abounds with great quantities of Pea Vine, Grass, and nu-
tritious Weeds of which Cattle are very fond, and on which
they soon grow fat. . . . For twenty two Chains and thirty
seven links further than the completion of one Mile, the
land is extraordinary good, and in some places it is too rich
for Wheat, where fine Meadow may be made. . . . At Fourteen Chains and forty links further the Line reached the top
of a steep narrow Ridge, its perpendicular heighth nearly
170 feet, the East side, like the East side of almost all the
other Ridges in this part of the Country, is very fertile, several parts of it is entirely faced with sand stone, some very
large of an excellent grit, and shaded with Oaks, Hickory,
Poplar, Mulberry, Chestnut, Dogwood, Grape Vines, Pea
Vines, Spikenard, sweet Brier, Rasberry Brier, and Golden
Rod, the latter when timely used, and properly applied has
been found very efficacious in curing the bite of the most
venemous Snake. . . . Thirteen chains further than the last
mentioned distance there is level land, the Line to this place
has a gradual descent along the side of the Ridge, over a thin
Soil, with yellow Clay, fit for Bricks, a few inches below its
surface, through a thicket of scrubby Dogwood, Oak, Chestnut, Aspen, and Hickory saplins and bushes, almost without
a single Tree, the whole of this distance was cut through for

the Chain carriers to pass. The Soil is nearly similar with that last described with the addition of a good deal of Sand stone."

The notes were full of references to oak, hickory, walnut, chestnut, a reassuring detail as the nut-bearing trees were considered a sure sign of the best soil. "The land between the above-mentioned distance and this Hill, is abundantly fertile, well adapted to the cultivation of Indian Corn, Wheat &c and is covered with Black and White Oaks, Hickory, Ash, Black Walnut, Mulberry, Shoemack and Grape Vines, and in several places it is tolerably free from brush or underwood."

In the winter of 1785-6 this exact and detailed report was zealously circulated by agents of the Ohio Company, then organizing in Boston. Other prospectors and speculators found it heady reading.

The following summer, 1786, when survey was resumed in the Seven Ranges, one of the men in Hutchins' company was young John Matthews of Braintree, Massachusetts, a nephew of General Rufus Putnam. As a fifteen-year-old boy he had served under his uncle in the Revolution; since then he had learned the science of surveying between terms of school-teaching in a New England town. Now he came out to the western country, a youth of twenty, alert and curious, recording his impressions in a detailed diary.

John Matthews arrived at the surveyors' camp on the east bank of the Ohio on July 31st, while the crew was waiting for troops to escort them to the field. After two weeks the soldiers arrived with some wagon loads of flour and a file of beef cattle. They crossed the river to the Indian side and while the troops fanned out in the woods the surveyors began running lines on the second range of townships. Matthews had a shrewd eye for terrain and soil. "Wednesday [August] 16th: Cloudy morning 9 A.M.—Decamped 11 arrivd at the end of the 1st raing [range] the land uneven but good for wheat rye Indian corn flax hemp &c. likewise in-

numerable specias of weads which make excelent food for
horses run this day on the E. and W. line 48 chain the land
in general good for wheat rye flax &c. except the tops of
some rid[g]es which is dry but good wheat land. Cloudy the
remainder of the Day."

Like any field man he had a close look at the country.
He knew its brush and briars, its flies, gnats, and mosquitoes,
its sun and rain, its stony slopes and boggy hollows. ". . . half
past 7, A.M. began to survey the 2d 20 chains of the 3d
mile through rich level land the timber all kinds of Oak
hickory Dogwood &c 3d 20 chains good wheat land and
Desending to the N.W. and rising ground on the Southward
which is light-soil'd except a bottom 8 rod wide with a brook
running through it and will make very good mowing the 1st
20 chains of the 4th mile a little desending to N.E. and
very rich the timber all kinds oak and hickory growing very
tall and will produce all kinds of grain likewise clover and
all other kinds of upland grass in the greatest abundance the
2d 20 chains poor and stony the 3d 20 chains level and
good wheat land."

He also learned the West's hostility. "Monday [Sep-
tember] 18th Foggy morning . . . General Tupper began
his raing and our camp moved to another large Branch of
the Tusarawas called Nineshilling After we had run 3/4 of a
mile an express arrived from Majr Hamtramchs Camp at
Little Bever and brought information that the Indians was
assembling at the Shawnees Towns and Intended making a
general attackt on the Surveyors. Capt Hutchins and Gen'l
Tupper thought it unsafe to procede any further. Information was immediately sent to Capt Morris who had got about
one mile and a half on the West boundary of the 7th raing and
we all returned to the ground from we left this morning
where we tarryed this night."

At this alarm Hutchins pulled his crews together and
under a tighter military cover proceeded to run the third
and fourth ranges. With their hunters called in from the
woods the surveyors shared the scant army mess—Major

Hamtranck's commissary was reduced to a few barrels of flour and eight scrawny bullocks.

At the end of October, with cold rains bringing down the last yellow leaves of the hickories and maples, Indians stole their horses. While the surveyors went on with Range Five the troops threw up a rude blockhouse. "The upland we run through the Soil is moist and stony fit for pasturing on our return to Camp we found the Block house in such order as to be a good shelter in case of an attack from the Indians."

John Matthews came out of the woods in November, having seen plenty of Indian sign but no actual Indians, and passed some weeks among friendly settlers on the Virginia side of the river. One cold day he sat in a shed husking corn with the convivial neighbors. "The inspiring Juce of rye had inlivened their Imaginations and given their Tongues such an exact ballance that they moved with the greatest alacrity while relating Scenes of Boxing Wrestling Hunting &c. at dusk of evening the corn was finished and the Company retired to the House where many of them took such hearty draughts of the generous liquor as quite deprived them of the use of their limbs. Some quarreled some sung and others laughed and the whole display'd a Scene more diverting than edifying at 10 o'clock in the evening all that could walk went home and left three or four round the fire huging the Whiskey Bottle and arguing very obstinately on Religion at which I left them and went to bed."

That winter he took a job as storekeeper at Fort Steuben, later Steubenville, Ohio, and sent parts of his diary back to New England, where his notes were read by agents of the Ohio Company to prospective shareholders and recruits. Meanwhile, a week before Christmas, John Matthews wrote in his journal: "This day I am twenty-one years of age and Free by the Laws of my Country. I am Near Six hundred miles from my native town and poor enough the whole pitance that I can call my own does not amount to more than 50 dollars but while I have my health I feal no anxiety about geting a living and hope to support by an honest Industery that Independancy of Spirit and Circumstances which is requisite to Happiness."

It was easy enough, or at least there was room enough, for a young man to get a living in the western country. There were millions of acres of new land to survey; soon there would be new towns to settle and a new society to grow with. After that first strenuous season in the Seven Ranges John Matthews was a confirmed Westerner. He surveyed for the Ohio Company along the down-curving river and ran townships in the United States Military Tract in the heart of the future state. Out of his twenty-seven dollars a month as an Ohio Company surveyor he bought a share, in partnership, in the Company. In 1820 he was elected to the Ohio Senate.

While the surveyors blazed their township lines and marked witness trees at the intersections, they sometimes came on beech or oak trunks already slashed with a squatter's hatchet. Their lines ran past lean-tos, three-sided camps and poplar cabins, over zig-zag fences and across fields of girdled trees. Survey, then sale, then settlement was the plan of Congress; the Ordinance described a logical and lawful process—the purchase of Indian title, the laying off of townships and sections, the sale of mile-square units in government offices at Pittsburgh and Philadelphia. In that orderly way the gate to the public domain would be opened and occupation would spread from one settled township to the next. But the frontiersmen saw no gate and they couldn't wait for word from Congress. They saw wild land, wild and empty save for roving Indians, and they wanted to live beyond the smell of a neighbor's chimney smoke. So the squatters came, floating down the river on rafts and scows, driving scrabbly pack horses through the woods, leading ragged families to a dry creek bed, with a hatchet ready to mark the trees where they found a trickle of spring water on a south hillside. This was a tomahawk claim, four corner blazes around the hut and cornfield a man would have; these were his witness trees. He had the right of discovery, of possession, of cultivation and improvement. He claimed squatter's rights.

Legal settlement could not begin until the first survey was recorded in 1788, but already the squatters were dug in. In 1784 General Harmar sent a detail of twenty troops to "drive off persons attempting to settle on the lands of the United States." They found squatter colonies on Little Beaver Creek, Yellow Creek, and Mingo Bottom, and on the Ohio shore across from Wheeling. The troops destroyed a few cabins—and the squatters promptly built again. At stronger settlements, where the squatters faced him with cocked rifles, the young ensign read his instructions in a loud voice and got a vague promise that the squatters would move on. On forest paths and river landings the soldiers tacked up their elaborately worded "No Trespassing," but back at Fort McIntosh Ensign John Armstrong made a glum report: "Notwithstanding they have seen and read those instructions they are moving to the unsettled countries by forties and fifties. From the best information I could receive, there are at the falls of the Hawk Hawkin [Big Hocking] upwards of three hundred families, and at the Muskingum a number equal. At Meravens Town [the Moravian mission to the Delawares] there are several families, and more than fifteen hundred on the rivers Miami and Scioto. From Wheeling to that place there is scarcely one bottom on the river but has one or more families living thereon."

Other expeditions went down the river to chase the squatters out of the woods. In 1785 Commissioner Richard Butler gave them permission to save their crops but insisted that they vacate the country before the next season. He reported that the squatters complied "with a degree of reluctance" to his orders, and he noted "they are fond of construing every indulgence in the most favorable and extensive manner for themselves, and seem to hint that saving their crops means feeding their cattle on the ground the ensuing winter, and of course giving them a footing in the Spring, and so on."

In 1785 a star-shaped stockade was built at the mouth of the Muskingum, across from the future site of Marietta. This was Fort Harmar, and its mission was not to repel Indians but to drive out squatters and hold back settlement till the lands could be surveyed and offered for sale. But the squatters were a more stubborn breed than any tribesmen, and quite as lawless. "I do certify," one of them announced to his fellow squatters and the world, "that all mankind agreeable to every constitution formed in America, have an undoubted right to pass into every vacant country, and there to form their constitution, and that from the confederation of the whole United States, Congress is not empowered to forbid them, neither is Congress empowered from that confederation to make any sale of the uninhabited lands to pay the public debt."

Most of the illegal settlers didn't bother to certify anything, but merely made their tomahawk marks on the timber. They came on year after year, poking into new country, the Hocking valley, the Scioto, the Little Miami and the Great Miami. In 1796 Governor St. Clair ordered intruders to withdraw from the public lands; six months later he observed that the countryside west of the Miami was dotted with the "hutts" of these trespassers. Many times a surveyor in wild country smelled woodsmoke and peered through thickets at a cabin with children playing round the woodpile and a man girdling trees to enlarge his cornfield. In every district warrant-holding settlers with lawful claim to the land found tomahawk claims already healing on their trees. When James Kilbourne led his friends to a townsite on the Olentangy in 1803, he found cornfields along the river and squatters' huts on the hillside. In the region west of the Scioto land sales lagged though men and families kept settling there. They ran their hogs and cattle in the woods, cleared a patch for corn, cut staves, hoop poles, and tanner's bark from the public lands. Dr. John Locke, one of Ohio's pioneer geologists, described these "bark cutters." "They erect a cabin toward the head of some ravine, collect the chestnut-oak bark from the neighboring hill-tops, drag it on sleds to points accessible by wagons, where they sell it for perhaps two dollars a cord to the wagoner. . . . Besides this common trespass, the squatter helps himself out by hunting deer and coons, and, it is said, occasionally taking a sheep or a hog, the loss of which may very reasonably be charged to the wolves. The poor families of *the bark cutters* often exhibit the very picture of improvidence. There begins to be a fear among the inhabitants that speculators may be tempted to purchase up these waste lands and deprive them of their present 'range' and lumber. The speculator must still be a non-resident, and could hardly protect his purchase."

The squatters were rebels within the Revolution, defying Congress and the United States Army as the colonies had defied the king. Wary and prolific, they lived like gypsies outside the law. They chose the wilderness for the purest reason, not because it would increase in value but because it set them free. They worried the lawyers, the land agents, the speculators and the judges, but they had one friend in Congress; Thomas Scott of Pennsylvania observed that the wilderness frontier "requires men of enterprising, violent, nay discontented and turbulent spirits. Such always are our first settlers in the ruthless and savage wild; they serve as pioneers to clear the way for the more laborious and careful farmer."

Meanwhile surveyors were roving the Scioto country, where the Virginia Military District was opened in 1790. Virginia, with claims to endless territory beyond the mountains, had been extravagant with her western lands. In colonial times the government had offered four hundred acres to any-one who would clear a plot of ground, build a cabin, and raise a crop of corn; a settler was also given preëmption right to purchase a thousand acres adjoining his improved land. At the same time great tracts of Kentucky wilderness were sold to Virginia gentlemen. As though the domain were boundless and everlasting, the colony issued quantities of land warrants, some by military authority and some by the treasury. Soon much of Kentucky was doubly appropriated, and confusion was increased by the indiscriminate system of survey which allowed any warrant-holder to locate his acreage for himself. The result was thirty years of disputing over land claims.

Before relinquishing its claim on the Northwest Territory, Virginia reserved a tract of Military Lands north of the Ohio, extending between the Scioto and Little Miami rivers. This was the old Shawnee hunting grounds, a well-watered and richly wooded country. In 1790, when Congress was convinced that public lands in Kentucky were insufficient to honor the military warrants of Virginia's veterans, the Virginia Military Tract was opened to claimants. Immediately the eyes of warrant-holders and of land speculators turned toward the Scioto.

Into this wild country in 1790 came Nathaniel Massie. He was already, at twenty-six, a veteran surveyor and locater of lands. In 1783 he had come home to Goochland County, Virginia, from the war, nineteen years old, lean and hardened by the Revolutionary campaigns. He gathered his chain and compass, level and transit, and rode off to the western country. Kentucky with its confused and conflicting land claims had endless work for a surveyor.

The Kentucky lands had been claimed by a primitive method of irregular and indiscriminate location, and young Massie had a rigorous initiation into his profession. Here is one of his early assignments: "I wish you to survey the entries that are on the heads of Grassy creek, in the name of Howard Lewis. If you find where Creuss was buried at a camp, you can easily find the entries. You must take the marked way from the camp up a ridge, westwardly course, about two miles, and the way is marked all the way of the two miles with a tomahawk; and then you will turn down a hollow to your left hand, until you cross a branch of

Grassy creek, and you will see some stumps, where there has been some firewood cut, on the east side of the branch; and continue the marked way the same course, perhaps two and a half miles, near the head of said waters, and there you will find some trees marked, as the entry calls for, on the west side of the black oak, and some small trees marked near the said oak; and you will return down to the same branch to the creek, and down the creek to the fork, and cross the forks and go a southeast course about four miles, until you come to a creek; then up said creek until you find a camp on said creek, in the bottom, where you will see trees peeled, and stumps, and an old camp, and there is Mr. Howard Lewis's entry of two thousand acres. You will find the beginning about fifty rods below the camp in a buffalo trace, on an ash tree, marked M. black with powder, the mark is facing down the creek; I peeled the bark off with my knife; and survey Stephen's above Meamy's and Young's preëmption; and that, I think, will be as much as you can do at this time."

With tasks like this Nathaniel Massie became an expert woodsman. He moved through rough country as silent as a fox, he took his course from a gray-textured tree trunk without ever opening his compass-case, his wind-narrowed eyes computed distances almost as accurately as his rod and chain. He could cheerfully tighten his belt when his stomach was empty and feast like an Indian when game was on the fire. He could travel all day and all night, if necessary, and his long loose stride never showed fatigue.

He saw a lot of wild country. Between surveying expeditions he traded in salt. In the winter of 1786 he took a flatboat down the lonely Cumberland, exchanging salt in Nashville for beaver, otter and raccoon skins, coming back overland with a string of pack horses. On this trip he was an agent for General James Wilkinson who reminded him: "You will remember you are going amongst a set of sharpers, and therefore you must take care of yourself."

Nathaniel Massie took care of himself very well. He soon learned that surveying was a hired job, and that the profitable business was in the hands of land locaters who chose valuable tracts for men with land warrants in their possession. Surveyors' fees were defined by law, but men who located choice tracts received a fourth, a third, or even half of the land they found for warrant-holders. By this means Massie acquired some thousands of acres in Kentucky. Then he moved on across the Ohio.

Late in 1790 he chose a site on the north bank of the Ohio, twelve miles above the Kentucky town of Limestone, and laid out the town that is now called Manchester. Next spring that river bank rang with ax and mallet. Twenty-five families, attracted by his offer of a hundred acres of land, raised cabins inside a picketed stockade with blockhouses at its corners. This was Massie's Station, the first settlement in the Virginia Military District and the fourth settlement in Ohio. Life at the station was pleasant, despite the Indian wars that raged in this year of St. Clair's disastrous expedition up the Miami. The men of Massie's Station cleared an island in the river and raised a bumper crop of corn. The river offered fish, the woods game, and occasionally a flatboat came down the river with a load of Monongahela whisky. "The inhabitants," wrote Massie's chain-man, John McDonald, "were generally as playful as kittens, and as happy in their way as their heart could wish. The men spent most of their time in hunting and fishing, and almost every evening the boys and girls footed merrily to the tune of the fiddle." Their nearest Ohio neighbors were at the village of Columbia, a few miles above Cincinnati, and at Gallipolis, opposite the mouth of the Great Kanawha. "Look at the map," suggests McDonald. "You will see the long and dreary waste, Massie and his companions, during their exploring expeditions through the wilderness of the present State of Ohio, had to travel, without roads or paths. They could not hear the agreeable sound of the plowman's gee-haw, nor the keen crack of the wagoner's or coachman's whip, nor the clink of the blacksmith's hammer, nor the pleasant clitter-clatter of the mill."

But Nathaniel Massie could foresee all this, and more. He was sure of the future of the Scioto country. During 1792-3 when the Indians were huddling in their winter camps, he explored the Scioto valley (where now an atomic plant spreads over thousands of acres) and followed the river's tributaries. This was rich land, rich as any district in Kentucky, and his field book filled with entries. He followed the three forks of Brush Creek, he mapped the bottoms of the Little Miami; he scouted both forks of Paint Creek, broke a trail through the thickets of Deer Creek, crossed the rough ridges to the East Fork of the Little Miami and found the rich bottoms of Caesar Creek.

It was a big country of tangled hillsides, spacious river bottoms, high ridges looking over green waves of forest, deep and sudden gorges, and streams as sinuous as the great serpent mound above Brush Creek. Massie learned it all. He surveyed all the way up the Scioto to Westfall. He ran lines along Paint Creek and up the Main and North forks. He followed Rocky and Rattlesnake creeks, crossed over to Buckskin, marked locations on Eagle Creek, saw prospective town sites on Paint Creek and the Scioto. He explored all the branches of the Little Miami and Tod's Fork, going up Massie's Creek and Caesar's to their headwaters, striking the head of Paint and Clear creeks, exploring, mapping all their branches. Between 1790 and 1801 Nathaniel Massie surveyed 750,000 acres of the Military Lands.

Some of this exploring Massie did alone, stealing through strange country, alert for Indian sign. On surveying tours he had an organized party, four teams of six men each, each team under an assistant surveyor and working a line of its own. Ahead went the lead man, or "hunter," keeping a lookout for game and Indian sign. He traveled light and moved silently, a quarter mile in advance of the others. The surveyor came next with his two chain-men and his marker, and crashing along in the rear came the pack horseman with the baggage. One other completed the party. The "spy" kept on the back trail, following at a half mile's distance, watch-

ing for signs of Indian pursuit. At intersections of the survey
the parties met and made a common camp. This was a festive
place, the men feasting around the fires, lighting their tobacco, trading songs and stories. But there was always danger, and Massie had the men separate, each group going into
its separate "mess" for the night. At daylight he would send
out a spy, looking for signs of ambush, before the men returned to the smoldering fire. This surveying was not all field
notes and mathematics.

At the close of a winter day in 1794, far up Caesar
Creek on the tangled height of land where its springs inter-
lace with those that feed Paint Creek, Massie found Indian
tracks in the snow. He sent two men to spy out the Indian
camp and two others to round up the surveying teams. His
men all came together just before the winter dusk closed
down. His scouts had found a noisy Shawnee camp of ten
tents in trampled snow. Massie, fearful of being followed
while snow lay on the ground, headed back for the home station on the Ohio. They traveled that night, and the next day
they came across another Indian trail, made by four horses
and ten men on foot, leading toward the Ohio. They followed this trail and at dusk crept up on a campsite where a
dozen Shawnees with thudding tomahawks were cutting firewood and tent poles. Massie decided to attack. His men stole
forward, single file, walking in the lead man's footprints in
the crusted snow. Then the white ground dropped away and
they looked across a gully to the Shawnees building up their
fire. A log bridged the ravine and the surveyors crept across.
When eight of them were over, the rotten log gave way. As
the Indians leaped up, Massie's men whooped and fired into
the camp and the Shawnees scattered in the snowy dark. The
surveyors ransacked the camp, taking "considerable booty"
and capturing four horses. Then they struck for home, hard
and fast, all night and the next day hurrying through the
snow to Massie's Station. While the men divided their Shawnee plunder, Nathaniel Massie copied out his field notes—
notations of uplands and bottoms, of thickets and forest, of

caves and cliffs, springs and creeks, ponds and waterfalls, salt licks and mill seats, of places where future roads might lead into towns and cities of the future. His mind was on the bigger plunder.

In all that spacious region Massie liked best the smiling country around the falls of Paint Creek. After the Treaty of Greene Ville had quieted the tribes, he was ready to found his town in the interior. At the end of March, 1796 he gathered a party at Massie's Station. Some of them he sent by water, paddling up the Ohio and the Scioto in dugouts laden with plows, grubbing hoes, axes, log chains, pots and kettles. The others went overland with cattle and horses, and the two parties met on the "Station Prairie" at the mouth of Paint Creek. On the first day of April three hundred prairie acres were plowed and planted to corn. Axes thudded in the woods and cabins grew up beside Paint Creek. Meanwhile Massie was selecting his permanent townsite. He found it four miles away, on a fertile plain with loam ten inches deep, between Paint Creek and the Scioto which there ran parallel. The natural prairie waved with long-stemmed fox grass and orange lilies; woods and meadows ran away to an arc of hills on the west side of the wide valley. Highest of those rounded hills was Mount Logan which would soon appear on the Great Seal of Ohio, and the town laid out on the pleasant prairie would be the state's first capital.

On this site Massie platted a handsome town, with in-lots six poles wide along the streets and twelve poles deep to the alleys. His two main streets he gave a generous six poles; the lesser streets, running back to the forest shade, were of four and five poles. When it was all laid out, with stakes striping the prairie and blazes leading into the shadowed woods, Massie chose a native name. He called his town Chillicothe, a Shawnee word for town or settlement. There were five previous "Chillicothes" in Ohio; now began a sixth and lasting one.

That summer the silence was gone from the Paint Creek prairie. With a clatter of log chain, a clamor of axes

and mallets, stores, shops and a tavern went up amid new
cabins on Paint and Main streets. That winter the settlers
cleared new land, piling brush and timber at the margins
of their fields. All spring the hills were hazed with woodsmoke from their clearings. In 1798 wagons came rocking in
over Zane's Trace newly opened from Wheeling on the upper Ohio. Two years later Massie's settlement became the
capital of the Northwest Territory, with sessions of the legislature meeting in a two-story log house built by Bazel
Abrams. The lower room was used as a legislative hall, a
court room, and a church. Its second floor was "a place of re-
sort for gamblers," with hand-hewn card tables and Ohio's
first billiard table. The town was flourishing on its rich
prairie. New settlers came, some in coonskin caps and faded
army blouses, some in silk hats and long-tailed coats of broadcloth. On hills outside the town rose Virginia mansions of
local sandstone, and fine Virginia horses drew gleaming carriages through the muddy village streets. Flatboats carried
grain, pork, turkeys down the Scioto and the Ohio. In 1803,
when Ohio became a state, Chillicothe was its capital.

By 1800 Nathaniel Massie had sold many thousands
of acres along the Scioto and his field days were behind
him. He married the daughter of Colonel David Meade of
Virginia and Kentucky. One of the largest land-owners in
the West, he could have chosen hundreds of sites for his own
home, but he stayed within sight of his Paint Creek settlement, building a mansion on a 3,000-acre tract above the
Paint Creek falls. Here he welcomed visitors from Virginia and his old comrades from the surveying seasons. One
of these former field-men was John McDonald, who later remembered that in Massie's mansion he first saw tea "handed
round for supper, which I then thought foolish business and
still remain of that opinion."

Under the new constitution of Ohio a militia organized and Massie was made Major General. A few years later
he was elected governor of Ohio, an office he declined in favor of Colonel Return J. Meigs who, though he had received

a small majority of votes, had been declared ineligible because of his absence from the state during the election. The old surveyor lived on quietly above Paint Creek, sitting on his veranda, looking over the spreading town he had founded and the ordered lands he had explored and measured. Perhaps he remembered how he had come to the West with nothing but a rifle and a set of surveying instruments. He died on a November day in 1813 and was buried beside Paint Creek where he had run boundary lines in the wilderness.

Massie had taught younger men the arts of surveying rough country and locating strategic lands. Now they were busy out-guessing and out-lawyering each other, and making fortunes. Duncan McArthur had driven pack trains over the Alleghenies in his youth; his first job in the West was salt-boiler at the licks near Maysville. Then he became Massie's chain-carrier. He was a burly man, strong as an ox, who learned slowly and never forgot. Under Nathaniel Massie he learned the land laws of Virginia and Kentucky, learned to judge farm lands, mill locations, future townsites. While the country filled up he made foolproof locations and detected the flaws in other men's entries. After years of controversy and litigation, crowding men off their claims by legal process, he was a great landholder, with a mansion on "Fruit Hill" above the Scioto a few miles northwest of busy Chillicothe. He became a general in the Ohio militia, and succeeded William Henry Harrison as commander of the Army of the Northwest. In 1830 he was narrowly elected governor of Ohio. In that contest McArthur's rivals made an issue of his land speculations, describing him as swindling illiterate farmers and turning widows and orphans out of their homes. Actually he had pursued bigger prizes—contending with other speculators for great tracts and buying up whole townships that had reverted to the government.

His speculations paid off, but McArthur came to a sorry end. One winter day in Columbus while he was passing a covered store front on High Street the snow-weighted

roof fell in. Battered and mangled he was pulled from the
wreckage; when he walked again one knee bent backward as
often as forward. That burly broken figure served his term
as governor while the canal was growing from Lake Erie to
the Ohio and the National Road was reaching west. Then he
ran for Congress and was beaten by a single vote. Back to
Chillicothe hobbled the old chain-carrier, a rich but shattered man. He died at Fruit Hill, above his endless acres, in
1839.

In 1795 thirty-five shareholders in the Connecticut Land Company bought from the State of Connecticut the
three million acres of its Western Reserve, the land Connecticut had withheld from cession to the federal government, and sent General Moses Cleaveland to survey that
country. Cleaveland, a lawyer in Canterbury, Connecticut,
was glad to get away from his Blackstone and *Nisi Prius*. He
had been a comrade of General Rufus Putnam in the Revolution and had bought two shares in the Ohio Company. He
was a veteran surveyor, he knew how to get along with Indians, and he had a lively interest in the West—lively
enough to buy $32,600 worth of shares in the Connecticut
Company. He was appointed the Company's agent in charge
of surveying the Reserve. In the spring of 1796 he led a task
force of fifty woodsmen, hunters, boatmen and surveyors,
along with thirteen horses and some cattle, to the Promised
Land.

At Buffalo on the way west General Cleaveland met
chiefs of the Iroquois nations. He was as swarthy as an Iroquois himself, a big burly man with a broad face and coarse
black hair. After several days of council he made a notable
bargain, giving the Indians two beef cattle, a hundred gallons
of whisky and five hundred dollars in trade goods in exchange for all the land extending from the Pennsylvania border to the Cuyahoga River. Then, with his ax-men, chain-
men, and rod men, he pushed on west in warm June
weather. Near the Pennsylvania border they met a party of

abject Massasaga Indians under huge Chief Paqua. Cleaveland bought them off with twenty-five dollars worth of knives, hatchets, mirrors and whisky, and Paqua presented Cleaveland with a long-stemmed pipe. After that day his men called the General "Paqua," a name that suited both his appearance and his preference.

On July 4th, when they were sixty-eight days out from Dover, Connecticut, surveyor Seth Pease, following the Lake Erie shore, came upon the monument marking the northwest corner of Pennsylvania. Rifle shots summoned the party, some splashing ashore from Mackinaw boats, others crashing through the thickets. They gathered round the marker, gave three cheers, and pushed on through the brush to the shores of Conneaut Creek where they made their first camp in the Western Reserve. Lake Erie washed steadily at the sandy creek mouth, the sun sank over the endless western forest. While the summer stars came out they fired salutes in honor of New Connecticut and drank some rounds of rum to the President of the United States, the Connecticut Land Company, and the future of the Western Reserve.

Before leaving Conneaut Creek the surveyors cleared an acre of land and built a sizable storehouse. Joshua Stow, the aptly named quartermaster of the party, stowed some tons of provisions under its low roof, and the first building in the Reserve was named for him. When the men moved on, Elijah Gun and his wife Anna (one of the two women in the party) were left in charge of "Stow's Castle" with its depot of corn, rice, salt pork, lead and gunpowder.

Now the surveying crews fanned out, seven men to a team—advance man, ax-men, compass man, chain-men, pack horseman. Day after day, week after week they traveled in wild country, across swamps and streams, over ravines and ridges, through brush and timber. The ax-men swamped out transit lines, the chain-men jabbed their pins into rough ground and stretched their links, the compass man jotted figures in his field book—while gnats swarmed round their heads and mosquitoes stabbed them. They laid out five-mile townships, range after range, across the lowlands of Grand River and the rough ridges above the Chagrin.

In mid-July Cleaveland led a party by boat along the shore in search of a likely site for a city. They found the broad mouth of the Cuyahoga framed by wooded bluffs. When they had clambered up to high ground they stood in a swath of fallen trees, the result of a windstorm of a few seasons past. New growth softened the shattered trunks, the soil was loose and dry. Beyond the Cuyahoga mouth Lake Erie stretched like a serene blue ocean. This looked like the place. It was the twelfth township from the Pennsylvania line and the seventh range above the 41st parallel.

In young oaks and maples the men marked out a ten-acre common and plotted the future streets around it. Behind homestead sites on the lake front they laid out rows of ten-acre lots, and on a line that later became Euclid Avenue they staked out hundred-acre farms. During the August days axes bit into the timber and the first buildings of Cleveland grew up between the Cuyahoga and the staked-out public square—a log bunkhouse for the surveyors, a storehouse for implements and supplies, a cabin for Job Stiles and his wife Tabitha Cumi who would winter there above the tossing lake. Moses Cleaveland called the town Cuyahoga, but his men overruled him and gave the place his name, misspelling it "Cleveland."

By the end of summer the men were grumbling about the heat and the rain, the long day's work and the short rations, the sandflies and mosquitoes. They wanted to head home to Connecticut. To renew their enthusiasm for the rigors of a surveyor's life, General Cleaveland offered them a stake in the new country. He drew up a preëmption for their joint purchase, at a dollar per acre, of a township fronting on the lake. Forty-one men signed the contract, agreeing, as Orrin Harmon noted, "to remain in the service of the company faithfully to the end of the year, and to perform certain acts of settlement, as follows:

To settle, in the year 1797, eleven families, build eleven houses, and sow two acres of wheat around each house—to be on different lots. In the year 1798 to settle eighteen more families, build eighteen more houses on different lots, and to clear and sow five acres of wheat on each. There must be also fifty acres of grass in the township.

In the year 1799, there must be twelve more families occupying twelve more lots, (in all forty-one,) with eight acres in wheat. On all the other lots three additional acres in wheat for this year, and in all seventy acres to be in grass.

With a rekindled interest in geometry, thinking about their own crops and cattle within their own section lines, the men named the prospective settlement "Euclid."

The survey was still unfinished in mid-October, when the men stored their gear in the warehouse at Cleveland and packed their field notes to take back to Connecticut. On a gray autumn day with a wet wind blowing down the lake they shoved their boats off the Cuyahoga sandbar and steered for Buffalo. Behind them in the leafless woods Job Stiles and his wife put a log on the fire.

Seven months later, on June 1st, 1797, a new surveying crew arrived, sixty-three men, bringing soap, candles and garden seeds among their supplies. They made a big garden on the bluff and lugged their stores up to the company warehouse. The pack horsemen went inland, along the winding Cuyahoga, building a chain of cabins and caching supplies for the survey parties.

Despite these systematic preparations the crews had bad luck. Seven men died that summer, four by drowning, three from disease. Dysentery and intermittent fever were harder obstacles than the swamps and gorges: every member of the party was ill at some time during the summer. But they kept the survey going—through rough country along the

Cuyahoga, across the tangled townships of the interior, over
the ancient beach ridges of the Erie shore. In October the
task was done. They took back to Connecticut the plots of
townships and the plats of towns—a blueprint of northern
Ohio's future.

Westward the government surveys proceeded, me-
thodically crisscrossing Ohio in the early 1800's, checked by
the War of 1812, then pushing into Indiana, Michigan and
Illinois, with a rash of squatters ahead of them and a rush
of settlers behind. During thirty years before 1815 the
federal government spent three quarters of a million dollars on western surveys; the same amount was spent in the
four years after 1816. Hard times beginning in 1819 slowed
the sale of land in the western districts, but survey went on.
In the Surveyor-General's office deputy surveyors
were sworn in, instructed in the government regulations, and
given contracts for a district survey. They hired their crews,
loaded their baggage onto pack horses, and took to the field;
a few months later they exchanged their survey records for
a season's pay. Many young men earned their first land payments in surveying crews—and chose their land from ranges
where they had marked the witness trees. Other surveyors
followed the trade for a lifetime. It was a hard life in lonely
country, but to some it was a luring life. It meant heat and
cold, thirst and hunger, sickness and accident, mosquitoes
and black flies. And it also meant wildness and freedom,
going first into unknown country, leaving a network of invisible lines in a land that had never been measured.
One February evening in 1821 young Hervey Parke,
a schoolmaster in Oneida County, New York, had a restless
urge to go West as a government surveyor. In March he set
out, walking five hundred miles to Detroit with food, blankets and surveying instruments on his back. He struck north
through the woods to Pontiac, a one-street village in the
hazel brush, and was hired as assistant to Horatio Ball who
had a contract for subdividing ten townships between the

Flint and Cass rivers. Parke soon learned the sorrows of a
surveyor. The section lines were supposedly completed, that
contract having been given to a footloose fellow named Hester. But Hester was found in a Chippewa wigwam making
moccasins with the squaws; a few weeks later he passed
through Pontiac on horseback with a dozen Indians, on his
way to the Surveyor-General at Chillicothe to claim his pay.

With a crew of six including a young Irish immigrant,
Hervey Parke went up the Flint River and began to run section lines. Before they had set up their transit, mosquitoes
came at them in a sticky, stinging swarm. In a week they
were back at the Pontiac trading post, red-eyed and swollen
from the torment. Even their horses were weak from loss of
blood. After the October frosts the crew went out again, with
little equipment and short supplies. They had no tents and
no shelter except a leaky tarpaulin, and for want of a kneading trough the cook used that piece of canvas to mix his
bread. "This was unfortunate," Parke reported, "for on our
first visit to the trading-house some swine, attracted by the
adhering dough, nearly devoured it, and we had no cover
besides our blankets." Camp was nothing more than a lean-
to facing a cooking fire. Food ran low; after long days in the
field the men returned to a supper of buggy peas. It was a
memorable day when they found an Indian squaw cooking
succotash in the woods. Without tents and mackinaw blankets, without pork, flour, beans, rice and coffee, the men took
small comfort from the absence of mosquitoes in the frozen
woods. "Nothing occurred worthy of note," Parke remembered, "except Chester Ball became frightened of what he
called a panther, and ran away from camp, and everything
came near being burned up during his absence, and Lucius
Hunt broke through the ice, three steps in my rear, when
drawing the surveying chain." They finished the last section
on the last day of December and crashed through frozen beds
of rushes to the trading post. In their pent-up hunger they
snatched half-cooked potatoes from a boiling kettle.

Hervey Parke volunteered to go with Surveyor Ball

to Chillicothe, far down in southern Ohio, to make his returns to the Surveyor-General. Through a thin snow
they tramped to Detroit, hitched a sailboat ride to Sandusky
with a farmer who had come up the river to sell his butter
and cheese, and "footed it" over two hundred miles of winter roads to Chillicothe. They turned over their plots and
field notes to an erect and vigorous man with keen brown
eyes and graying hair. This was Edward Tiffin, former Governor of Ohio and United States Senator. He had been the
first director of the National Land Office and was now
Surveyor-General of the western territory. He promised young Parke future contracts as a government surveyor.

A few days later Parke walked on back to Oneida
County, having been away eleven months. He had served his
apprenticeship and a few months later he was in the field
again. During the next sixteen years he walked twenty thousand miles in unmapped country, laying out townships all
the way to the Mississippi.

After the War of 1812 when land sales northwest of
the Ohio passed a million acres a year, a new phrase entered
the American language. "A land office business" became a
popular expression and the government land office was national news. In January, 1815, *Niles' Register* published a
letter headed "Unexampled Sale of Public Lands" from the
district agent at Canton, Ohio: "As you are a friend to the
western country you will be delighted to hear of its rising
importance. Our monthly returns from the several land offices in Ohio and Indiana Territory, exhibit an unparalleled
sale of public lands, since the pacification of the Indians in
that quarter. In some districts the sales have been *doubled in
the last six months*. In the Canton district, for instance, the
sales in November (the last account received) is upwards of
45,000 acres, nearly all in quarter sections. When I came into
the office in May last, the monthly sales were only about
17,000. In the Cincinnati district the sales exceed Canton.
The emigration to the state the last summer, also, has been

beyond all example, great. The main road through the state, I am told, has been almost literally covered with waggons moving out families."

Not only the land office but the land itself was news. Government surveyors were thrusting into new tracts of wild country, and even seaboard citizens followed the mapping of new ranges and sections on the frontier. For the American public Josiah Meigs, former Surveyor-General in the West and now Superintendent of the General Land Office, reported regularly on the progress of the surveys. In 1819 in a widely reprinted statement in *The National Intelligencer* he took a long look ahead, explaining the five principal meridians and extolling the system of rectangular survey. "The principles of this system . . . will unquestionably be adhered to until the public surveys shall reach *Astoria* at the mouth of the *Columbia* river, in longitude 48 degrees west of the capital. It has been said that 'man brings down the Heavens to the earth, for his convenience.' A few geographical positions on the map of the public surveys being accurately determined by astronomical observations, with very little difficulty the longitude and latitude of every *farm,* and of every log-hut and court house, may be ascertained with great precision. . . . About sixty million acres (twice the extent of England) have been surveyed. . . . So wise, beautiful and perfect a system was never before adopted by any government or nation on earth. It is . . . the 'divided feast' of Homer. The government with a temper and spirit truly *paternal,* has divided, for the children of the republic, that patrimony in which they all have a right and an interest."

Josiah Meigs, a native of Middletown, Connecticut, and a classmate of Joel Barlow and Noah Webster at Yale, had left a chair of Astronomy at Yale in 1812 to become Surveyor-General in the western territory. In 1814 he exchanged offices with Edward Tiffin and took over the General Land Office in Washington. While he kept records of the public domain, the field men hacked their way into new tracts of wilderness, wolves in the western country mysteriously diminished—some surveyors thought they were carried off by hydrophobia—and the frontier moved on toward the Mississippi. In hundreds of new counties settlers located their claims—a specific quarter of a specific section in a specific township in a specific range (NW¼ S14 T32N R29W)—by invisible lines that the chain and compass men had drawn, straight as light, over the rough hills and the wandering valleys.

CHAPTER FIVE

THE HERMIT AND THE LAND SHARKS

Man rode up from the Tidewater: over the Gap:
Turned into men: turned into two-day settlers:
Lawyers with the land-grants in their caps:
Coon-skin voters wanting theirs and getting it.
                              —ARCHIBALD MACLEISH

The public lands are in reality the property of the people.
                    —JAMES FLINT: *Letters from America*

THE WESTERN country gave men large ideas. Before
1840 they had cleared fifty million acres of forest, dug a
thousand miles of canals, launched hundreds of steamboats on
the western rivers, laid a highway from the Alleghenies to the
Mississippi. But the first expansive ideas were of land—land
claims and land possession. From Pittsburgh westward
stretched the huge, dim, silent woods, all the way to the far-
off Wabash; beyond the Wabash spread the huge, bright,
silent grassland. It was an empire without walls or guardians,
and despite the tribes who had lived there for a thousand
years, the adventurers who found it called themselves dis-
coverers. At first they claimed it for their kings across the sea.

Later, when men had a closer look at it, they thought of themselves.

Signatures were not yet fixed to the parchment sheets of the Greene Ville Treaty in 1795 when a little group of men made a fantastic grab for the whole peninsula of Michigan. News of Wayne's peace with the tribes started an idea in the minds of three shrewd and avid Easterners. Ebenezer Allen and Charles Whitney of Vermont and Robert Randall of Philadelphia made a contract with five traders in Detroit to purchase from the Indians the entire country between Lakes Michigan and Huron. For this domain, as big as all of Ireland, they were willing to pay Congress half a million dollars, in addition to their deal with some sulking chiefs who had stayed away from Wayne's council. The promoters formed a stock company of forty-one shares—each share representing half a million acres—and divided them, five shares to the Detroit traders and twelve to Allen, Whitney, and Randall. This left twenty-four shares to be handed to Congressmen who would vote for the cession. Whitney approached northern Congressmen with this luring proposal while Randall worked on Congressmen from the southern states. But Congress was not easily bought as the disgruntled Detroit chiefs. Three days before Christmas, 1795, the chairman of the Land Office Committee exposed the attempted bribery, and the promoters were under arrest. The woods and waters of Michigan remained for forty-two years in the national domain.

There had been earlier land schemes on the same grand scale. In 1766, while bonfires burned in Boston to celebrate repeal of the Stamp Act, General Phineas Lyman of Connecticut, in the interests of veterans of the French and Indian War, asked the English Board of Trade for a grant extending six hundred miles along the Mississippi, above and below the Ohio, and reaching westward for "a great extent." In the same year Governor William Franklin of New Jersey and Sir William Johnson, the British Indian Agent in the northern colonies, petitioned the king for a grant south of the

Ohio and as far west as the Kentucky River—a vast tract of twenty million acres. They proposed to placate the Indians with gifts. Shares in this "Vandalia Company" were distributed to thirty-two influential men in London and Philadelphia. After extended discussion in the British cabinet and the Board of Trade, the grant was approved. But by then the year was 1775 and the colonies were rebelling. The envisioned Vandalia became a part of the western territory.

Meanwhile land-conscious planters of Virginia were looking avidly across the Alleghenies. As early as 1750 they had sent leathery, landwise Christopher Gist on a tour of the Ohio country. He found his way by Nemacolin's Path to the Monongahela and so to Fort Pitt; from there he tramped the Indian trails through the dark Ohio woods, through the Delaware towns and past the Great Buffalo Swamp, then down the Scioto and north and west again all the way to Pickawillany on the Miami, the most remote of the English trading stations. When he returned from this long tour of land-looking his report was rosy: "Nothing is wanting but cultivation to make it a most delightful country." The Ohio Land Company of Virginia petitioned the king for a grant of 500,000 acres on the banks of the O-hy-o.

In 1773 Judge Richard Henderson of North Carolina organized his Transylvania Land Company, with Daniel Boone as his trail-blazer. By purchase from the chiefs of the Cherokees, Henderson took title to half the present state of Kentucky. In offering his Transylvania lands to prospective landlords and settlers, he wrote: "The country might invite a prince from his palace, merely for the pleasure of contemplating its beauty and excellence, but only add the rapturous idea of property, and what allurements can the world offer for the loss of so glorious a prospect?"

"The rapturous idea of property" went on exciting men north of the Ohio. In 1773 William Murray, a trader in the Illinois country, acting as agent for the "Illinois Land Company," bought from the Indians a vast tract between the Illinois, Ohio and Mississippi rivers. Murray followed that deal with another equally lordly, purchasing for the "Wabash Land Company" in 1775 a huge domain on both sides of the Wabash. If his purchases overlapped, that was better than overlapping some other man's purchase, as was commonly the case in Kentucky. He bought from some Piankeshaw chiefs a prairie empire 279 miles long and 210 miles across, paying them three horses, fifteen barrels of flour, a wagonload of knives, mirrors, blankets and ribbons, files and hatchets, jew's-harps, bells, and whistles. Thirty-seven million acres were involved, but the Indians got the better deal. They had their trinkets, and events at Concord Bridge and Bunker Hill prevented the Wabash Company from taking possession of the prairie. However, during the Revolution, the proprietors, including Philadelphia merchants and colonial officials of Virginia, sold shares in the combined "United Illinois and Wabash Land Companies" and laid out two strategic towns, on paper, one at the junction of the Ohio and the Mississippi and the other at the mouth of the Illinois. In 1781 Robert Morris, financier of the Revolution, bought an interest in the United Companies. Most of the speculators had not seen the great slow rivers of the West, but they thought of them possessively as boundaries of their lands.

A more limited petition was made in 1775 by three clergymen—"Myles Cooper, LL. D., President of King's College in the City of New York, John Vardill, A.M., Professor of Divinity in the same, and Thomas Bradbury Chandler, D.D., Rector of St. John's Church, Elizabethtown, New Jersey." These divines sought a grant of a hundred thousand acres between the Muskingum and Hocking rivers, since their concern with the "principles of Religion, Virtue, Loyalty and just Subordination to Government" did not allow them to make adequate provision for their families. The events of 1776 gave the British Board of Trade more pressing problems and their petition was not acted on.

Another group who thought themselves deserving were members of the law court at Vincennes, on the Wabash. The court, established by Virginia, was instructed to grant land to new settlers according to their needs. They followed, as they said, the law and their duty, and before dissolving the court in the 1790's they granted to each other all the public land, some six million acres, claimed by the town. Speculators later bought these unconfirmed claims, had them officially recorded, and sold the titles to gullible settlers. It must be said they sold land cheaply, giving as much as a thousand acres for a horse or a gun.

In 1776 Silas Deane of Groton, Connecticut, secret agent for the Continental Congress in France, proposed a way of paying for the Revolutionary War by sale of western lands which he was confident the war would win for the American nation. He wrote to the Secret Committee of the Congress in December, 1776: "You may smile, and recollect the sale of the bearskin in the fable, but at the same time must be sensible that your wants are real; and if others can be induced to relieve them, it is indifferent to you whether they have a consideration in hand or in prospect."

Then he outlined his bold proposal: "I trace the river *Ohio* from its junction to its head; thence north to *Lake Erie,* on the south and west of that lake to *Fort Detroit,* which is in the latitude of *Boston;* thence a west course to the Mississippi, and return to the place of my departure. These three lines, of near one thousand miles each, include an immense territory in a fine climate well watered and by accounts exceedingly fertile; it is not inhabited by any *Europeans* of consequence, and the tribes of *Indians* are inconsiderable, and will decrease faster than the lands can possibly be called, for cultivation. To this I ask your attention, as a resource amply adequate, under proper regulations, for defraying the whole expense of the war, and the sums necessary to be given the *Indians* in purchase of the native right. But to give this land value, inhabitants are necessary. I therefore propose, in the first place, that a grant be made of a tract of land at the mouth of the *Ohio,* between that and the *Mississippi,* equal to two hundred square miles, to a company formed indiscriminately of *Europeans* and *Americans,*

which company should form a distinct State, confederated
with and under the general regulations of the *United States
General of America*. . . . These are the outlines of a proposed grant, which you see contains more than twenty-five
million acres of land, the one-fifth of which, if a settlement
is carried on vigorously, will soon be of most prodigious
value. At this time a company might be formed in *France,
Germany,* etc., who would form a stock of one hundred
thousand pounds sterling, to defray the expense of this settlement. By such a step you in the first place extend the circle
of your connection and influence, you increase the number
of your inhabitants, proportionately lessen the common expenses, and have in reserve a fund for publick exigencies.
Further, as this company would be in a great degree commercial, the establishing commerce at the junction of these large
rivers would immediately give a value to all the lands situated on or near them . . . and further grants might admit
of larger reserves, amply sufficient for defraying the expenses
of the war. . . . It may be objected, this is not a favorable time for such a measure. I reply, it is the most favorable
that can happen. You want money, and by holding up this
early view a certain fund, on which to raise it, even the most
certain in the world, that of land security, you may obtain
the loan and engage the moneyed interests of *Europe* in your
favor. . . . I will now dismiss this scheme . . . only add-
ing, . . . that a large and generous allowance ought immediately be made for the officers and soldiers serving in the
present war. . . . This will make the Army consist literally
of a set of men fighting for freehold; and it will be a great encouragement to foreigners, with whom five hundred or a
thousand acres of land has a great sound."

    This confident plan overlooked two obstacles: the war
was not yet won, but only beginning; and the seven eastern
colonies with western claims had not relinquished their
trans-Allegheny lands to the Continental Congress.

    A somewhat similar plan was advanced by Thomas
Paine in 1780, proposing a western state between the Ohio

River and the North Carolina line and extending to the Falls of the Ohio (Louisville). Paine thought twenty million acres could be sold through land offices established in Europe, bringing a revenue of four million pounds, which would meet the cost of war for three years.

To this proposal the most vigorous reply came from shrewd and salty old Pelatiah Webster of Philadelphia. Said this retired clergyman and economist: "Some people think we ought to *sell* or *mortgage them* [the western lands] *to foreign States,* for money in our present distress. But I have many reasons against this method. The first is, that it is capable of the most demonstrative proof, that *no importation of money* can help us, even if it was *given to us,* much less if our lands are to be *mortgaged* for it. . . . Our salvation must arise from the *wealth* and *virtue* which abounds *in the country,* not in hunting *abroad for money.* Besides, I abhor the very idea of *strangers* having their *paw on any of our lands* in any shape whatsoever; and further, they would bring *mighty little in* this way, i.e. very little *present* benefit, tho' enough of *future* trouble; it would be like killing the goose that laid an egg every day, in order to tear out at once all that was in her belly."

Often from the lawns of Mount Vernon George Washington let his gaze wander to the West. As a young man he had first seen that country, and it never failed to inflame him. He had fought there; at the age of twenty-two he raised Fort Necessity on the Great Meadows and stood off the French. A year later he was again in the forest of the West, with Braddock and his redcoats. He knew the vastness and beauty, the danger and promise of the western country. In 1770 he made a "hunting trip" on the Ohio; he drifted three hundred miles down the river in a canoe and then paddled up the Great Kanawha. He marked out his corners on 41,000 acres of river-front land. He also did some hunting, killing several buffalo and a number of deer. Later, at Mount Vernon, he tried raising buffalo, thinking that herds of domesticated bison might supply meat for the future nation; at his death in

1799 a buffalo cow was listed among the cattle at Mount Vernon. In 1784, after the West was won from the British, Washington made another journey across the mountains. Again his mind was on the future nation; he looked for a route that might eventually connect the Potomac River with the Ohio. He found the post-Revolutionary West rushing into life, and men talking always about the prospects of western lands. On his return he wrote: "Such is the rage for speculation in and forestalling of lands on the northwest of the Ohio that scarcely a valuable spot, within a tolerable distance of it, is left without a claimant. Men in these times talk with as much facility of fifty, an hundred, and even five hundred thousand acres, as a gentleman would formerly do of one thousand."

Early in the Revolution Congress had passed a G.I. bill promising officers and men in the Continental Army a share of the new territory which it hoped that the war would win. This prospect of rich bounty lands led to the forming of the Ohio Company of Associates which asked Congress for one and a half million acres on the upper Ohio; and through political necessity the Ohio Company became a front for the shadowy Scioto Land Company whose members aimed to grab some three million acres of Ohio Land. The direct and patriotic motives of the Ohio Company and the devious scheme of the Scioto promoters will appear in later chapters. Now, in passing, it can be observed that the Ohio Company planted a sturdy colony on the banks of the Muskingum while the Scioto Company dissolved into thin air after luring a company of helpless French émigrés to the Ohio wilderness.

As dispenser of western lands Congress had other applications. Royal Flint, a New York merchant and member of the Scioto Company, and his partner Joseph Parker asked for two million acres on the Ohio. Other groups sought tracts along the Mississippi, proposing to make their own deal with the Indians. But Congress resolved that no land should be sold until the Indian title had been obtained and that no grant should have a frontage greater than a third of its depth along the Ohio, Mississippi, Wabash, or Illinois rivers. In 1785 Nathaniel Sackett asked Congress for half of future Ohio, all the country between the Muskingum and the Scioto northward to Lake Erie, proposing to pay the United States "an ear of corn annually, if demanded, as an acknowledgment of their sovereignty." Every family man who came to settle in this tract would receive a thousand acres for himself and a hundred for each of his children; a single settler would receive five hundred acres, with a hundred-acre bonus for getting married. This grant, Sackett argued, would secure the interior country from hostile invasion, encourage a general settlement of the public domain, and so increase the value of the remaining public lands, "thereby rendering them more speedily a more productive fund for the discharge of our national debt." Congress was not persuaded that the way to raise revenue from the public lands was to give them away.

At Trenton, New Jersey, on November 26th, 1787, there was issued "To the Respectable Public" a pamphlet describing a tract of a million acres of Ohio land between the two Miami rivers which was now open to sale and settlement. It contained some glowing language: "This land bordering on the river Ohio . . . is supposed to be equal to any part of the federal territory, in point of quality of soil, and excellence of climate. . . . Its situation is such as to command the navigation of several fine rivers, as may be seen by maps of that country; boats are frequently passing by this land, as they ply up and down the Ohio. . . . A larger portion of the lands on the Miami are supposed to be of the first quality, and the whole equally good, compared generally with those of Kentucke. The titles to the Miami lands will be clear and certain, and no possible doubts can arise. . . . It is expected that a considerable settlement will be begun on the land early next spring. . . . The subscriber intends going out himself, and shall make it his duty to en-

courage and superintend the settlement of this purchase."
The circular was signed by John Cleves Symmes.

Two months later advertisements in the New Jersey
papers described the Miami lands as the best tract in the
Northwest Territory, stating that cattle, horses, and hogs
could find abundant forage in the woods, wild game and fish
were there for the taking, cotton and indigo would flourish
along with all grains and vegetables. Millstones and grind-
stones could be picked up on the hillsides and the country
offered the finest of timber of a great many kinds. Three navigable rivers were ready to carry vessels loaded with Miami
produce and freighted [apparently by way of the Gulf of
Mexico] to New York. To prospective settlers Symmes offered free lots in his projected city on the Ohio, timber
enough to build a log house, and a six months' ration of
Indian corn. He predicted that thousands would emigrate
to the Miami country, "especially young men, and others
who have little or no land." Land warrants, he added, could
be had from his agents in New York, Philadelphia and the
chief towns of New Jersey.

Response to this notice was prompt and eager. It
seemed, indeed, that thousands were ready to start for the
Miami wilderness.

John Cleves Symmes, Judge of the Supreme Court of
New Jersey and a former member of Congress from that
state, had been introduced to the Ohio country by his comrade of the Revolutionary campaigns, Benjamin Stites. Major Stites had made a trading trip down the Ohio in 1786.
Below Limestone he joined a party of Kentuckians who were
pursuing marauding Indians into Ohio. So he saw the Miami
country, and he could not forget its richness and beauty. His
ardor for the Miami lands induced Judge Symmes to make a
journey in the spring of 1787 to see that country for himself.

On his return, Symmes formed a company, including
Jonathan Dayton, a Congressman from New Jersey who was
later to become Speaker of the House, Elias Boudinot, another New Jersey Congressman who had formerly been Pres-

ident of the Continental Congress, and John Witherspoon, a signer of the Declaration of Independence and President of Princeton University, and sought from Congress a tract of two million acres, to be paid for at a dollar an acre, between the two Miamis. Congress approved the purchase, though reducing the tract to one million acres fronting for twenty miles on the Ohio between the Great and the Little Miami rivers.

For himself and his colleagues Symmes reserved some 40,000 acres bordering the Ohio and including the future site of Cincinnati. Some shares in this district he sold even before he started west with a company of sixty settlers. They crossed the mountains in the summer of 1788—a caravan of thirty-one horses, six freight wagons, and a stage wagon; in the party were three carpenters and a stonemason. Confident and careless, Symmes had not taken forethought of the seasons. The settlers arrived late. While Symmes impatiently went exploring in the interior, shrewd Benjamin Stites had his men hacking forest trees beside the Ohio in the chill November air. Before the snow came he had raised a group of cabins and a blockhouse. He called the settlement Columbia.

Another group was led by Matthias Denman of New Jersey and Robert Patterson, who nine years before had founded Lexington, Kentucky. With them was John Filson, a Pennsylvania schoolmaster who had been pioneering in Kentucky. They located a townsite opposite the break in the Kentucky hills where the Licking River pours into the Ohio. Here the Indian trails came down from the Ohio hills; for centuries tribal hunters had crossed the Ohio and paddled up the Licking. For the new town classical-minded John Filson coined the ingenious name Losantiville. He did not live to see the name changed to Cincinnati; within a few weeks he disappeared from a surveying party up the Great Miami and was never seen again. At Losantiville in the last days of December the men broke up their flatboats to build huts. Next spring a cluster of cabins and a log stockade rose above

the steep river bank. Later that year General Harmar came
down the river with a garrison of troops; they enlarged the
stockade which then became Fort Washington. Governor St.
Clair moved to the village, renamed it Cincinnati in honor
of the Order of Cincinnatus, an organization of Revolutionary officers, and made the rude little station capital of the
Northwest Territory.

In mid-winter Judge Symmes located a third settlement, North Bend, twelve miles below Cincinnati on a handsome site high above a great crescent of the river. Within a
few months he had twenty-four settlers whose cabins extended a mile and a half along the Ohio. This village
Symmes hoped and believed would grow to be "the city."
But North Bend has remained a village to this day, while
Cincinnati, with the Little Miami and Mill Creek leading
to the interior, became the Queen City of the West.

As a land-jobber Symmes was no more successful. He
sold lands that were not included in his purchase, and for
years he was embroiled in controversy and litigation. In
New Jersey as well as in the new Miami country his agents
were pushing land sales and promoting settlement, but troubles outran the success of his speculation. An English visitor,
Thomas Ashe, described him in 1806 living on his fine site
above the lordly river. "The banks of the River were settling
with unparalleled success and the title to all the adjacent
lands is bought up by individuals and speculators who propose selling again at an advance in price. Most of the prairie
grounds are now as high as from twenty to fifty dollars per
acre, and the woodland adjoining the river at from five to
sixteen dollars per acre." Symmes' total patent amounted to
a third of a million acres, for which he paid a total, in cash,
of somewhat less than $50,000. But the profits did not come
to him; his own lands were seized to reimburse men to whom
he had unknowingly sold locations outside his purchase.
During years of dispute and litigation settlers in the Miami
Valley called Symmes "the greatest land-jobber on the face
of the earth," and the government considered him a trespas-

ser on the public lands—the grandest squatter of them all. But he died, in 1814, a poor, lonely and defeated man.

Symmes' Purchase was the last land contract made with private interests. Though many petitions had come to Congress, just three grants had been made—one and a half million acres to the Ohio Company of Associates, three and a half million to the corrupt Scioto Company, and a million acres to John Cleves Symmes. Two extensive tracts in Ohio, Connecticut's Western Reserve bordering Lake Erie and Virginia's Military District between the Scioto and Little Miami rivers, were dispensed by those states; a prospective settler in the Reserve could buy land from the partners in the Connecticut Land Company, and a settler in the Virginia district claimed his ground with Virginia military warrants which he had acquired through army service or by purchase from a warrant-holder who was not lured by new land. Most of the rest of Ohio, some fifteen million acres, was public domain, open to purchase in the various land offices. When, during the early years of the nineteenth century, Indian treaties brought into the federal domain the wilderness beyond Ohio, the huge Indiana Territory, comprising the future states of Indiana, Illinois, Michigan, and Wisconsin, would be open to public sale and settlement.

In 1796 Congress passed a highway bill, creating the first road in the Northwest Territory. Ebenezer Zane was instructed to slash through the woods from the Ohio River opposite Wheeling to a point on the river across from Maysville, Kentucky, cutting the southeast quarter of Ohio and opening up the interior. In two years Zane's Trace was ready, a rough and narrow road walled in forest and ribbed with the roots of giant trees. Soon wagons came rocking through the woods and cattle splashed across the fording places. In 1799 Zane and his partner John McIntyre laid out the village of Zanesville, first called Westbourne, at the junction of the Licking and Muskingum rivers. Here Zane

operated a ferry—two canoes with a log lashed across them—
for travelers on the Trace, but some saw no reason to travel
farther. Zanesville soon had a store and a tavern, a weaver
and a shoemaker, and a growing cluster of cabins around the
meeting of the rivers.

A landmark on Zane's Trace was an upthrust cliff of
sandstone above the Hocking River, called Standing Stone
by the Shawnees. Here, at the "crossings of the Hockhocking," Ebenezer Zane laid out another townsite. Soon German
voices called across the prairie under Standing Stone: families from Lancaster County, Pennsylvania, made a settlement there in 1799, and the town was named Lancaster. In
1800 a mail route was established, the mail coming over
Zane's Trace on horseback once a week in every kind of
weather.

In 1797 Lucas Sullivant of Virginia, with a wagonload
of supplies and surveying instruments, creaked up toward
the head of the Scioto and laid out the village of Franklin-
ton, which later became Columbus. In 1803 Colonel James
Kilbourne brought a hundred settlers from Connecticut to
begin the town of Worthington ten miles up the Olentangy.
In 1804 a land company formed by citizens of East Granville, Massachusetts, bought up military warrants for 28,000
acres and located their town of Granville on the upper waters
of the Licking. At the same time towns were springing up on
the two Miamis.

After the War of 1812 Ohio spawned villages like
mushrooms, not all of them real enough to settle in. On the
walls of stores, stables, taverns, blacksmith shops and coach-
ing stations travelers found notices of new townsites. Here is
a broadside which greeted strangers in Newark, Mount Vernon, Zanesville, and at crossroads in Knox, Coshocton, and
Licking Counties:

CLARKSVILLE

The subscriber is laying out a NEW TOWN, on the
waters of Wakatomica Creek, of the name of *Clarks-*

ville, and will offer about sixty of the lots, at Public Auction, on the ground, on the

20TH OF MARCH *next*

The conditions of the sale will be as follows . . . ¼ of purchase money to be paid in hand . . . ¼ in six months, notes with interest to be given for the last two payments. . . . If the purchaser builds a house or a stable of wood, brick, or stone within two years from the time purchase is made, sixteen feet by twenty and one story high, or larger, on each lot purchased . . . he will be given a FULL WARRANTEE DEED, with a provision that the actual owner or occupant shall pay one dollar a year forever to be appropriated for the support of a school; but if the house or stable is not built, at the end of two years then the lot shall be forfeited, together with all the improvements and payments made.

The scite of the town possesses nearly as many advantages as the most flourishing towns of the state of Ohio . . . and will, probably, before long become a county seat. . . . The local advantages of this place are peculiarly promising. The ground on which the town is to stand, is a large hill, of a gentle ascent on every side, and on the center of the hill two important roads intersect each other in parallel lines of north, south, east, and west. There is a large spring of excellent water within a few rods of the centre of this hill, and an extensive bank of stone coal within 100 rods on each side of the above hill. Within one fourth of a mile runs streams of durable water, which, after running about ¾ of a mile meet each other and form the Brushy Fork of Wakatomica Creek. This brushy fork has a rapid descent of about one mile and a half, forming several good mill seats, and then enters into the main Creek.

A grist mill and saw-mill are within two and one half miles of this place. . . . Within three miles is one of the best seats for a furnace in the state, with abundance of iron ore. . . . Within six miles there are not less than 10 good mill seats—the country is generally filled with stone coal—there are immense bodies of fine clay suitable for manufacturing glass, stone and earthenware. In addition to all this the country is uncommonly fertile, producing all the comforts of life in the greatest abundance, and the country is nearly settled with industrious, enterprising farmers.

A lot each will be given for a Court-House, a Market-House and an Academy. Every reasonable encouragement will be given by the proprietor to industrious, peaceable mechanics, who will come and settle in the town; *but no countenance will be given to overgrown speculators in any shape.*

THE SUBSCRIBER IS NOW ERECTING BUILDINGS FOR A STORE, TAVERN AND OTHER PURPOSES, WHICH WILL SOON BE COMPLETED. HE WILL GENERALLY BE FOUND AT THE ABOVE PLACE, BUT IN HIS ABSENCE DANIEL ASHCROFT, RESIDING NEAR THE PREMISES, WILL GIVE ALL NECESSARY INFORMATION.

FEBRUARY 1, 1817   J. CLARK

This heady notice did not catch any settlers. Another Clarksville grew up in Clinton County, a hundred miles away, and ultimately reached a population of four hundred and ten. But Mr. J. Clark's town never existed except in his expectation.

Meanwhile on its river bank Cincinnati grew like the bottom fields of corn, and land values multiplied year after year. Nicholas Longworth, arriving from Newark, New Jersey, in 1803, saw the promise of the spreading city. A young and far-sighted lawyer, he bought town lots and farm tracts as fast as his fees came in. Once he successfully defended a man accused of horse-stealing, and his penniless client offered in payment two copper stills which belonged to a friend of his. Longworth, learning that the owner of the stills also owned an empty lot at the edge of Cincinnati, suggested that he take the land and the distiller keep his equipment. This was a happy arrangement. The distiller went on making whisky and Longworth had a piece of land that before his death was worth two million dollars. A few years later Longworth paid $5000, on time, for Jacob Burnet's cow pasture, and saw it rise to a value of $1,500,000. He went on acquiring land up Mill Creek and the Miami valley and all the way to the Maumee and Sandusky districts on Lake Erie.

"His books were nothing," wrote a Cincinnati banker who first knew Longworth in 1817, "for he never used them; the same may be said of his office for he was never in it. He carried his law in his head and his papers in his hat. 'Tis useless to add that he was successful at the bar. But independently of his professional abilities he possessed two different and distinct kinds of talent. The one was for *getting* and the other for *holding on*." At his death Nicholas Longworth was one of the richest landowners in America.

Settlement in the Ohio country ebbed with the financial troubles of the 1820's and then swelled again. A mania of townsite speculation made men imagine cities at every fording place and river landing. Recorded maps showed towns on the empty, swamp-bordered Maumee—Manhattan at the mouth of the river, Oregon, Austerlitz, and Marengo a few miles above. Each of these towns was advertised as superior to the others: Manhattan commanded the meeting of the river with Lake Erie, Oregon was described as having unique advantages for the pork business, Marengo claimed the advantage of being at the falls and so at the head of navigation on the Maumee. With this advertising hundreds of hopeful young men flocked into the country. Eleven towns were mapped and platted on the Maumee, but the hopeful emigrants found only the dim forest with charred circles of old Indian camps. The Maumee towns, with lots sold by their eastern agents, were towns on paper only.

An English traveler, Joseph Briggs, described this process of town speculation: "A speculator makes out a plan of a city with its streets, squares, and avenues, quays and wharves, public buildings and monuments. The streets are lotted, the houses numbered, and the squares called after Franklin or Washington. The city itself has some fine name, perhaps Troy or Antioch. This is engraved and forthwith hung up in as many steamboats and hotels as the speculator's interest may command. All this time the city is a mere vision. Its very site is on the fork of some river in the far West, five hundred miles beyond civilization, probably under water or surrounded by dense forests and impassable swamps. Emigrants have been repeatedly defrauded out of their money by transactions so extremely gross as hardly to be credited."

This was precisely the experience through which Charles Dickens, after his tour of the Ohio country in 1842, put his fictional Martin Chuzzlewit.

The English were intensely aware of speculation on the frontier. There was an American land office in Threadneedle Street, London, in the shadow of the Bank of England, and as early as 1794 John Dewhurst had published a pamphlet saying that purchase of American land was the best financial opportunity in all history. The English colonist Morris Birkbeck, who looked for town locations all the way to Illinois in 1817, exclaimed: "Gain! Gain! Gain! Gain is the beginning, the middle, and the end, the *alpha* and *omega* of the founders of American towns." He described the process of town-jobbing: "On any spot where a few settlers cluster together . . . some enterprising proprietor finds in his selection what he deems a good site for a town; he has it surveyed and laid out in lots, which he sells, or offers for sale by auction. . . . The new town then assumes the name of its founder:—a store-keeper builds a little frame store, and sends for a few cases of goods; and then a tavern starts up . . . as the boarding house of the weary traveler; soon follows a blacksmith; a schoolmaster, who is also a minister of religion, becomes an important accession to this rising community. Thus the town proceeds, if it becomes the metropolis of the neighborhood. Hundreds of these speculations may have failed but hundreds prosper."

Another Englishman, H. B. Fearon, sent in 1817 as an agent for thirty-nine families to find what part of the Ohio country would offer them the best residence and the brightest prospects, had another caustic word to say: "With regard to the western country . . . there are many men of real, but more of fictitious capital. All are speculators and each man anticipates making a fortune."

That wasn't quite true. Many were speculators, but not all. Look at the Hermit of the Scioto. For fourteen years while the Ohio towns were spreading, he lived in a cave under a shelving rock eleven miles south of Chillicothe. He was a Virginian, it was said, who had shot his wife's lover and fled to the wilderness. He lived on game and dressed in the skins of animals. Occasionally he visited Chillicothe, stalking down the middle of Paint Street to trade furs for powder and rifle bullets. He planted an orchard on government land which was later sold, and when the fruit was ripe he asked the owner's permission to pick a portion of it. He lived as neatly and simply as a woodchuck, making a secure stone entry to his cave and fitting it with a snug timber door. When he died his neighbors refused to forget him. They buried him in his cave and raised a stone monument above it:

WILLIAM HEWIT
The Hermit
occupied this cave 14 years, while all
was wilderness around him.
He died in 1834, aged 70 years.

Others lived in the wilderness without purse or scrip, wanting nothing but freedom and their own footpath to the moss-lined spring. Almost every county had its legend of a man who shared his hut with a horse or a dog, or of a hunter who lived alone. To them the rise and fall of real estate, the gain or loss in land transactions, meant less than nothing.

Squatters were of several kinds—some merely ahead of the law, expecting to secure their land by legal process when it was surveyed and put on sale, some outside the law and meaning to stay there. But they were all alike in their indifference to the kind of gain pursued by land-jobbers and townsite speculators, and in their superiority to laws of trespass. When John Amberson, squatting in "Amberson's Bottom" on the upper Ohio in 1785, declared that all men "have an undoubted right to pass into every vacant country . . . and Congress is not empowered to forbid them," he spoke for the generations which have passed into wild land all the way from the forks of the Ohio to the coasts of Oregon.

Some squatters grew tamed while they subdued wild land. Having made a farm in the wilderness they took root on it and sought preëmption rights to the land they had improved. Others moved on from their rude clearings, ahead of the ragged wave of legal settlement. They left their tomahawk blazes along the Muskingum, the Hocking, the Scioto, the Miami, the Wabash. They squatted in Ohio, Indiana, Illinois; then they rafted the Mississippi and made their camps beside eastward-flowing water. They were a raffish, tenacious, indestructible tribe.

They have their prototype in Ishmael Bush of Fenimore Cooper's *The Prairie*—Ishmael, "the outcast," who had come from the woods of the Ohio to the great grasslands of the Missouri. There were no trees in the windswept country to witness his lawless claim, but he hacked the ground with his tomahawk and dropped his grains of corn. In England a hundred years after Cooper's tale was written D. H. Lawrence, troubled by the triumph of the machine, was fascinated by these untrammeled and primordial men.

"Into the prairie enters the huge figure of Ishmael, ponderous, pariah-like Ishmael with his huge sons and his were-wolf wife. With their wagons they roll on from the frontiers of Kentucky into the savage wilderness. . . . They entrench themselves in isolation on a hillock in the midst of the prairie. There they hold out like demi-gods against the elements and the subtle Indian. The pioneering brute invasion of the West." Here, said Lawrence, is the myth of the essential America. "All the other stuff, the love, the democracy, the floundering into lust, is a sort of by-play. The essential American soul is hard, isolate, stoic, and a killer. It has never yet melted."

But essential or not, the squatter had to go. He was as natural to the country as wolves, but he had to be driven on. The army, the courts, the surveyors, the speculators and warrant-holding settlers were his natural enemies. Here and there a few of them might stay, in backwoods, on barren land, or like the harmless hermit in a hole on a river bank. But not ten thousand families finding a branch or a spring, clearing a field, standing off the law. They had to go—not out of existence but on farther into wild country. The squatter was stronger and more enduring than the law. Eventually the law accommodated itself to him, making his settlement legal since he would settle anyway. Here was a dirt-road demonstration of democracy. The law shaped the people less than the people shaped the law.

Yet for a while legislation favored the squatter, encouraging the outlaw by discouraging the title-holding farmer. The first federal land law was an instrument for raising revenue to pay the national debt. The minimum purchase of government land was 640 acres at two dollars an acre, half the price to be paid in thirty days, the remainder within a year. (Few frontier farmers could count out that money—twelve hundred and eighty dollars—in the land office. Speculators had the money. They bought land, gave terms to settlers, foreclosed when payments lapsed, and sold the land again) Until 1800 the federal land laws were an obstacle between farmers and the public lands. That year the West was heard in Congress, in the voice of William Henry Harrison.

After the treaty was signed at Greene Ville, Lieutenant Harrison reported at Fort Washington, Cincinnati, to take command of the one remaining company at the post. Twelve miles down the Ohio, at North Bend, John Cleves Symmes had founded the town which he expected to become the metropolis of the Miami country. Fort Washington made small demands on its commandant, and Harrison frequently rode down to North Bend with pack-horse trains carrying supplies to Symmes' settlement. It was a pleasant half-day's journey through the autumn hills, with the great river curving away in distance and with dark-eyed Anna Symmes waiting at North Bend. On November 25th Harrison did not ride back alone. They were married that day in the log house of Dr. Stephen Wood, who was a Justice of the Peace, as well as doctor, storekeeper, and proprietor of a sawmill. Through leafless woods, under the gray November sky, Harrison and his small bride rode back to Fort Washington where their married life began.

After morning inspection on the parade the young commandant tended to paper work in his office, with its map of the Ohio River on the wall and a glimpse of the gray river through his narrow window. While Anna Harrison went to the public market across the trampled mud of Broadway, he read military science and history—*Memoirs Upon the Art of War, Military Guide for Young Officers,* and the four-volume *Portable Military Library.* Sometimes at officers' mess he entertained his new friends Jacob Burnet and James Findlay; occasionally he was host to an old comrade or an old adversary in Wayne's campaign. In 1797 he had a notable guest. Chief Little Turtle, returning from a visit to the President in Philadelphia, passed a few days as a guest at Fort Washington. He sat down to dinner with the Harrisons, wearing the sword that President Washington had presented him and the pair of pistols from General Kosciusko.

With Jacob Burnet, recently arrived from Princeton University, Harrison walked the streets of Cincinnati, the young lawyer in his fine Philadelphia clothing dodging the mud from hoofs and wagon wheels. He was Harrison's first friend in Cincinnati. They differed in politics but they agreed on the prospects of Cincinnati. It was a restless town, farmers creaking in with potatoes, corn and pumpkins, drovers herding hogs through the streets, some days a dozen flatboats at the landing and men and families trudging up the steep slant of Broadway. The public market was alive with people, the taverns buzzed with talk. Already a center of frontier life, Cincinnati was a place where squatters jostled land speculators and Indians brushed past army men. Through the motley market crowds, past silk hats and coonskin caps, broadcloth capes and linsey-woolsey, army blouses and deerskin jackets, went the spare young captain and his dressy friend, arguing about land laws, public revenues, and the national debt. Burnet upheld the policies of Federalism against the views of Thomas Jefferson which Harrison admired. Forty years later they would be on the same side; at the Harrisburg Convention in 1839 Jacob Burnet made the speech that nominated Harrison for the presidency.

In 1796 Harrison purchased 160 acres at North Bend at three dollars an acre, buying it from Congressman Jonathan Dayton, a partner of Judge Symmes in the Miami speculation, and the next year he bought a four-room cabin at the edge of his land. He was a family man now—two children had been born in the fort—and thinking about civilian life. In 1798 he resigned from the army and took the job of Land Office Register, keeping records and receiving payments, when purchasers appeared, for lands in the Miami tract. His father-in-law had posted handbills on the river landing, in Cincinnati taverns, and at crossroads up Mill Creek and beyond: "It is hoped that all who want to become purchasers, will not longer suffer themselves to be amused with the idle reports against the contract [with Congress] but purchase immediately from some Persons who have a right to sell. And those Gentlemen who have already contracts for the Miami Lands, are desired to make payment as soon as possible to William Henry Harrison. . . ."

Then came a larger office. In June, 1798, President John Adams was "pleased to appoint . . . William Henry Harrison to be Secretary of the Territory of the United States North West of the River Ohio."

In his log office on the Cincinnati river bank Harrison kept the Territorial records—changes of county boundaries, militia rosters, ferry licenses, cases against squatters, land disputes, the sessions of the Territorial court. There he watched land-hungry speculators and farmers, while in Congress Hall in far-off Philadelphia men were debating the federal land policy.

Two years later, elected Congressional Delegate from the Northwest Territory, Harrison raised his voice in those discussions. For eight impressionable years he had been in the West. His memories of Virginia, with manor houses dominating great plantations, had been dimmed by fresh knowledge of squatters and settlers girdling the forest trees, hacking out clearings, and chopping the ground with an ax blade to start a crop of corn. As a Territory man he was placed on the Committee of the Public Lands. There the lean young Westerner, twenty-seven years old, told veteran lawmakers that the West must offer a future not for speculators and landlords but for hopeful and ambitious settlers. He proposed a land act which became law on May 10, 1800, when cornfields along the Ohio were being plowed and planted.

The Harrison Land Law provided for sale of half sections—320 acres—at the established price of two dollars per acre, to be paid in installments over four years. Amended four years later, the law allowed a settler to buy a minimum of 160 acres for an eighty-dollar entrance fee, followed by annual payments of eighty dollars for the next three years.

The new land act was electric news on the frontier.

Published in the *Western Spy,* Cincinnati's pioneer newspaper, it was read and re-read in crossroads inns and forest
cabins, on flatboat decks and river landings, in blacksmith
shops and gristmills. Now a young farmer could buy land
from the government instead of from the speculator who
had entered public land and resold it in lots at an inflated
price. The new law offered smaller tracts on easier terms; at
the same time it assured the settler of a clear title. A writer
in *Niles' Register* remarked that "probably as much money
is annually expended in Kentucky and Tennessee in *land
title litigation* as would defray their taxes for the support
of the severest war. . . . What a contrast between occupying
land by a doubtful title and purchasing from the United
States."

Under the new law land offices were established in
the midst of the wilderness for sale. Land could be purchased from government agents at Pittsburgh, Marietta,
Chillicothe and Cincinnati. Back to Ohio Delegate Harrison sent a message: "this law promises to be the foundation
of a great increase of population and wealth to our country."
It was the beginning of a policy of public land for the public,
a policy which was liberalized in the Old Northwest during
the next forty years, and then continued to be enlarged in
new frontiers beyond the Mississippi. Under the old law, allowing no purchase of less than 640 acres, sale of public land
had been slow as summer smoke; less than fifty thousand
acres had been purchased by 1800. In the first eighteen
months of the new law four hundred thousand acres passed
into private hands, and three quarters of a million acres were
sold by the end of 1802.

Under the Harrison Land Act counties filled up,
surveys were pushed into new regions, district land offices
were opened in Vincennes, Kaskaskia, Detroit, then in Canton, Jeffersonville, and Shawneetown. By 1820 there were
fourteen land offices north of the Ohio. Though townsite pro-
motions continued, wild land speculation all but disappeared
in the Ohio country. Sale of small claims on installment

terms opened the common domain to the common man. The Harrison Land Act looked forward to 1862 when Lincoln would sign the Homestead Bill, indicating his belief in "settling of the wild lands into small parcels so that every poor man may have a home."

The installment plan, always popular in America, seemed to western settlers a good way to buy land. One quarter down-payment, the rest within five years—it was a cheerful system and sadly unrealistic. By nature a frontier farmer was hopeful and ambitious, always expecting a better season, a bigger crop, a higher price for his produce. The West attracted young men who had not learned doubt and caution, and the unfenced land enlarged their hopes. So a settler took all the land on which he could make the first payment. It was more land than he could clear and farm, and he would be lucky if he could meet the second, third and fourth payments. All the West was opposed to eviction and Congress dared not deal harshly with delinquent settlers. So the farmer stayed on his unbought land, waiting for the better season and the bigger crop. When hard times darkened the West in 1819 the errors of the credit system were as plain as daylight. By 1820 the government had sold forty-four million dollars' worth of land and had collected twenty-two millions. Half of the land claimed in the West was not paid for.

In Congress debate went on—eastern men arguing that public land should produce revenue, western men crying for cheaper land and the sale of smaller tracts to encourage frontier settlement. Eastern Congressmen feared that cheap land would depopulate the older states; Westerners wanted to open wider the domain. But both sides saw the evils of the credit system.

The new land law of 1820 offered eighty-acre tracts at $1.25 an acre, cash. Now a man could buy a small farm instead of going in debt for a large one; if he prospered he could add another eighty acres, owning it outright. The auction system was continued, land being opened to bidding before it was offered at the $1.25 figure; district auctions were scheduled for three weeks a year at the various land offices. A speculator could travel from one auction to another, bidding on the best locations and hoping to resell at a profit. But when a man with a hundred dollars in his pocket could get clear title to eighty acres, the speculators had new competition from the federal land agents.

Still the newcomers pressed on ahead of legal entry. They wanted land of their own choosing and they could not wait for the slow processes of law. Indian purchase meant a summoning of the chiefs, a ceremonious presentation of gifts, a deliberate council; it was a drawn-out business. Survey was still slower. The chain-men had to traverse all the country, measuring ponds and marshes and hardscrabble hillsides as well as rich bottom lands and meadow openings. The settlers scrambled on to the best locations. They were a population on the move, ahead of the law rather than outside it, hacking out tomahawk claims on Indian lands, clearing a field before the surveyors had come. Thousands of frontier farmers found their land, improved it, and made their first harvest before their claim could be identified in the land office. They expected to buy it at the government price and they wanted assurance that no land-jobber could stand in their way. They wanted squatter's rights.

The settlers were numerous as well as headstrong, and since they would not yield to the law, the law must yield to them. In 1807 Congress had passed an Intrusion Act, penalizing and dispossessing squatters on the public domain. But law could not catch up with men overrunning the wild lands, and the Intrusion Act was soon forgotten. In 1830, considerably wiser in the realities of the West, Congress enacted a preëmption law which made "intrusion" legal. Settlers who had cultivated land in the public domain were allowed to purchase as much as a hundred and sixty acres at the $1.25 figure. This was a temporary law, renewed throughout the

1830s. At last came the Preëmption Act of 1841, which permanently legalized settlement before purchase. Squatter's rights were established.

In fifty years land policy had reversed itself. The original land laws sought revenue for the federal government, but the western people, growing in numbers and power, saw the wilderness as opportunity. The spreading of settlement became more important than the raising of revenue, and the squatter changed from an outlaw to the American pioneer. Wild land was not for the speculator or even for the national treasury; it was for the man who would tame it and gather its harvest.

CHAPTER SIX

FOUR ROADS TO OHIO

The possession of land is the aim of all action, generally speaking, and the cure for all social ills, among men in the United States. If a man is disappointed in politics or love, he goes and buys land. If he disgraces himself, he betakes himself to a lot in the West.

—HARRIET MARTINEAU: *Society in America*

SOMEONE said that if an Ohio town built a Congregational Church and a college, it was certainly of New England origin; if it had a Presbyterian Church and a distillery, it had been settled by Virginians. Both Yankees and Southerners carried their household goods, and their institutions, over the mountains. Beside them came people from all the other seaboard states and from lands across the sea. An emigrant from England described his fellow travelers on the road: "The New Englanders . . . may be known by the cheerfulness of the women advancing in front of the vehicle; the Jersey people by their being fixed steadily within it; whilst the Pennsylvanians creep lingeringly be-

117

hind, as though regretting the homes they had left." In no other American region did so many different peoples meet.

Before its history began America was a country of migration. The Indians were a roving people, with long trails for hunting, trade, and war, and the great game animals ranged with the seasons. The ancient trails, cut by hoofs and hardened by the tread of moccasins, were the natural ways through wild country. They followed the streams, climbed the easy grades, found the gaps and notches in the mountain walls. In the years of the great migration of folk from the East these wild trails became the paths of history. There were four of them: the Genesee Road through the Mohawk Valley from Albany to Buffalo; Forbes' Road from Philadelphia over the mountains to Pittsburgh; the Cumberland Road from Baltimore along the Potomac through old Fort Cumberland and on to the Ohio at either Pittsburgh or Wheeling; and the Wilderness Road down the great valley of Virginia over Cumberland Gap and up through the woods and meadows of Kentucky. Four roads fanning into the Ohio country brought the future to the West.

The oldest was the Wilderness Road. This ancient Indian path formed a lazy U, starting from the Potomac just above Harper's Ferry, following the Shenandoah Valley down to Cumberland Gap, and then striking up through Kentucky to the Ohio at the site of future Louisville. It was the path Daniel Boone had followed, traveling wary, cheerful and alone, into wild green country. He found the westward flowing rivers—the Shawnee which some called the Cumberland, the winding Cuttawa that was also called the Tennessee, the rock-walled Chenoa, the River of the Great Salt Lick that was later called the Licking, the green and gentle Pigeon River and the boisterous Chatteraway.

In 1775 Judge Richard Henderson's Transylvania Company bought most of present Kentucky from the Cherokees, and Henderson sent Boone ahead to mark a trail for colonists to follow. He blazed Boone's Trace from Cumberland Gap along the Kentucky River that flowed into the

Ohio, and he led the first risky caravans to Boonesborough and St. Asaph's Station. In 1776, while Washington was driving the British out of Boston and Tom Paine was fuming at the thought of a new continent overshadowed by an island three thousand miles away, that western land was organized as Kentucky County. But Indian war parties armed by the British at Detroit crossed the Ohio, besieged the frontier stations, and drove the Kentuckians out: by 1777 just two western towns, Boonesborough and Harrodsburg, remained. In that "year of the bloody sevens" George Rogers Clark planned his bold campaign north of the Ohio. His capture of Kaskaskia and Vincennes secured Kentucky, and settlement poured in.

Over the Wilderness Road came hunters, land-lookers, pioneer farmers and families. Down the Ohio from Pittsburgh and Wheeling came the Kentucky boats, boarded up against arrows and bullets from the Indian side. At Louisville whole households came ashore—master and slaves, mother and children, horses, oxen, sheep, and pigs. Through Cumberland Gap passed a great procession—pack horses laden with flour, salt, gunpowder; freight wagons bulging with bags of seed corn, rye, malt and bundles of blankets and booting; farm wagons bristling with plow-handles, scythes, cradles, and spinning wheels. Campfires twinkled beside the fording places, hogs and cattle foraged in the woods, hens laid fresh eggs under the wagon beds. Soon the valleys were hacked with clearings and dotted with cabins; along the rivers new towns sprang up. In 1792, when four anxious settlements clung to the north bank of the Ohio, Kentucky, along the south bank, became the fifteenth state.

After the Treaty of Greene Ville, with the Indians out of the way, Kentuckians crossed the river to squat on Ohio land or to make a clear, sure purchase from the federal government. When the Virginia Military District was open to settlement, Virginians trooped into the Scioto valley where land waited to be claimed by men with military warrants. Not all the Virginia veterans came west to claim their bounties. Many of them had no experience of frontier life and the prospect of a tract of wild land did not lure them over the mountains. They gladly exchanged their wilderness claims for a few dollars in cash. So Nathaniel Massie and Duncan McArthur, as we have seen, came into the wild District with warrants for hundreds of thousands of acres.

In the last years of the 1790s caravans of Virginia adventurers creaked up the Scioto to Massie's town of Chillicothe. Two notable arrivals in the spring of 1798, with a troop of freed slaves shambling beside their wagons, were Thomas Worthington and his brother-in-law Edward Tiffin. In his portmanteau Tiffin had a recommendation for public office, addressed to Territorial Governor St. Clair and signed by George Washington. He would become the first governor of the state of Ohio, the first director of the National Land Office, and Surveyor-General of the Northwest. Thomas Worthington had been a surveyor. He looked shrewdly at the hills and valleys, the woods and meadows of the Scioto; perhaps he pictured roads and waterways of the future. He would become one of the first two Senators from Ohio, its sixth governor, and a leader in its first canal commission. He would build mills on Paint Creek and a mansion above the Scioto—a country mansion in the manner of tidewater Virginia, designed by the elder Latrobe and furnished with glass, marble and mahogany from Baltimore and Philadelphia. There he would walk with his friends in an English garden while his ten children played under the maple trees.

But first he learned the silence and solitude of the western country. As deputy surveyor he ran township lines between the Ohio Company's purchase and the Scioto River. In the back country he saw trees blazed with the squatter's tomahawk claim and he talked with men who wanted legal farms but could not pay for a section of government land. Remembering those poor and hardy farmers he went to Philadelphia in 1800 and helped William Henry Harrison push through Congress the act which opened half-sections to sale and settlement, and so made honest citizens out of trespassers on the public lands.

Hill farmers in Virginia and the Carolinas, plowing a steep field and running cattle in a hacked-out pasture, heard of land a-plenty across the Ohio. When a horseman rode through the Miami valley, it was said, his legs were splashed with the juice of strawberries. This was a traveler's tale, but Ohio was indeed a beckoning and fruitful country. It had tiny wild berries, sweet as honey, plump dark mulberries, wild grapes, dewberries, red and black raspberries, juicy persimmons, pawpaws yellow as gold and rich as butter. It had uplands and bottoms, timberland and grassland. And it offered secure titles without prior and conflicting land claims.

From the great valley of Virginia the Cumberland Mountains stood up against the sky, softly blue, smoke blue, hazed with light and distance. Nearer they grew dark, slate-colored under a clouded sky, green if the sun was on them. From the Powell River valley they looked hard and hostile, lifting steep forests and naked cliffs across the west. Then the Gap appeared, a gunsight in the barrier hills, and the sky was bright in its cleft of green. The road staggered and climbed. It passed under the looming rock and the roar of water. It pitched up, into the notch, and there the emigrants stood, looking into new country before they set the wagon brakes for the long descent.

What they saw was more hills, long green ridges tumbling on to the horizon. Ahead of them, to the north and west, over the last diminishing hills lay the bluegrass meadows of Kentucky, and farther yet the winding Ohio and the wild lands beyond. Cumberland Gap was a gateway before Wheeling, Pittsburgh and Buffalo heard the creak of movers' wagons. But no city grew there. It was a lifeless landmark, without navigable waters though streams flowed in three directions from its lofty caves, and with other hills ahead. As its name suggests, the Wilderness Road was the most strenuous way to the West—across the Clinch River and over Clinch Mountain, past Shelby's lonely fort, over Moccasin Gap and across the Powell River, then past Martin's Station and up the steep pitch to the pass. It was the first route to be traveled, and the first to be abandoned. When other ways were opened its traffic dwindled; the clangor of cowbells and the rattle of trace chains died away in the hills. Now U.S. 25 climbs through Cumberland Gap, taking fishermen to the Tennessee Valley and winter tourists on their way to Florida. But it brings few travelers to the West.

At Baltimore began the Cumberland Road, which took its name from Cumberland on the Potomac, three hundred miles northeast of Cumberland Gap and wholly unrelated to that strategic gateway. From Baltimore the road ran nearly due west for a hundred and fifty miles to the head of navigation on the Potomac; then it struck across the lifting green Allegheny ridges to Redstone on the Monongahela. It forked there, one route turning north to Pittsburgh and the other continuing westward to Wheeling on the Ohio.

This was the road, originally an Indian path, which Braddock's men had widened to carry the wagons of war. Over it in the early years came George Croghan the trader, George Washington the soldier, Christopher Gist the landlooker for Virginia gentlemen, Conrad Weiser the Indian Agent. This way, in 1772, came nineteen-year-old George Rogers Clark when the West was British and the road was crossed by the track of bears and panthers. Its ruts were deepened by emigrant wagons when the West became American. In 1790 it brought the hopeful French emigrés on the long rough journey to their Scioto lands. Thousands of emigrants knew its bruising roots and boulders before the road crews smoothed it out. As the National Road, opened to Wheeling in 1817, it was the first macadamized highway in America, graded and graveled and ground by the wheels of frontier commerce. Then stages rattled west on daily schedule and six-horse teams hauled the big Conestoga freighters. Now the old Cumberland Road is part of U.S. 40 which spans the continent from Atlantic City to San Francisco.

West from Philadelphia ran the Pennsylvania State

Road, originally Forbes' Road, through Lancaster, Carlisle, and Bedford to the forks of the Ohio. Once it was a pack-horse trail, carrying trade goods to the Black Forest and bringing back the Indian peltry. In 1758 Colonel Bouquet and young George Washington with a hundred grunting ax-men opened it to wagon traffic across Laurel Ridge and on to Pittsburgh. Blockhouse forts were raised along the way to guard the movement of troops, arms and supplies. Over this military route in the fall of 1791 came William Henry Harrison with a file of eighty men; his pack, bulging with Cicero's *Orations* and a book of rhetoric besides his army gear, grew heavy on the long hills. This was the road that brought John Cleves Symmes, with seven wagons, thirty-one horses and a company of sixty colonists, on his way to the Miami country. It brought Blennerhassett to his island of beauty in the Ohio and Aaron Burr on his quest for a western empire.

"A pile of people are on the road," said tavern-keepers in the Pennsylvania valleys. They came from New York and New Jersey, from the eastern counties of Pennsylvania and from immigrant ships in the docks of Philadelphia. Striking straight west from the central seaboard the Pennsylvania Road was worn by wagons, carts, carryalls, traps, flies and buggies, a motley procession of wheeled vehicles. It brought George Rapp's Württemberg Germans on their way to Harmonie in Indiana, the English colonists on their way to Albion in Illinois, the cosmopolitan band of scientists and fanatics on their way to Robert Owen's brave new world of social equality on the Wabash. "A powerful parcel of people are headin' for the 'Hio country," said Pennsylvania mountaineers, and some of them loaded their farm wagons and went along. The road ended under the hills of Pittsburgh at the trampled river landings. There the movers sold their horses to travelers going east and loaded their goods onto flatboats. The broad Ohio carried them on to the wilderness.

When the Erie Canal was opened across New York in 1825, the Pennsylvania Road could not compete with that smooth waterway. But there was business in the West, more business every year, and Philadelphia's merchants were not content to watch the traffic dwindling overland. They could not cut a canal through the watershed of the Alleghenies, but they could approach the height of land by water and cross it by a wagon portage. In 1825 when the first barges ran from Albany to Buffalo surveyors measured a proposed canal from Harrisburg to Pittsburgh; it called for a total lockage of 1782 feet, requiring 220 locks, and a twenty-mile portage road over the highest barriers. In describing this prodigious work the Pittsburgh Gazette grew urgent; "Now is the important time—let not folly, infatuation, party spirit or local jealousy deprive the west of this grand improvement. . . . The *west* expects every man to do his duty." In 1826 the Pennsylvania legislature passed an act calling for construction of a "waterway" from Philadelphia to Pittsburgh.

So the work began, at both ends of the line, and in 1834 a new way was open to the West. The "Pennsylvania System" was a 363-mile combination of railroad, canal, horse car, and stage coach—a marvel of transportation in its time. The route lay north of Forbes' Road, along the old Kittanning Path of the colonial pack horsemen. A pioneer railroad was built from Philadelphia to the Susquehanna. There a canal began, following the Susquehanna and Juniata rivers to the forbidding rise of the Alleghenies. For forty miles the way was barred with looming ridges and deep valleys, but by horse power and steam engines the Pennsylvania System got across. Wooden "inclined planes" carried rail cars up and down the slopes, with horses plodding around a capstan at the top of the grade and ropes easing the cars down the other side. Stages dashed across the valley to the next inclined plane over the next mountain wall. At the foot of the long hill to Johnstown a western canal began. After passing sixty-four locks, ten dams, two tunnels, and sixteen aqueducts, the traveler arrived at Pittsburgh. Passengers could step from railroad car to canal boat, from horse car to stage coach, but freight must be transferred at all these points. To

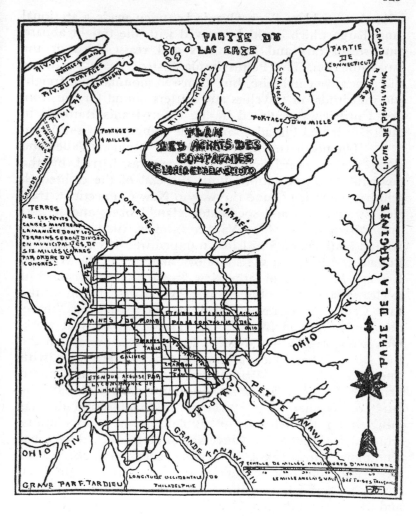

The above is a copy of the map published by the Scioto Company in Paris in their *Prospectus*. It was intended to show the respective situations of the Ohio and Scioto companies' tracts of land. Note the inscription, "Etendue acquis par la Compagnie de la Scioto, . . ." Water routes especially are shown, rivers and portages being given to show the easy means of communication with the United States, the south, the Great Lakes, and Canada. Notice also the mines and salt springs given.

solve that problem Pennsylvania boatmen made a sectional canal barge which could be moved with the freight aboard onto steam cars and horse cars and reassembled at the canal junction. The Pennsylvania System was a strenuous and expensive enterprise, but it carried mountains of freight and multitudes of travelers and settlers bound for the frontier. Until it was replaced by the Pennsylvania Railroad in the 1850s it tied Philadelphia to the commerce of the West.

The northern route, through the Mohawk Valley and along the westward-flowing Genesee, was barred by the powerful Iroquois nations until the end of the eighteenth century. Then it became the way to New Connecticut, traveled by surveyors and speculators, land-lookers and settlers in northern Ohio. Many Yankee farmers, tired of plowing around boulders on a hillside, tramped west from Albany to Buffalo and followed the shore of Lake Erie to the Western Reserve. Many sons of large New England families came out to clear a farm in the Ohio forest. When work began on the Erie Canal the Genesee Road became part of a "three-thousand-mile road from Cork." Thousands of Irish workmen swung axes in the Mohawk forests and shoveled out the Big Ditch. They made a smooth new western way, with canal boats leaving Albany every hour of day and night, bringing Yankees, Yorkers, and immigrants from all the lands of Northern Europe. A dozen tongues and dialects mingled on the wharves of Buffalo as new populations crowded into boats for Cleveland and Detroit. The canal sent plows, anvils, axes, horseshoes, sugar, tea, rice, calico seed grain, and new settlers to the West; it brought back corn, oats, and wheat, pork, beef, and wool, apples, cheese, and whisky from the new clearings.

"The old America seems to be breaking up and moving West," said Morris Birkbeck in 1817. Behind the travelers on the roads were the same pressures that have sent people to every new region in America. Population was growing in the older states; the native population of America doubled every generation in the fifty years after the Revolution. Fifteen children of a Yankee farmer could not all inherit the family farm. Some of them went to work in the cotton factories, others went to the frontier. During hard seasons in New England, or when Southern farmers watched the price of cotton falling, there was a special brightness in the West. Economic hardship pushed people from the older regions to a new beginning beyond the mountains. But most important was the American restlessness and optimism, a habit of mind which carried settlement across the continent in a few decades. In the beginning of the American experience people lived on the shore of an empty continent, on the fringe of unmapped and unmeasured land, on the edge of endlessness. The vastness of the country came to them gradually and it worked on the national consciousness.

There was room in the West; there was a new chance over the mountains; beyond the horizon waited the unknown and untried. Most Americans had no long family tradition, no home for generations past. With new country to be claimed they felt little sentiment for the older country. Land was to be possessed, not to be possessed by. A home could be sold, like a horse or a harvest, and a new home found. There was a hazard of new fortunes on the road ahead. Said William Faux, an earthy English farmer on tour in the Ohio country, seeing how lightly a man could load his wagon and leave the past behind him: "The American has always something better in his eye; he lives and dies on hopes, a mere gypsy in this particular." And Birkbeck concluded his reflection: "Americans are a migratory people."

The same motives that sent emigrants from the seaboard states brought immigrants on a longer journey. Birkbeck himself was seeking a site for an English settlement in the Ohio valley when he remarked on the American migration. Harriet Martineau said, as though it were peculiar to the United States, "The pride and delight of Americans is in their quantity of land. I do not remember meeting with one to whom it had occurred that he had too much." What was peculiar was not the pride of ownership but the wholesale opportunity for that kind of pride. No dukedom in France or England lay open to ambitious farmers. The opportunity for landless men to become landed men drew people across three thousand miles of ocean and over the long roads to Ohio. The West was a new name for the good chance.

As in every land boom the newcomers were lured by dishonest claims and unscrupulous advertisement. Many became victims of fraud and swindle—"town lots" in the middle of a swamp, mill sites on a dry creek, "fertile farm lands" covered with impenetrable forest. But behind the speculator and land-jobber was a rich country, millions of acres of wild land full of promise for those who could tame it. Many came ill-prepared—who can prepare for fever and ague, for draught and famine, for bad luck and bad management? Some settlers failed, many died early, a few returned to the land of steady habits and small expectations. All new countries are settled by unprepared people, but this vanguard learned in time. They made the West over in a generation.

Migration to the Ohio valley went on for forty years, a tidal movement with surging rhythm and power. The first big wave swept in after 1800 when the Harrison Land Act opened the public territory to ambitious farmers. Movers came on despite the War of 1812, but the end of the war was the signal for a new surge of western settlement. The Great Migration filled five expanding years, 1815 to 1819, with the thud of the settler's ax and the haze of his brush fires. Forests became farms, Ohio villages grew into towns, wild territory became the states of Indiana and Illinois. This urgent inrush came by the Ohio River, filling the southern counties while northern districts of the new states were still wild and empty. The panic of 1819 halted the migration and hard times curbed it for a decade. But a bigger surge came in the 1830s, when new highways and canals carried new multitudes to the West. These years brought settlement to the northern districts, and the Great Lakes became a waterway as vital as the Ohio. Speculation and expansion reached a crest in 1836 and the panic of 1837 ended the greatest land boom in the old Northwest. But it did not end the growth of the western states. By 1840 they were strong enough to elect an Ohio President over a New York man. Then the Ohio country was no longer a new region. The West had moved on across the Mississippi.

CHAPTER SEVEN

THE FIRST FORTY-EIGHT

No colony in America was ever settled under such favorable auspices.

—GEORGE WASHINGTON

TWO HUNDRED miles below Pittsburgh on a table-land along the Muskingum's west shore stood Fort Harmar, a pentagon of logs and timbers with a blockhouse overlooking the meeting of the rivers. Built in 1785 to keep squatters from Indian lands west of the Seven Ranges, it was the first fort on the "Indian side" of the Ohio and the only fort ever built in America to protect the rights of red men. But when surveyors cut their way into the Seven Ranges, troops from the garrison scouted the woods around them. Fort Harmar was no longer on the Indian side.

After some weeks the surveyors left their witness trees and pulled back up the river, but the men at the fort stayed on. Three dollars a month was a soldier's pay; his life was mostly empty. For desertion a man received a hundred lashes on his bare back, unless he got far enough away for the Indians to find him. Sometimes scouts and hunters came on signs of violence in the woods, a bloody jacket or a body gnawed by wolves, or a canoe caught in the willows containing a pair of shoes and some parched corn. For drunkenness a man got the same hundred lashes, except on special days like the First of May and the Fourth of July when the whole company had extra rations of whisky. May Day was a big day, with drinking and whooping and firing of guns in honor of St. Tammany, patron saint of this boisterous festival. A soldier could get safely and completely drunk under the aegis of the affable Tammany, a Delaware chief remembered for his friendliness to white men when the colonies were young. Otherwise, the days were much alike. The sun rose out of the Virginia hills and the flag went up in the compound. The garrison moved through a morning drill. A detail of men stalked out to hunt deer and turkey for the mess, the rest lounged on the riverbank or hacked at the weedy garden beyond the stockade walls. The sun sank into the woods and the flag came down, the bugler's last note fading over the hills. Fort Harmar was an outpost in far country, and if a man got to wondering whether any life was left in the world, his eyes searched the rivers.

Sometimes a long canoe, hacked and burned out of a poplar log, came down the Muskingum. There would be a grave, monosyllabic deal in trader Gibson's storehouse—a pile of peltry for a pair of blankets and a skinning knife—and the canoe would creep back up the river toward the straggling Wyandot camps. Sometimes a flatboat came down the Ohio. That was more lively—men shouting and waving from the roof, horses whinnying with pointed ears, women shading their eyes to see a white man's station in that savage country. Long oars worked the clumsy craft to the landing. They wanted fresh fodder for the animals and a fresh side of meat if the quartermaster could spare it. They wondered about the Indians down river and the distance to Limestone Creek. They talked about Redstone, Kittanning, and Pittsburgh, about the roads over the mountains and the place in Kentucky they were seeking. When they pushed out and the current carried them away, there were new figures to add to the record of river traffic.

Most of them came in spring, when the river was high and there was yet time to find a location in Kentucky and get a crop of corn into wild ground. But some straggled down the river in the shimmering heat of summer, and a few in the soft haze of fall. The tally from June to December, 1787: one hundred forty-six boats, three thousand one hundred ninety-six souls, thirteen hundred eighty-one horses, one hundred sixty-five wagons, one hundred seventy-one cattle, two hundred forty-five sheep, twenty-four hogs—all bound for the Kentucky settlements, though some of them would surely steer into the forbidden rivers north of the Ohio and squat on Indian land.

All winter the river was empty save for sullen slabs of ice drifting past gray shores. Snow outlined the lifeless mounds across the Muskingum—steep-sided burial cones, abrupt earth platforms, flat-topped pyramids, ceremonial squares joined by raised avenues. Those ghostly earthworks would remain on the riverbank long after all signs of Fort Harmar had vanished. And if that melancholy realization did not occur to the men in the stockade, they had no thoughts more cheerful.

Winter was a long and lifeless season, but at last the wind came with a softness from the south. Spring brought high water, strewing the shores with brush and driftwood, washing the last gray slush ice from the willow thickets. It brought Indians down the Muskingum, eager for the bright taste of the white man's molasses and the quick fire of his whisky. Soon it would bring flatboats down the Ohio.

On the misty morning of April 7th, 1788, the river was a vague gray silence under Harmar Hill. But through the mist came voices, and out of the blur grew shapes of two broad flatboats and three long canoes. They groped in to the landing and men stepped ashore—forty-eight men under Rufus Putnam, ready to begin settlement of the Ohio Company's lands and to build their town on the Muskingum shore. There was a noisy welcome at the fort, and amid the general hubbub Ebenezer Sproat, Anselm Tupper and John Matthews renewed acquaintance with soldiers they had known in the survey camps eighteen months before. Putnam's men had been making for the east bank of the Muskingum mouth but had missed it in the thick weather. Later that day the soldiers towed them across the Muskingum, where a party of wondering Delawares watched them unload. While their winter-starved horses and cattle grazed on lush pea vines and buffalo clover, the men began hacking at the woods. That night the sentry at Fort Harmar could look at camp-fires flickering in the rainy dark.

Marietta, like most other cities, was not founded in a day. It had begun five years before, in 1783, when the Revolutionary army was camped in winter quarters at Newburgh on the Hudson. The war was over, and what was there to talk about? In their smoky tents the men talked about women, about home, about the years ahead, about the shinplasters that were a soldier's pay and the land warrants that were a soldier's bonus. They talked about wild lands beyond the mountains, the Ohio country rolling westward toward the Mississippi. Military warrants were good for land in the public domain—eleven hundred acres to a major general, five hundred to a colonel, one hundred to a private. Out there beyond the mountains men might form a soldiers' state which would enter the Union as a new and equal commonwealth. The talk quickened. Looking into the fire they saw pictures of a green new world, of towns beside the rivers, of forest clearings where chimney smoke went up to the Ohio sky.

At last Timothy Pickering of Salem, Massachusetts, Quartermaster-General of the Continental Army, acting as scribe for his fellow officers, wrote out a proposal for a colony north of the Ohio River, a colony which in time would become a state. As chairman of the officers' organization General Rufus Putnam framed the Newburgh Petition, asking Congress to mark off such a district and to allot army bounty lands in this territory. Two hundred eighty-eight officers signed, most of them from Massachusetts and Connecticut where land was already crowded and the fields were strewn with rock. They had a dream of rich land in a wild new country.

General Putnam, who had driven the British out of Boston, rebuilt the fortifications at West Point and fought at the battles of Verplanck and Stony Point, sent the petition to his friend President Washington, stating that he considered the western lands "of great consequence to the American Empire." He went on to prophesy: "The country between Lake Erie and the Ohio, will be filled with inhabitants, and the faithful subjects of these United States so established on the waters of the Ohio and the lakes as to banish forever the idea of our western country under the dominion of any European power." He added that the army men were opposed to large individual grants of land, for "it throws too much power in the hands of a few."

Washington gave the petition a prompt recommendation, but it was pigeon-holed in Congress; the hard-pressed legislators were not ready to settle the future ownership and administration of a territory six times the size of England. A year later, however, a Congressional committee headed by Thomas Jefferson offered a plan of government for the western country. This Ordinance of 1784 called for a division of the western territory into some sixteen or eighteen states, ten of them north of the Ohio. These states would be bounded by lines of latitude two degrees apart, intersected by meridians drawn through the mouth of the Great Kanawha and the Falls of the Ohio; they were to be named Sylvania, Michigania, Cheronesus, Assenisipia, Metropotamia, Illinoia, Saratoga, Washington, Polypotamia, and Pelisipia. The Ordinance, though approved by Congress, was not put into action.

Before western settlement had begun it was superseded by the Ordinance of 1787.

The Continental Army was disbanded, but the dream at Newburgh smoldered in men's minds. In the spring of 1784, when snow water ran off in the brooks and the first green showed on Massachusetts hillsides, General Putnam wrote again to President Washington: "The settlement of the Ohio country, sir, engrosses many of my thoughts . . . and if I am to form an opinion on what I have seen and heard on the subject there is thousands in this quarter will emigrate to that country as soon as the honorable Congress makes provision for the granting of land."

The next year Congress passed the Ordinance of 1785 which called for the commencing of a systematic survey of the public lands and authorized their distribution to Revolutionary troops in exchange for land warrants. But it failed to provide for organization of a new state and it required minimum land sales of 640 acres. That minimum would be a barrier to many potential settlers, but Congress, burdened with war debt, was more concerned with raising revenue from the public lands than with offering a future to poor men.

The western survey, as we have seen, began on the far boundary of Pennsylvania with the measuring of seven ranges running forty-two miles west of the up-curving Ohio. The western meridian would run south over the wooded hills to a point near the confluence of the Muskingum and the Ohio. Townships six miles square would contain thirty-six sections of six hundred forty acres each. So began the rectangular survey which eventually was carried all the way to the Pacific.

Rufus Putnam was appointed a surveyor of the Seven Ranges, but he was already in charge of a survey of Maine lands owned by the state of Massachusetts. In his place he recommended General Benjamin Tupper, whom he had known in the war and who had signed the petition at Newburgh. Tupper went west in the fall of 1785 and worked with Thomas Hutchins in the Seven Ranges. He brought back an exciting account of the wild country, along with the field descriptions made by young John Matthews. All one winter night he sat before Putnam's fireplace at Rutland, Massachusetts, talking about the western lands. The forests were magnificent and vast, with lofty roofs of branches and hollow trees big enough for a man to live in. One hunter could keep sixty men supplied with meat. In open places the soil, thinly scratched by Indian women, yielded crops never heard of in the rocky valleys of New England.

The dream at Newburgh leaped up again, but Congress had not yet opened the Northwest to settlement. The land-hungry veterans needed an organization and a plan. A few weeks later newspapers in Boston and Worcester carried an item of "Information," advising all officers and soldiers eligible to claim land in the Ohio country, as well as other citizens who cared to become "adventurers in that delightful region," to meet locally and send representatives to an organizing meeting in Boston on the first day of March, 1787.

On that day eleven delegates met at the Bunch of Grapes Tavern, two streets below the Old South Meeting House. After three days of discussion the Ohio Company of Associates was formed, and plans were made for raising capital of one million dollars in Continental certificates. This it would use to purchase Ohio land and locate a settlement.

But they must still wait upon Congress. The Reverend Manasseh Cutler, one of the Associates, was sent to New York to lobby for the project. Cutler was a big and buoyant man, versatile as a Franklin. Botanist, lawyer, merchant, he had become a Congregational minister and had served as chaplain during the Revolution. On a radiant June day in 1787 he hitched his horse to a two-wheeled cart and drove away from his manse in Ipswich Hamlet, Massachusetts. After stopping at New Haven to lecture on Botany at Yale College, he arrived in New York (then the temporary national capital) and began his calls on the Congressmen. A proposed ordinance for the government of the Northwest Territory was pulled out of the committee file. Cutler made some suggestions, including the general principle: "Religion, morality, and knowledge, being necessary to good government and the happiness of mankind, schools and the means of education shall forever be encouraged." On July 13, 1787, the revised ordinance became law. Cutler then pressed for approval of the Ohio Company's contract. Congress wanted a minimum of one dollar an acre for the one million acres, payable three months after the purchase. Cutler could not agree to these terms, and the prospect dimmed. But at that point he was approached by Colonel William Duer, Secretary of the Board of the Treasury. Duer was later to engage in many speculations; now he proposed that the "Scioto project," hastily organized by a group of promoters, be included in the Ohio Company's contract, but that it be kept a "profound secret." Over an oyster dinner in Brooklyn, with a procession of fine wines, Cutler agreed to Duer's plan. Accordingly he enlarged his application to four million acres, of which three million would be assigned, it was unstated but understood, to the Scioto Company. Duer proceeded to use his influence and that of his associates in the federal Treasury to win over reluctant Congressmen. At the end of July Congress approved the purchase by the Ohio Company of Associates of a tract covering five to six million acres, to be paid for at a dollar an acre. Four months later at Ipswich, Massachusetts, with a cold wind blowing from the ocean, twenty-two men listened to Manasseh Cutler's farewell words. They cracked their ox whips and started west, striding beside a wagon covered with black canvas and lettered in Cutler's bold hand FOR THE OHIO COUNTRY. Nearly four years had passed since the men at Newburgh had signed the petition, but now they were on their way.

Some notable men took possession of bounty lands, made available to veterans through military warrants, in the years after the Revolution. Like any other veteran, George Washington was entitled to land warrants—from Virginia for duty in the French and Indian War and from the United

States for service in the War for Independence. Though he claimed no bounty lands (he had already taken title to forty-one thousand acres along the Kanawha in Virginia and the Ohio into which the Kanawha empties) he bought warrants from other veterans, one for three thousand acres issued to Captain John Rootes by Governor Dunmore of Virginia and another for a hundred acres issued to Thomas Cope by the federal government. These warrants were located in the Little Miami valley, near Cincinnati; but like many less informed men Washington failed to record them properly and never received title to the land. John Paul Jones was rewarded for a naval victory off the stormy coast of Scotland by ownership of five shares in the Ohio Company's purchase; it gave him nearly six thousand acres of hill-and-hollow land in the Hocking valley. General Thaddeus Kosciusko, the Polish patriot who built fortifications at West Point and led American cavalry at Charleston, used his bounty warrants to claim five hundred acres in Franklin County, near present-day Columbus; funds from the sale of that land, after his death, were used to found a pioneer Colored School at Newark, New Jersey. Baron de Steuben, drillmaster of the American forces, was granted eleven hundred acres in the Muskingum valley. At the same time multitudes of anonymous veterans took their land warrants as a soldier's pay. Some came west to claim land for themselves; some sold the warrants, made transferrable in 1788, to settlers and speculators; some put them on the cupboard shelf and forgot about them. The forty-eight men bound for the Ohio country in 1787 were the only group to use their military warrants in a common venture.

Out of Ipswich on that December morning marched twenty-two men, including a shipwright, Jonathan Devol, who would direct the building of flatboats when they reached the western waters. (Twenty years later at Marietta he would build tall-masted ships to carry Ohio wheat down the rivers and across the sea to England.) A second group of twenty-six left Hartford, Connecticut, on New Year's Day, 1788; they included four surveyors who would lay off the Ohio Company's lands—huge Ebenezer Sproat and three young men, Return J. Meigs, Anselm Tupper, and John Matthews. All but the scholarly Meigs had worked on the survey of the Seven Ranges under Thomas Hutchins a few years back; they were returning to familiar country. Rufus Putnam, after settling some company business in New York, overtook the party in the Pennsylvania mountains where they were struggling through fresh snow. When more snow fell they left the wagons in the drifted road, lashed their gear onto sledges, and pushed on to the Youghiogheny. They found the advance party at Sumrill's Ferry, thirty miles southeast of Pittsburgh. Snow had kept the boat-builders idle, but Putnam could not wait. In the short February daylight axes rang on the frozen trees, the whipsaw sang through heartwood, oxen dragged logs to the river bank and the adze-men hewed out timbers. When snow ran off and the river rose, the boats were ready, their framework solid as a blockhouse and slitted windows peering from walls heavy enough to turn a shower of arrows or a spatter of lead. They were eight days on the Ohio, the river running high between shores softened with the green of April. It was a kinder season than the cold New England spring, and the country seemed inviting. They heard no thud of bullets on the walls, though a party of Delawares gathered on the Muskingum shore to witness the unloading. Curious as children the Indians admired the big tent raised for Putnam's headquarters, watched the first board huts go up, and looked on with uncomprehending interest while the surveyors marked out eight-acre lots along the river. Colonel Ebenezer Sproat, six feet four in his surveyor's boots, they promptly named "Hetuck"—Big Buckeye; they did not know his chain and compass would measure all their land. They shook hands with the Big Buckeye and went back up the river.

It was a busy season on the Muskingum shore. Trees crashed down in a square laid out for the fort, a hundred

acres of corn were planted in a girdling of woods beyond the
Mound Builders' earthworks. Houses went up behind a log
palisade on the Point—where now the throbbing diesels push
their huge tows of oil, steel and coal past the weedy stones of
Marietta's landing and around a far bend of the Ohio. On
the second of July, 1888, agents and directors of the Company,
meeting in Putnam's airy tent, named their town Marietta,
in honor of Marie Antoinette, and drew on their Latin
School days to name the fortified square "Campus Martius."
On July 4th two newly-appointed judges of the Territory
made speeches under the trees, the soldiers across the river at
Fort Harmar trooped the colors, and a salvo of thirteen guns
rolled back from the Virginia hills across the Ohio. The roar
of cannon startled the onlooking Indians but did not drive
them away from a long table laden with barbecued venison, turkey, bear meat, roast pork and a huge broiled pike,
six feet long, that had been speared in the Muskingum. A
week later a twelve-oared barge flying the American flag
steered in to Fort Harmar, and Governor St. Clair stepped
ashore. He was received by a parade of troops with drums
rattling cadence and colors flying—also by a burst of thunder
and a soaking shower. In better weather a few days later the
Fort Harmar officers escorted him across the river while signal cannon boomed from the hill. The men of Marietta led
him to blockhouse quarters in their uncompleted fort. Before the month was over Governor St. Clair had proclaimed
creation of Washington County, a wild tract extending to
the Scioto and Cuyahoga rivers and covering half of present
Ohio. Law had come to the western country.

In the middle of August the first boatload of families
arrived on the Muskingum, landing at the Sacra Via where
an ancient people had marched from their temple mounds
to the river. Marietta was no longer a camp. Women took
charge of the new cabins and children ran over the old ceremonial mounds. There was talk of a church and a school.
That month at Ipswich, Massachusetts, the Reverend Manasseh Cutler hitched his horse to a sulky and started for the

Ohio. He found the settlement thriving and preached a sermon of hope and thanksgiving under the thinning trees.

On September 2nd the community gathered, men, women and children, for the first court session in the Territory. A procession formed at the Point between the rivers and marched through dappled sunlight to the Campus Martius and back to the commons on the Muskingum. After Cutler's deep-voiced blessing, huge Sheriff Sproat boomed "Oyez, oyez!" and declared that a court was convened to administer justice in the light of law and without respect of persons. A party of Indians, come down the river to make a treaty, stood wondering at this ceremony.

It was something to wonder at, for there were no cases on the docket, and no docket. The record reads: "There being no business before the court at this term, it was adjourned." The first community had held court without a case, and in that aimless act it had done a simple and majestic thing. Forty-eight adventurers in savage country had reminded themselves that they were civilized men, the bringers of institutions. Already it was agreed that one blockhouse of Campus Martius would serve as a schoolroom, another as a church. In timbered walls slitted for rifle barrels people would raise their prayers and children would learn their letters. Religion, learning and morality had come to the somber woods and the ancient waters.

That evening while a blue dusk darkened the rivers and stars grew white in the September sky, the settlers must have had some long thoughts. The first summer was ending. Soon frost would wither the cornfields and the forest would stand bare. But their cabins were sound, grain was heaped in the storeroom, pumpkins, squash and cabbage were piled at the kitchen wall. Children played in the dooryard, women carried water from the well, from their chimneys woodsmoke drifted up to the Ohio sky. This was the dream fulfilled— fields and fences, homes and harvest. And dimly in the back of the mind was another knowledge. The land would change past recognition. In time to come the forests would be fields,

towns would grow at the creek mouths and the fording
places, the rivers would carry the commerce of cities not yet
founded. But the first men had something that no other men
could know. They came to a timeless land and began its history. To silence and darkness they brought songs and firelight. They knew the country's loneliness and grandeur, its
promise and danger, as their descendants in times of progress
and confusion could only dimly picture it in the wistful-
ness of historic memory.

The Indians were curious about the white man's camp
on the Muskingum. They understood the cabins and the cornfields, the picketed Point at the meeting of the rivers and
the log-walled Campus Martius. But they were puzzled by the
one-room building with two sloping desks and a long plank
table strewn with big rolls of paper and ruled record books.
No family lived there, no clothes hung on the wall, no
smell of cooking came from the blackened fireplace. But men
went gravely to that house, pondered its papers, counted
out money, and signed their names. It was a small room
where the white man made big medicine. The first Land
Office, with its plots and transfers of their Muskingum country, was beyond the Indians' comprehension.

The second season brought more flatboats on the rivers, more axes thudding in the woods. New settlements began at Belpré, Waterford, Plainfield. Mill wheels were splashing on Wolf Creek and Deer Creek, roads crept through the
forest. The tribes began to see that something alien and omi-
nous had come. They stopped their trade with the settlers,
remaining in camps up the Muskingum. But they would be
back.

In the fall of 1790 thirty-six men, disregarding Rufus
Putnam's counsel, went thirty miles up the Muskingum and
began a settlement on the fertile Big Bottom, a bench of
land along the river opposite the Indian war path from Lake
Erie. They were young men, careless and confident, with no
experience of Indian warfare. They threw up a blockhouse
on the river bank and began clearing lots for their cabins.

They kept no lookout. One winter evening while they were eating supper by firelight, the blockhouse door flew open. They looked up at a Mohawk warrior, with dusky forms behind him. Muskets roared in the room and the settlers fell by their fireside. The Indians ate the unfinished suppers and set the place on fire. Its green logs smoldered all night long.

Next day troops from Fort Harmar hacked a hole in the frozen ground and buried the blackened bodies. The Indian wars had begun.

For four years the Ohio valley was disputed country. Alarm over the growing white invasion had spread through all the tribes, and Indian resistance was fanned by British aid from Canada. Governor St. Clair called a group of chiefs to Fort Harmar and made a new treaty, but the proud Shawnees and the stubborn Miamis stayed away. American settlers wanted more land, the Indians wanted the white man driven across the Ohio. In the Miami country war parties attacked outlying farms, stole horses, shot down hunters and surveyors, took prisoners to their camps in the interior. St. Clair's treaties had not purchased the Ohio valley. It would have to be won by war.

There were just six hundred troops in the whole northwestern territory, and in a dozen villages the Indians were painting themselves for war, when Congress ordered the militia of Virginia, Kentucky and western Pennsylvania to muster at Fort Washington, at the site of present-day Cincinnati. With this makeshift force, undisciplined and scantily equipped, General Harmar advanced into Indian country in western Ohio; he was soon driven back to Cincinnati. New troops, picked up from the streets and prisons of the eastern cities, were shipped down the Ohio, and Governor St. Clair took military command of three thousand men. Orders from the War Department directed him to build a series of forts north from Cincinnati and to strike the Indians "with great severity." In September, 1791, he moved north with his rag-tag army, cutting his own supply roads through dense country. He built Fort Hamilton, twenty-five miles up the Miami, and Fort Jefferson, another twenty-five miles north. Then the time ran out. In the gray daybreak of November 4th, where St. Clair was camped on a tributary of the Wabash a hundred miles north of Cincinnati, the bare woods exploded with Little Turtle's warriors. The Indians struck with stunning force, and less than half the troops got back to safety at Fort Washington where, as we have noted, St. Clair sat in his dim blockhouse room and wrote a bleak report to the Secretary of War.

The tribes were still exulting when Mad Anthony Wayne was charged with defense of the West. Disproving his name for rash and headlong action he established headquarters at Pittsburgh, gathered recruits and began their training. There Ensign William Henry Harrison, called up river from Cincinnati, reported to his new commander and was assigned to drilling raw recruits. In the spring of 1793 Wayne brought a disciplined and equipped army down the Ohio, debarking them at Cincinnati. He marched into Indian country that autumn, built Fort Recovery on the site of St. Clair's disaster, and raised the bastions of Fort Greene Ville around his winter camp. Eighteen months later, as we have seen, the chiefs assembled there to surrender twenty million acres of their tribal lands.

PART III

"WHAT PART OF THE WORLD
DO YOU COME FROM?"

CHAPTER EIGHT

CITY OF THE FRENCH

ON TIIE evening of October 16th, 1890, a special train on the old Hocking Valley railroad pulled in to the river town of Gallipolis. It brought the General Assembly of Ohio, headed by Governor James E. Campbell, and a delegation including the Honorable Charles H. Grosvener, Judge R. A. Safford, and the Reverend Dr. Washington Gladden. All the way from Columbus a cold autumn rain had pelted the windows, but when the party stepped onto the wet platform at Gallipolis a half moon showed through torn white clouds and a Hallowe'en tingle was in the air. They marched through glimmering streets to the public square on the river front. There a reception tent and a dozen committee tents were scattered around a huge auditorium tent with a stage accommodating four hundred and seats for two thousand people. This was the site of the first clearing in the Scioto forest, where four rows of huts had huddled in the wilderness.

For three days visitors swarmed the streets of Gallipolis and sat under the big top hearing the Governors of Ohio and West Virginia, college presidents, Congressmen, and judges extol the first settlers of the town. Between lectures there were stereopticon picture shows, excursions on the steamboat *Bostona* to Point Pleasant where one October day the Virginians had fought Chief Cornstalk's warriors, and displays of fireworks on the river. On Sunday morning, October 19th, Washington Gladden preached a sermon in the Opera House—"Migrations and their Lessons"—and trains brought thousands of people for Centennial Day. That afternoon the grand parade formed on Third and Court Streets—regimental bands, National Guard companies, the governors and their staffs, visiting firemen in red shirts and polished helmets, citizens in carriages, visitors on foot. They marched from Second Street to Olive, from Olive to Third, from Third to Grape, and finally disbanded on the riverfront.

As they wandered the leaf-strewn streets or sat in the airy auditorium tent the visitors had pictures in their minds. An Indian summer haze softened the river and the smell of leaf fires hung over the town. It was easy to call up the vanished scene—a fleet of flatboats steering in and a colony of strangers staring at a stump-filled clearing, four dark blockhouses peering over the barracks, an olive grove withering at the edge of the Ohio woods and a vineyard straggling down to the river, an old man in a doorway making plaintive sounds on a silver flute while shadows crept across the stumpland, a little doctor humming a French air as he bent over his mortar and pestle.

Before the day was over the visitors filed through the Centennial Relic room. They saw a miscellaneous exhibit—

rusty wolf traps and silver French snuff boxes, candle molds and the ax used by Colonel Robert Safford to cut down the first tree on the town square, the Bible of Mad Ann Bailey and Cornstalk's blackened pipe, a petrified russet apple and a pen portrait of Voltaire, a set of ivory dominoes from France and a box of chips used when the settlers played Boston on winter nights, the horn of a buffalo killed on the public square, a piece of the flagstaff raised by General Wayne at Fort Recovery, a copy of the *Prospectus pour l'établissement sur les rivières d'Ohio et de Scioto en Amérique* which had lured five hundred hopeful settlers from Paris to the wilderness.

Gallipolis in 1890 was celebrating the centennial of the Ohio country's most pathetic colony and its greatest swindle.

In Paris in 1789 a young man from Connecticut was selling land. Joel Barlow was a Yale man, a classmate of Noah Webster; already, at 35, he had been an army chaplain, preaching to ragged soldiers, and later a poet, preaching to his readers the florid patriotism of *The Vision of Columbus,* as well as a busy young lawyer in Hartford. He was an ambitious man; he wanted to be both rich and famous, and he knew that Boston, New York and Philadelphia were buzzing with great land speculations in the Ohio country. In Hartford he had been an agent for the Ohio Company of Associates, to whose contract with Congress the greedy Scioto Company's speculation had been attached. Manasseh Cutler, prime mover of the Ohio Company project, knew and trusted Barlow, and when Colonel William Duer proposed selling Scioto lands in Europe, Barlow went abroad as the Scioto Company's agent. He carried a bundle of letters of introduction and blank contracts for the sale of western land. For his labors he was to receive 50,000 acres of that wilderness.

Joel Barlow was a man of honesty and romantic ardor; he believed in liberty and democracy, and in the prospects of the American frontier. But he did not know the shaky structure of Duer's Scioto Company and he was no business-man. For ten months he wandered about Paris, trying in banking houses and drawing rooms to stir up interest in lands he had never seen. Before a year was over he was dis-heartened and ready to return to America. Then things changed.

Barlow met a fellow American, a Colonel Blockden of Massachusetts, who was also a land agent—selling Kentucky lands to French speculators. Blockden introduced Barlow to an Englishman, William Playfair, who had been in business in Paris for years. Playfair struck Barlow as a man "of a bold and enterprising spirit and a good imagination." He thought he could find buyers for the Scioto lands, and Barlow wel-comed a partnership with this amiable and knowing man.

One of Barlow's difficulties was that he could sell only preëmption rights in the Scioto country. Since Duer's com-pany had made no payment to Congress they owned not an acre, and Barlow's task was to sell land to which his company had no title. He had concluded that he needed to find a French company that would make a payment on a large tract, for which, after their payment was received, Duer could provide a deed of ownership. Public confidence in France would then lead to other sales, the American Congress could be paid, and the French purchasers could be given titles, never knowing that they had originally bought nothing but an option.

In August, 1789, Playfair and Barlow formed the Compagnie du Scioto in Paris. The eight members of the com-pany, including a delegate of the French National Assembly, several merchants in Paris, and the Comptroller of the Pay Office of the Domain of the King, proposed to purchase, im-prove and re-sell three million arpens of American land be-tween the Ohio and Scioto rivers. They issued eight thousand shares, valued at one thousand livres each. They then ap-pointed Barlow and Playfair their agents to sell portions of the tract. Up to this time not a sou had changed hands. No money had been paid by the Compagnie du Scioto, but it now appeared that there was a substantial French company from which the French public could buy American land.

It was a good time to advertise American real estate— the best time in all the history of France. For this was the momentous summer of 1789 when M. Fénelon, prelate of the church, informed the king that all of France was "simply a great hospital, full of woe and empty of bread." In June the National Assembly formed in defiance of the king. The king massed troops around Versailles to overawe the Assembly. Paris was in turmoil. A provisional government took form; the National Guard organized with Lafayette at its head. Then rumor went like a wind through boulevards and alleys: the guns of the old Bastille were being trained upon the city. On July 14th a mob streamed through the streets and razed the Bastille. In the first week of October crowds marched out to Versailles, sacked the palace, and brought King Louis into Paris where he was imprisoned in the Tuileries.

In this dark season Parisians flocked to the American land office. On the wall hung a large map, handsomely engraved and colored, of the Scioto tract. It showed a region of many rivers bordering on cleared and cultivated lands, with nowhere a sign of wilderness or barrier mountains. It showed quarries, salt springs, lead and coal mines, and on a bend of La Belle Rivière was marked the *première ville* of the Scioto Company.

Printed pamphlets described the tract more fully. For the speculator there was an assurance that the soil was fertile, resources abundant, climate ideal; in eight years, at most, the land would double in value. The wild Hockhocking River was portrayed as "much frequented" and richly endowed; on its banks were "inexhaustible quarries of building stone, great beds of iron ore, and some rich mines of lead." Prospective settlers read that "no territory in the United States offers so many advantages . . . —the most salubrious, the most agreeable, the most advantageous, the most

fertile land which is known to any people in Europe, whatsoever." It was confidently expected that the colony would soon
export wheat, hemp, indigo, silk, flax, iron, and potash. There
were "vast fields of rice, which nature here produces spontaneously," waiting to be harvested. Hogs would flourish in
the forests without care. A couple of swine would multiply a
hundredfold in a year or so, and the colony could export
thirty thousand barrels of pork by the end of the first season.
Everything existed on a grand scale in the luxuriant Scioto
country. A black walnut tree had been measured twenty-two
feet around, a sycamore forty-four feet. Maple trees dripped
sugar, a swamp plant yielded candles, custard grew on a
shrub in the underforest.

To this land of plenty five hundred "cultivators" were
being sent, according to the announcement, to prepare the
way for thirty-five hundred land-owning settlers. The first
town was already begun; houses were now being built for
future colonists. The town, being located at the confluence
of two great rivers, the Kanawha and the Ohio, would soon
be the center of a vast settlement and would probably become the capital of the United States. Altogether this region
must be considered "the garden of the universe, the center of
wealth, a place destined to be the heart of a great Empire."

Now Joel Barlow had a land-office business. Aristocrats and tradesmen, court officials and Paris merchants, artists and artisans clamored for Scioto lands. Families brought
their savings and housewives sold their possessions to buy
some piece of paradise. Said the philosopher Volney: "Nothing was talked of, in every social circle, but the paradise that
was opened for Frenchmen in the western wilderness, the free
and happy life to be led on the blissful banks of the Scioto."
King Louis himself, according to his barber, remarked that
all Paris was talking about the Scioto lands.

By the end of the year 100,000 acres had been sold. A
fortune was in the hands of Playfair and his French associates,
though Barlow never managed to examine their accounts.
In shaken Paris, American land seemed a promise of secu-

rity. People paid their money, took their worthless titles, and dreamed of a French Eden on the Ohio.

In January, 1790, five hundred eager emigrants, men, women, and children, assembled at Havre de Grace. Some were of rank, small noblemen and courtiers; some were professional men; many were artisans—jewelers, watchmakers, gardeners, wood-carvers, wig-makers. Some were indentured servants, engaged to clear the forest and farm the fields: at the end of three years' service they would receive fifty acres and a house and a cow.

During February and March five vessels sailed with the emigrants—*Recovery, Lady Washington, Nautilus, Pennsylvania,* and *Scarborough.* In the month of May they arrived at Alexandria, seventy-five miles up the Potomac. After three months at sea the pilgrims looked eagerly at the bright New World. What they saw was a cheerful, substantial town, brick and clapboard houses facing the water, carts and carriages passing under the oak and maple trees, the river busy with sloops, cutters, and longboats. The newcomers trooped ashore, up Prince Street and along Royal and Fairfax under the summer trees. Their minds and muscles expanded after the long weeks in close quarters. The first sight of America was reassuring and they were eager to start for the Ohio country. But no company agent appeared with a caravan for the journey. Instead they were met by news of disaster and deceit.

The Scioto Company, having made no payments to the government, had no claim to a single acre in the wilderness. The Ohio Company of Associates agreed to locate the colony on its lands, but now, for the first time, the homeless Frenchmen learned that their prospective homes were still a long journey distant, beyond forbidding mountains, in deep woods inhabited by hostile Indians. The Scioto paradise that was the talk of Paris had become a never-never land.

In this plight the immigrants wrote to President Washington and sent a committee to New York to find Colonel Duer, the shadowy founder of the Scioto project. Action was

slow, but finally it came. By the first of July it was agreed
that board and lodging of the immigrants at Alexandria
should be paid for, at two shillings a day, by the Company;
the colonists were allowed an extra year to make the second
payment on their lands; the party would be guided to the
Ohio, with wagons for their baggage and carriages for the
women and children.

Meanwhile axes were thudding on the Ohio river bank
four hundred miles away. The homes which Playfair had described in Paris, as awaiting their new owners, were rising
in a stump-filled field. In the windy month of March, when
the emigrant ships had sailed away from France, General Rufus Putnam as agent for the Scioto Company had hired John
Burnham of Essex, Massachusetts, to recruit a construction
crew. Burnham mustered fifty young farmers from Danvers,
Ipswich, Rutland, and started west. They arrived in the Ohio
woods at the end of May and began their work. For twenty-
six cents a day they were to clear the tangled river bank and
build a village for five hundred people. Then they would
clear the lands adjacent, hunt game for the community, and
keep guard against the Indians. Four men of the fifty deserted in the Ohio country; the rest began hacking at the ancient Shawnee woods.

From Alexandria the French immigrants headed westward, under direction of two skilled woodsmen, Major Isaac
Guion and James Backus. It was a motley caravan—high-
wheeled, canvas-topped freight wagons loaded with axes, mattocks, log chains, burlaped seedlings and crates of chickens,
along with the chests and pormanteaus, musical instruments
and silver teapots, chess sets and chafing dishes from Paris
and Lyons; lighter wagons for the women and children; a
file of saddle horses, hogs and cattle. They straggled out for
two miles on the dusty wagon road.

James Backus, who had been in the first party of settlers at Marietta, kept a diary, writing by firelight at the end
of a long day's travel, and what he recorded was a tedious
and trying journey. They followed the valley of Virginia a

hundred and fifty miles to the town of Winchester; from there to Fort Cumberland, then northwest on the rough road over the looming ridges. Thomas Cresap with his Indian friend Nemacolin had opened the path, sixty miles from Will's Creek to Redstone Old Fort—which was merely a mound builders' moated site on the Monongahela. Christopher Gist had traveled it in 1749 on his tour for the Virginia speculators. Now the French toiled over it on the way to paradise.

The summer of 1790 was hot and sultry. Through breathless days they traveled, wagons swaying, lurching, grinding, horses slipping and sliding, men hauling at the stay ropes. Some days the hot sky clouded; thunder rumbled in the mountains and rain streamed down. The thunder rolled away and the sun burned down again on a steaming caravan. Often they made their camp on wet ground, horses stamping in the thickets, wagons settling in the mud. (*The land transit is about thirty miles,* the Prospectus read, *but will very probably be diminished in a little while, by means of a plan which is actually in contemplation for opening a communication between the Potomac and Ohio rivers.*) Over the smoky supper fires they asked the guides again—How far to the Ohio?

When they arrived at the Monongahela, summer was fading. They made a camp under thinning sycamores while Guion and Backus went downstream for boats. The boats came, ponderous and silent, nosing in to shore. Men staggered under baggage, led horses and cattle up cleated runways and tied them to ringbolts on the deck. Women and children found the shelter of the cabins. The worst, they thought, was over.

Mooring lines cast off, the boatmen swept their long steering oars and swung into the current. In a string of clumsy "arks" the French moved westward. At Pittsburgh their eyes sharpened. It was still two hundred miles to the Scioto lands but they were on the O-hy-o. Sitting on the cabin roofs in golden October weather they watched the colored

shores slip by. They swung around leafy headlands, along
dense islands, past tawny river meadows, through sunlight
and starlight on the river. At Marietta, a town now three years
old, named for their own Marie Antoinette, they stopped for
hay and grain, for fresh meat and corn meal and fresh water
in the casks. They saw the walled Campus Martius of the
town, the earthwork avenue of the mound builders, the blockhouses of Fort Harmar across the Muskingum with a flag
rippling above the parade. That glimpse of life in the wilderness was cheering. On their way again, they saw deer swimming the current and migrant birds passing over. The river
ran gold in the sunset. It carried them on in the silent and
beautiful country, deeper and deeper into the mysterious new
world. Paris, with its tumult and terror, seemed on another
planet. Here was a world as innocent and fresh as from the
first creation, with the future all before it.

But the future was gloomy. Under a wet gray sky on
October 19, 1790, two miles beyond the mouth of the Great
Kanawha, the flatboats swung inshore and were moored to
stumps on the landing. The French pilgrims looked at paradise. What they saw was a high, steep bank, then a square of
cleared land ending in a frame of forest. In the clearing
crouched eighty low dark cabins—four rows of log barracks,
each broken into twenty one-room dwellings. At the corners
of the clearing stood two-story blockhouses with loopholes
peering from the heavy walls. At the upper end of the stump
land two short rows of cabins were surrounded by a log stockade—a storehouse and a refuge for the colony when the Indians should come. The French had traveled four thousand
miles to this new Eden.

Yet it had a kind of grandeur: the great silence of the
forest, the great sweep of the Ohio, and the Kanawha leading
southward through the Virginia hills. Silently the French
moved into the cabins and unpacked their things—their ivory
dominoes and silver candlesticks, their flutes and violins.
That night, according to legend, they gathered in one of the
blockhouses for a celebration. They tuned their violins and

danced a minuet on the puncheon floor. Bravely they named their town Gallipolis—City of the French.

Winter came like an enemy. Though the prospectus in Paris had said: *A climate wholesome and delightful, frost even in winter almost entirely unknown,* the ground turned to iron, snow raged across the clearing, the river froze solid to the Kentucky shore. The colonists huddled around their fires. No provisions could come down the river, but a few hunters left from Burnham's crew kept Gallipolis from starving. In early spring the townsmen began to clear a garden tract. Ohio produced the greatest ax-men in history, but these Frenchmen were still strangers. They hacked away, a circle of puny figures swinging their blades at a tree trunk while a dozen others pulled at a rope attached to the lower branches. A few were killed in that way. When they had a tree down, the Marietta hunters said, they tried to dig a trench to get it out of sight.

Somehow they cleared a garden space and planted grapes and berries, artichokes, peas, and beans, olive and almond trees. Hunters from Marietta kept them supplied with turkey, venison, and bear meat. The river was plentiful with fish, their gardens flourished. Once a week they dressed in their fading Paris clothes and danced on a puncheon floor.

Summer brought clouds of mosquitoes and a hovering miasmal air. The prospectus read: *There is very little bad land in this territory, and no marsh,* but at the lower edge of town Chickemage Creek ended in a morass of slough grass and cattails. The French soon shared with other western settlers the wretchedness of malaria. They shook with ague and burned with fever. Their faces grew sallow and their minds forgot the glowing hopes that had brought them here. Even this dismal village did not belong to them; they had no title to it and would have to pay for their land again. Some discouraged families went back to France, some moved to the eastern cities, some went on down the Ohio to Louisville and Vincennes, a few to their countrymen in far-off New Orleans.

In 1795 Congress made the French colony a grant of 24,000 acres on the Ohio River near the mouth of the Scioto, forty miles west of Gallipolis, each settler over eighteen being entitled to a share in the distribution. But this generosity did not attract many from Gallipolis. A few moved to the new "French Grant," but more stayed on in their little town, tending their gardens, working in their shops, playing French airs on their flutes and violins.

For fifteen years life dwindled in Gallipolis, while a great current of new settlement floated past to the lower Ohio. The French remnant lived in their rude cabins and worked at their crafts. They carved wood, chiseled stone, made fine compasses and sundials; one of them made a parlor lamp out of bear and buffalo bones dug up at the salt lick. As time went on, new settlers from Pennsylvania, New Jersey and Massachusetts came to the "City of the French," and more of the French colonists moved away. But a few Frenchmen stayed to the end, and were buried in the old cemetery on the hill where the stones are worn smooth by the wind and the rain.

The best remembered of all the French settlers was little Dr. Antoine François Saugrain. He stood four feet six and walked with a limp, and he had a restless nature that belied his ancestry of booksellers and librarians. He was twenty-seven when the emigrants landed at Gallipolis, but he had already had a career as naturalist, scientist, physician and philosopher. At twenty-two he was sent by the king of Spain to examine mines in Mexico. Two years later he was in Philadelphia, a close friend of Benjamin Franklin, with whom he discussed deism, electricity and inoculation for smallpox. In the spring of 1788 he made a trip down the Ohio with two French companions, looking for sites for a French settlement. While exploring the valley of the Great Miami they were attacked by Indians. His companions, M. Raquet and M. Picque, were killed, and Saugrain was wounded and captured. He escaped from the Indians and made his way through deep country to Louisville, but he lost part of his right foot from frostbite. Back in Paris he heard excited talk about the Scioto lands, and he was ready for another venture.

In Gallipolis the little doctor fitted up a log room as a laboratory and hummed to himself while working with his blow pipe and crucible. He made ink and sold it up and down the river. He made thermometers and barometers with the scale neatly painted and the frames deftly carved. He devised a phosphoric light for hunters in the woods. One of the wonders of the West was his invention of phosphoric matches, tiny tubes which jetted a bright flame when the glass was broken. To amuse himself and amaze others he had a full-grown peach inside a narrow-necked bottle. This was a wonder that had taken all summer to accomplish, for he had tied the bottle to the tree when the fruit was no bigger than a marble. Busy as a cricket, he still had time to talk with anyone who came—traders, travelers, Indians from the woods, flatboatmen from the river. Gallipolis was not too harsh or too remote for him, but after six years the town was no longer new and he grew restless. He went on to St. Louis and was appointed surgeon at the army post. When Lewis and Clark outfitted there he supplied them with a medicine chest, thermometers, barometers, matches. He would have liked to go along.

For a year in Gallipolis Dr. Saugrain and his young wife had a boarding patient. In 1794 ten-year-old Henry Brackenridge was brought ashore from a keelboat, shuddering with chills and wan from fever. They tended him and mended him, the boy following the little doctor around the settlement, and at last Henry Brackenridge was well enough to take passage on a keelboat to his father at Fort Pitt. In the years ahead he became a noted lawyer, a diplomat and an explorer; with Manuel Lisa he made a long voyage up the Missouri for the Missouri Fur Company. But he did not forget the cheerful little doctor in the dwindling French settlement between the woods and the water. Years later he came down the Ohio on a steamboat, eager to see the remembered place and people. "As we passed Point Pleasant, and the little island below it, Gallipolis, which I looked for with anxious feelings, hove in sight. I thought of the French inhabitants— I thought of my friend Saugrain, and I recalled in the liveliest colors, the incidents of that portion of my life which was passed here. . . . I hastened to the spot where I expected to find the abode, the little log house, tavern, laboratory and garden of the Doctor—but they had vanished like the palace of Aladdin. I took a hasty glance at the new town as I returned to the boat. I saw brick houses, painted frames, fanciful enclosures, ornamental trees! Even the pond which had carried away a third of the French population by its malaria, had disappeared, and a pretty green had usurped its place, with a neat brick Court House in the midst of it."

Like the other rude settlements Gallipolis changed into a thriving comfortable town. A few French balconies and doorways distinguish it from the other river towns, but it became American. When Lafayette stopped there in 1825 he was met by a cheering crowd of Virginians and Yankees; among them were a few old settlers who remembered when Scioto lands were the talk of Paris in the stormy year of 1789.

In 1890 at the Centennial celebration thousands filed through the relic room. One item on the exhibit tables was a pamphlet sketch of the life of Dr. Antoine François Saugrain, along with an engraving of the monument of his great-grandfather in the cemetery of Père-Lachaise in Paris. The visitors on Centennial day quickly forgot the other relics—the button worn in the War of 1812, the flask of water from the River Jordan, the iron key to the first Gallipolis jail. But they remembered the little doctor who had lived cheerfully in the wilderness that seemed so long ago.

Colonel Duer, the author of the Scioto project, died in debtor's prison in New York in 1799. William Playfair went back to England, with some millions of livres that had been paid for the Scioto lands. In London he opened a "security bank" in 1795. It soon collapsed, and he took up the pen that had so brightened the Prospectus on the Ohio country.

This time it didn't pay so well, though he made a precarious living with pamphlets and translations. Joel Barlow became a citizen of France and stayed abroad till 1805. Coming back to America he rewrote his poem *The Columbiad* in seven thousand lines, dedicated to Robert Fulton. In 1824 he went to Poland on a mission for the French government. He fell ill there and died on the day before Christmas in a desolate village near Cracow. He was buried in Polish ground.

On Centennial Day there was no display of the promoters' relics: no photograph of Colonel Duer, no autograph of William Playfair, no lines from Barlow's grandiose poem. Only that fading Prospectus that had lured French dreamers to the wilderness.

CHAPTER NINE

YANKEES GOING WEST

Half a mile from the old town of Granville, Massachusetts, lived these great-grand-parents of mine, on two acres of good garden land with a small orchard in which there were six famous Seek-No-Farther apple trees. . . . My grandparents Bancroft and Howe were both born in Granville, Massachusetts; the former died in Ohio, the latter in Kansas.

—HUBERT HOWE BANCROFT

IN THE summer of 1795, while the tribes were trudging home from the great congress at Greene Ville, thirty-five men, among them Moses Cleaveland whose Ohio surveying exploits we have already followed, traveled the Connecticut roads to Hartford for a council of their own. They organized the Connecticut Land Company and bought from the state its "Western Reserve," three million acres bordering Lake Erie, for forty cents an acre; actually they made no cash payment but gave mortgages on the lands they meant to purchase. Revenue from the Western Reserve was assigned to the Connecticut School Fund, and so the Nutmeg State had an interest in Ohio's future. Thirty-five years later when the

first canal boat passed with band music and bunting from
Akron to Cleveland, the Commissioner of the Connecticut
School Fund rode with the Governor of Ohio and the canal
commissioners. Eventually twelve hundred thousand dollars
was paid to the fund; the income from the sale of Ohio land
still helps to keep Connecticut school doors open.

In that historic summer Oliver Phelps, Roger New-
berry, Samuel Mather, Moses Cleaveland and other shareholders bought land assigned to the colony by an English
king who had never heard of Lake Erie or the Ohio country.
The charter of Connecticut, granted by Charles II in 1662,
showed the Merry Monarch's disposition and his ignorance
of New World geography. He fixed the royal seal to a docu-
ment which described Connecticut as extending from Narra-
ganset Bay to the South Seas. That gave the colony a Pacific coastline, though in 1662 no one in Europe knew
of a "Pacific Ocean," and it would be seven years before the
first vague reports could be made of a westward-flowing river
called O-hy-o.

Connecticut clung stubbornly to the charter. When Sir
Edmond Andros came to Hartford in 1687 to recall it, debate
rang in the Assembly Hall while daylight dimmed to candle-
light. Someone threw a window open and the candles went
black; when they were re-lighted the disputed paper
was gone from the speaker's table. For two years the charter
was hidden in a hollow oak at the foot of Wyllys Hill on
Main Street. It did not reappear until Hartford was quiet
and the threat to Connecticut had passed.

A hundred years later Connecticut clung as stubbornly to its charter lands. By 1787 the Ohio valley had been
won from the French by the English, and from the English
by the Americans. The American boundary extended to the
Mississippi, if not to the South Seas, and Connecticut insisted on its claim to western lands. Under pressure of the
other states that claim was finally surrendered to the federal
government, but Connecticut reserved the spacious tract between the 41st and 42nd parallels of North Latitude, bor-

dering on Lake Erie and extending 120 miles west from the
Pennsylvania line. This Western Reserve was thought to
comprise three and a half million acres. Five hundred thousand acres at its western end, designated as the "Firelands,"
Connecticut granted to families, chiefly of Danbury, Fair-
field, Norwalk, New Haven, and New London, whose homes
had been burned and pillaged by British troops during the
Revolution. The rest of that wilderness was for sale.

Rival bids were made by Oliver Phelps, representing
the Connecticut Land Company, and John Livingstone; both
these men had previously speculated in western New York
lands. Phelps bought off Livingstone by agreeing to turn over
to him all the Reserve in excess of three million acres; this
was a pure gamble, as the acreage could not be known until
the surveyors' work was done. In a further feverish deal the
Excess Company, organized to receive the surplus, was sold
for fifty thousand dollars to William Hull, state senator in
Massachusetts and a general in the state militia. General
Hull was an unlucky man; in 1812 he surrendered Detroit
to the British without resistance and was sentenced by court-
martial to be shot. The intercession of President Madison
saved him from that end. But nothing could save his land
speculation. When the final survey showed that the Western
Reserve contained slightly less than three million acres, his
Excess Company owned exactly nothing.

The Connecticut Land Company fared better. As we
have seen, Moses Cleaveland's survey crew found a rich and
spacious realm with a lake-tempered climate and a dozen
creeks and rivers winding into the interior. An inviting country, it had no natural barriers and few disputing Indians.
When the survey records were complete the gratified stock-
holders drew lots for their land; the thirty-five of them owned
an average of nearly ninety thousand acres each. The next
thing was to find purchasers and settlers.

The western country had a lively press in all the seaboard states. Ohio was news, as California and Colorado
would be news two generations later. Newspapers on the

Connecticut shore and in the stony Massachusetts valleys printed reports of travelers and settlers in the fabled Ohio country, and soon booksellers were stocked with Western Gazetteers and Emigrants' guides. So the Yankees knew some of the wonders of the West: corn at the Marietta colony grew fourteen feet tall, the soil in Trumbull County was as black and fine as gunpowder, the land at Berea was as level as a barn floor, a seven-acre farm on the Ohio River had produced seven hundred bushels of corn, cattle fattened on the wild grass of the Mahoning meadows, hogs flourished on the rich mast in the woods, potatoes in Lake County along Lake Erie grew as large as Connecticut pumpkins. Captain Hamilton Carr had found a hollow sycamore on the Ohio which was used as a dwelling. In January, 1815, a letter to the editor of *Niles' Register,* published in Baltimore and read throughout the states, exclaimed over the fertility of northern Ohio and its natural pastures. "We are in the culture of Merino sheep and have a beautiful flock of nearly five hundred. We have named our plantation after the celebrated plains of Estramadura in Spain." In October, 1825, *Niles' Register* described a mushroom on the farm of David Hudson in Portage County; it weighed twelve pounds and was bigger than a Connecticut washtub.

New England had thin soil, steep hillsides, everywhere a glacial drift of boulders. Wayne's Treaty, the Ohio River settlements, and Cleaveland's survey all told of a kinder country, and the Ohio fever ran like a contagion through the New England states. It went from one town to another, one crossroads to the next, one rocky farm to the neighbors up the valley. It spread through old seaports on the Sound, up the long Connecticut River, through the Berkshire valleys, into the White and Green Mountains. It began with a flush of fervor, an excitement of heart, a purpose burning in the mind. It sent men and families and whole communities toward the luring light of the West.

By 1800 the migration was underway. Farmers drove herds of cattle from Connecticut to Ohio, men rode horse-

back through the Mohawk valley and along the Erie shore,
families rocked in ox-drawn wagons over the rough Genesee
Road to Buffalo where they boarded sloops for Conneaut,
Grand River, Cleveland or Black River. Caravans creaked
over the "Pittsburgh Pike" on their way to interior counties in
Ohio. Connecticut river towns were deserted while new
towns sprang up on the Scioto and the Cuyahoga. In 1804 a
new "Scioto Company," wholly different from and probably
ignorant of the organization that had horned in on
the Ohio Company's contract seventeen years before, was
formed at Granville, Massachusetts; the next autumn two
hundred thirty-four persons trekked out of East Granville,
leaving empty houses and lifeless farms behind them. On
September 14th, 1815, Elisha Niles of Chatham, Connecticut,
watched forty of his townsmen creak off toward the Western Reserve, and Chatham disappeared from the U.S. census.

1816 was a dark time in New England, a year without a summer. "Eighteen hundred and froze to death" the
Yankees called it after frost had withered the fields in
June, July, and August and left the orchards bare. "Thousands feared or felt that New England was destined, hence-
forth, to become a part of the frigid zone," wrote Samuel
Goodrich ("Peter Parley") in his *Recollections*. "At the
same time, Ohio—with its rich soil, its mild climate, its
inviting prairies—was opened fully upon the alarmed and
anxious vision. As was natural under the circumstances, a
sort of stampede took place from cold, desolate, worn-out
New England to this land of promise."

By the summer of 1817 thousands were on the way.
Peter Parley described them—some families in covered wagons, some on foot, some in ox-carts laden with kettles, grid-
irons, feather beds, crockery, Bible, Watts' Psalms and
Hymns, and Webster's spelling book. It was a population
moving from a land of trouble to a land of hope, and
spreading the migration fever like a plague. Connecticut Assemblymen, seeing their towns depleted and farms abandoned, considered a bill to prohibit emigration.

Law could not cure the Ohio fever, but print had spread it and perhaps print could check it now. In 1818 Peter Parley published a tract, *T' other Side of Ohio,* written by a young Connecticut physician who had made a disillusioned visit to the West. It showed a painful picture of the migration—steep Pennsylvania roads strewn with the ruins of carts and wagons and the carcasses of oxen and horses; families huddled at night in miserable sheds called taverns, mothers frying, children crying, fathers swearing— and a bitter ending of the journey. Arrived at new homes on the Muskingum or the Scioto, the whole family began shuddering with intermittent fever. Here in Ohio they "mourned the land they had left, with its roads, schools, meeting houses; its hope, health, and happiness!"

After a year in the Western Reserve the Connecticut doctor was glad to return to the Land of Steady Habits and felt it "a duty incumbent upon me . . . to undeceive the community respecting a portion of the Western country, which has been represented as an *earthly* paradise, where everything necessary, everything convenient, and almost everything which has been considered a luxury, might be had almost without care, labour or exertion." His letters were printed in order "to prevent the evil effects that may arise from the high sounding recommendations (in most cases totally unfounded in fact) of land speculators. These evils are, persons selling their property in Connecticut and other Eastern States at a great loss in many cases, the expense of moving to Ohio, which swallows up a great portion of their property, incapacitating them to pay for their farms, disappointments of all kinds, on arriving at the place of destination, in most cases an inability to return, in consequence of the impossibility of procuring the means." He fervently hoped that his experience might deter restless and deluded people from emigrating to "fabled Ohio."

Other anti-Ohio writings followed. Jedediah Morse, clergyman, geographer and Commissioner to the western Indians, declared that "the best mowing land in Connecticut produces about twice as much clear profit as the same quantity of the best wheat land in New York or Ohio." Letters in the newspapers described the hardships and disappointment of deluded emigrants. Pairs of engravings showed healthy happy families heading west in laden wagons, and haggard families—"I Have Been to Ohio"—dragging back to New England in broken and empty carts. In 1819 a Boston printer brought out the curious *Journal of Doctor Simpleton's Tour of Ohio.* This disillusioned emigrant declared that after a hideous journey he had looked in vain for the much advertised town of his destination. He found the place infested by mosquitoes and swamp flies, wolves and wildcats. Now he was thankful for old Massachusetts and a meal of codfish and potatoes.

Another caustic report came from Zerah Hawley, a forty-year-old physician who spent the year 1820-21 in Ashtabula County of the Western Reserve. He found the settlers wanting in manners and morals, as well as in the comforts of life. "On Sept. 30, [1821] I crossed the State line and entered Ohio, the *fabled region* of the West. I say *fabled region,* because more, much more, has been said about the State, than has any foundation in truth. It has been called the *Garden* of America, and many other high sounding titles have been given to it, which it is needless and superfluous to mention."

Wherever he went he found wretched roads, crude, dirty, and drafty houses, shiftless people. "Every year a part of their pumpkins, corn and potatoes remain in the fields until snow falls, and so are lost, for the want of a little more industry."

All the settlers were called Judge, Squire, Senator, Colonel or Major—a detail which led Dr. Hawley to give "some account of *titled men and their habitations.* In riding through the country, you come to a log or block house; on enquiring to whom it belongs, you are surprised to hear that it belongs to Judge ————. The whole establishment consists of one room, in which all the family, with

their guests, eat, sleep, and perform all the domestic oper-
ations. You proceed a little farther, and arrive at a similar mansion, and are informed that it belongs to Esquire
————, who you find is a miller, and a man who has had
no other advantage for acquiring information than an or-
dinary school education. Soliciting information respecting
another residence, you are told that it is the property of a
Representative or a Senator of the Legislature of the State
of Ohio. In this villa, containing also but one room, is
found a bed in two corners, in another a cup-board, in the
fourth a swill-barrel, and on one side of the room a wooden
clock without a case, and by one window a three-cornered
piece of looking-glass, set in a little wooden frame of domestic manufacture and on the other side may be seen the
Major Z———— at work at shoes. You will find another
similar residence belonging to Colonel such a one. These
things are well enough; but if such are the residences of
the Honourable, what must be those of the vulgar."

Dr. Hawley could not observe that the older settlers,
with the first lean seasons behind them, were any better
off than newcomers. After seventeen years in Ohio a family
at Harpersfield had no table ware: one member ate with
a shoe-knife, another with an old razor blade fitted to a
wooden handle. "For want of a glass, or other convenient
vessel, from which to drink, if you are offered whisky,
(which is the principle drink here,) the bottle is presented
to you, or a bowl, or tea-cup containing the liquor." In this
Garden of America people commonly went barefoot for
want of leather. Dr. Hawley visited a Methodist preacher
who shuffled about in shoe-soles bound to his feet by tow
strings.

The fabled Ohio vegetation he found no different
from that of New England. "I was made to understand, before I came to the Reserve that vegetation was wonderfully
luxuriant here, almost beyond a parallel; so that grass growing by the road-side, was equal, if not superior to the best
pastures in Connecticut. But to my surprise, I found not

only roads, but the pastures almost destitute of vegetation. Some allowance must be made for the drought, which has continued for a number of weeks. But making all the concessions of this kind which the nature of the circumstances require, I do not think that vegetation is much more if any more luxuriant than in the old settled Eastern States. Indeed, I know many towns in Massachusetts and Connecticut, which naturally produce as much, and by the present mode of cultivation, more than the best lands in this part of the country."

The shiftless settlers, he reported, endlessly gossiped about their neighbors—"each of whom is a drunkard, a cheat, or a swindler." A Justice of the Peace told him of twenty-eight men married to women here who had left their wives living in the Eastern States, and he heard of many others living in bigamy and adultery. It seemed to the Connecticut doctor that missionaries were "as much needed here as in the Islands of the Seas; and as these people are our own brethren according to the flesh, there appears to be a duty incumbent on those who possess the means, an *urgent necessity,* to send them well instructed teachers, who may lead them in the way of heaven." But most of the settlers would have been satisfied with Connecticut. Wherever he went he found emigrants who "sigh for the land of their nativity but cannot go back because they are ragged and penniless and ashamed of their failure." If people were bound to go west, Hawley concluded, they would do well to stop short of the Ohio country. "To those who are desirous of relinquishing the privileges of the Atlantic States, for the sake of removing to an unsettled part of the country, it is my advice that they should stop in the Western part of the State of New-York, in preference to going any farther West."

Still the Ohio fever burned in New England. Connecticut children played a game called "Going to Ohio," and every Yankee knew the lilting song:

Says I, my boys, we'll leave this place
For the pleasant O-hi-o.

Countless young villagers and farmers dreamed of land on the Ohio River or the shores of Lake Erie. Instead of pondering the regrets of disillusioned travelers they read Kilbourn's *Ohio Gazetteer*—a new edition appeared every second or third year—*The Emigrant's Guide or Pocket Geography of the Western States*, and the *New Guide for Emigrants to the West*. "Such an extent of forest was never before cleared,—such a vast field of prairies was never before subdued and cultivated by the hand of man. . . . Cities, and towns, and villages, and counties, and States never before rushed into existence and made such giant strides. *Who hath heard such a thing? Who hath seen such things? Shall the earth be made to bring forth in one day? Or shall a nation be born at once?*" There was a Biblical wonder about this exodus to the Promised Land.

The emigrant books were full of beckoning phrases —"thriving villages and settlements . . . land of the first quality . . . valuable and unsettled lands . . . flourishing towns . . . prosperous settlements . . . fertile and empty country." More specifically: "Ross County . . . is well watered by Paint Creek on the west side of the Scioto, and Kinnikinnick and Salt creeks on the east. The inhabitants are in general wealthy, have elegant buildings, and large and improved farms, well stocked. The land is fertile and suitably diversified with meadow and upland, the latter of which is well adapted to the production of grain." . . . "Richland County is watered by the head branches of the Huron, east fork of the Sandusky, Clear Fork, a branch of the Muskingum, Muddy Creek, etc. The soil is rich and particularly fertile, and the county contains large bodies of unsettled lands of good quality." . . . "Wayne County has Apple Creek, Sugar Creek, the Chippeway, Mohican and Johns creeks, all of them good streams for mills. The creek bottoms are extensive and fertile, producing immense crops of corn." One description of Ohio culminated with: "The cultivated farm and decent mansion occupy the dreary haunts of savage cruelty, while magnificent cities and numerous villages are springing up, as by magic art, on the ruins of the cheerless wigwam." Through a dozen editions of his *Gazetteer* John Kilbourn repeated: "Without boasting, we aver, and challenge the world to contradict the assertion that this great and growing state (Ohio) possesses more of the essential ingredients of future greatness, and more self-sustaining and self-creating principles than any other territory of equal size on the face of the globe."

To verify the printed word there were letters from settlers who had found the promises coming true. One man in the Ohio country drew others after him—his brothers, his wife and children, his parents, his former neighbors in a rock-strewn New England town.

Here is one family, out of thousands:

Joshua Stow of Middletown, Connecticut, was a member of the Connecticut Land Company, having invested $6,000 in the speculation; eventually he received five thousand acres in what became Stow Township of Summit County in the Western Reserve near the future city of Akron. In 1796 he came west with General Cleaveland's party, in charge of the commissary. He doubled as a flagman for Augustus Porter's survey crew, making the traverse of the Lake shore. Going ahead of the others Stow killed a lot of rattlesnakes, and though there was salt meat stored away in "Stow's Castle," the surveyors' storehouse on Conneaut Creek, he frequently provided fresh meat for his crew. "During almost any day while on the lake shore," Porter recalled, "he killed and swung over his shoulder and around his body from two to six or eight large rattlesnakes, and at night a part were dressed and cooked and eaten by the party with a good relish."

Back in Middlesex County, Connecticut, Joshua Stow's sister Jemima had married Daniel Kelley. Throughout their boyhood her sons heard their uncle's stories of the Western Reserve and thought of Ohio as their future. In 1810 Alfred Kelley, aged twenty-one, packed law books in his saddlebags and rode west beside his uncle, arriving in the hamlet of Cleveland at the end of June. His brother Datus arrived a year later. In 1812 their younger brother Irad Kelley joined Captain Cobb's company of the New York militia and was assigned to guard duty at the frontier post of Ogdensburg on the St. Lawrence. That was a dull routine, and young Kelley kept thinking about the Ohio country. He hired a substitute and started off to join his brothers in Cleveland.

In 1813 Cleveland had a scant one hundred inhabitants but war was making it a busy town. A company of regulars was stationed there and hundreds of Ohio militiamen were gathering. Irad Kelley joined the staff of Samuel Huntington, ex-governor of Ohio and now Paymaster of the Northwestern Army, and was told to report at headquarters. There he found a straight, lean, long-nosed man with two gold stars on his shoulders and a wing of coarse hair falling down his forehead—a man who had been in the Ohio country since Wayne's campaign, who had traveled its roads and trails and rivers, who knew the Indian chiefs, the politicians, and the land speculators. William Henry Harrison was now a major general, commander-in-chief of the Army of the Northwest. In the second week of July Irad Kelley rode with General Harrison to Fort Meigs on the Maumee, where he was instructed to pilot a company of militia over a road "half a leg deep" through the Black Swamp to Fort Stephenson on the Sandusky. The commandant there, Major George Croghan, twenty-one years old and a nephew of George Rogers Clark, commissioned him to buy a thousand dollars' worth of supplies at Cleveland. A month later, fortified with the new provisions, Major Croghan with a single cannon and a small garrison stood off an overwhelming force of British.

His purchasing mission showed young Irad Kelley

the opportunity that waited for a well stocked merchant in Cleveland. That fall, 1813, he went to New York state and bought a wagonload of goods. He brought it back in mid-winter, over frozen and drifted roads, and stored it in Alonzo Carter's warehouse on the Cuyahoga. Then, with his brothers Irad Kelley bought a ten-acre lot on Superior Street between the public square and the river and made plans to raise the first brick building in the city.

This first merchant of Cleveland spent weeks sailing a sloop on Lake Erie, bringing merchandise from Presque Isle and Buffalo and delivering powder to frontier posts. On a purchasing trip to New York City he heard news from Washington: the British had captured the city and burned the White House and the Capitol. It was a somber summer, 1814, with American ports blockaded and foreign trade cut off. But the Ohio country was just beginning. The young merchant bought his goods, consigned them to Buffalo, and stopped at Lowville to help his parents move to Cleveland. The older generation had succumbed to the western fever.

After she had arrived in Cleveland and could look back at the journey, Jemima Kelley recalled: "It rained almost all the time. Irad grew more and more unwell. We lost our way. I never saw anyone so sick as he, keep about. Our waggon broke down three or four times. Once in a place that was just like a bed of mortar, knee-deep. I had to walk sometimes three and four miles. I was so overcome by fatigue and so unwell, I felt as if I could proceed no farther."

Buffalo was a shambles, destroyed by the fighting of a year ago. But it was a relief to leave their broken-down wagon and load their goods on a sloop. They waited eleven days for a favorable wind, which blew up into one of Lake Erie's sudden storms. "We at last set sail in the evening. The next morning there came up a heavy blow which tossed the vessel all day and all night in such a terrible manner that everything in the cabin was tumbling about and we were too sick to have any fears. The next day we went ashore at Erie and came to Cleveland in a waggon. If you could know how much I suffered in this journey, you would wonder that I am alive."

In January 1815 the Kelley brothers opened their store at Superior Avenue and Sixth Street, and two months later news of peace reached Cleveland. In that year Cleveland was incorporated as a village and its first election was held: twelve votes were cast and Alfred Kelley was chosen president. The next year the first pier in Lake Erie was constructed by the Cleveland Pier Company, the Kelley brothers proprietors. In 1817 Daniel Kelley was elected president of the village. Irad Kelley became Postmaster, and the U.S. mail was handled at the Kelley Brothers' store, along with salt, gunpowder, crockery, tea, calico, and lime juice.

While sailing to Detroit with merchandise Irad Kelley sometimes stopped for shelter at Cunningham's Island, the old Island Number Six of the Firelands survey. When the agent for its Connecticut owners offered the island for sale, Irad and his brother Datus bought the three thousand acres of limestone ledge and cedar forest. It became Kelley's Island, and Datus Kelley settled there in 1833. From the island quarries the Kelley brothers shipped stone to build the Soo locks at the foot of Lake Superior and cedar crossarms for the first transcontinental telegraph line. Meanwhile their brother Alfred had become a leader in the Ohio Senate and the chief proponent of the Ohio canal system.

The country that Joshua Stow had surveyed, killing rattlesnakes and hacking out township lines, was another country now. All the way from Pennsylvania to the Maumee River farms were cleared, roads built, towns laid out. The Ohio Fever brought 150,000 people in ten years—a great inrush of people—farmers, lawyers, merchants, preachers, teamsters, millers, blacksmiths. At the Unionville crossroads, between Ashtabula and Cleveland, the New England House opened its doors in 1805. During the next thirty years it sheltered thousands of Yankees on their way to new counties of the Western Reserve. Over its oak tables and beside its blackened fireplace they traded information about townsites and land locations, about future county seats, shipping ports and flour mills. The new country stretched a man's stride and widened his conceptions. So Irad Kelley sailed a sloop the length of Lake Erie to keep goods on the shelves of a pioneer store, and Alfred Kelley pushed a canal from Lake Erie to the Ohio River.

Return J. Meigs, one of the pioneer settlers at Marietta, had come west from Middletown, Connecticut, in 1788, giving a young wife that long journey as a wedding trip. From clearing timber on the Muskingum he went into the strenuous life of frontier politics, becoming the first Chief Justice of Ohio, then governor of the state, and for nine years United States Postmaster General. He increased the number of Post Offices from 3,000 to 5,200, and the mileage of post roads from 41,000 to 85,000.

In the spring of 1799 Judge Eliphalet Austin of New Hartford, Connecticut, came west with a hired man, driving 150 cattle through the woods. He founded the town of Austinburg and saw the first church in New Connecticut established there in 1801; its first sermon was preached by the Reverend Joseph Badger who had come west to be a missionary to the Indians. ("We live the same as the Injuns," said one of the settlers, " 'ceptin' we take an interest in politics and religion.") In the same year young Benjamin Tappan, who had studied painting with Gilbert Stuart and law under Gideon Granger, came out from Weathersfield, Connecticut, to be the first settler in Portage County. At the end of a long June day he climbed through thickets to the crest of land where waters flowed toward the St. Lawrence and the Gulf of Mexico. He hired a man, cleared a road from the Cuyahoga and brought a load of farm tools to his settlement. Until January he lived in a bark lean-to; then he moved into his cabin on a site which became the seat of Portage County. Benjamin Tappan became a judge, an Ohio Canal Commissioner, a U.S. Senator.

David Hudson of Goshen, Connecticut, fell in with Tappan on the way to the Reserve. They came by boat to the

Cuyahoga, with a copy of Morse's *Geography*, which told them the river was navigable by sloops. Three miles from its mouth they found the Cuyahoga just eight inches deep. They left their boat on a mud bank and scrambled through the forest. After six days' search they found the surveyor's line that led to the southeast corner of what was to be Hudson township. It was a wet gray day and that night David Hudson slept under a dripping oak "with the grateful pleasure of resting on his own land." The village that he founded on that wild land became one of the distinguished settlements of the West, being the seat of two female institutes and of the pioneer Western Reserve College.

To New London, Connecticut, John Walworth came home after five years at sea, and promptly he caught the Ohio fever. In 1799 he bought two thousand acres in Painesville township and set out with his family in midwinter. From Buffalo they traveled in sleighs over Lake Erie's ice and along the snowy shore to Painesville. That spring General Edward Paine arrived from Bolton, Connecticut, with seven hired men to clear his land. All summer axes sounded in the Painesville woods.

In 1800 Samuel Huntington mounted a horse in Coventry, Connecticut, and started for the Reserve. A small but tireless man with a scholar's mind and courtly manners, he became governor of Ohio eight years after that long horseback ride. In 1804 Samuel Pomeroy, "an enterprising merchant of Boston," came out, looked around, and bought 262 acres on the Ohio River. When a coal bank was opened in his steep hillside he put a thousand bushels of coal into boxes and loaded them on a flatboat for New Orleans, to be sent round to Boston. The boat foundered before it got out of Pomeroy's sight, and the coal was lost. Samuel Pomeroy built another boat and loaded more coal. Eventually he employed two hundred men, dug two million bushels of coal each year, and operated twenty-five boats and barges on the Ohio. In 1804 Gideon Granger of Suffield, Connecticut, Postmaster General in President Jefferson's cabinet, sent Eldad

Smith to look at his lands in the Reserve and to lay out a town to be named Jefferson. Smith cleared a six-mile bridle path from the townsite to Austinburg and sowed ten acres of wheat. Six years later the Ashtabula County Courthouse was built in his wheat field.

No other inland region in America has had so pure a New England population as that of the Western Reserve in its first half century of settlement. Its towns, with white spires above the village green, looked like Connecticut, and there were fifty New England names, from Amherst to Windsor, on the map of the new counties. But it was not a new New England. The Ohio country changed its Yankee settlers as they changed the western land. It relaxed their Calvinism and enlarged their interests and undertakings; it made Yankee farmers into Ohio merchants, builders, politicians and industrialists.

Half a mile outside the village of Granville, Massachusetts, on two acres of garden land lived the great-grandfather of Hubert Howe Bancroft—a strict old man who wore his hat indoors and out, only baring his head to say grace, standing at the table, and who took great pride in his Seek-No-Farther apple trees. But Azariah Bancroft, the historian's grandfather, settled a hundred-acre farm at Granville, Ohio, and in his hay-strewn barn held the first anniversary meeting of the Ohio State Anti-Slavery Society. He was eighty when his youngest son was born. Azariah Ashley Bancroft built the first locks on the Ohio Canal, went to Missouri for a land purchase and to California for gold. Hubert Howe Bancroft toiled with his father in the Sierras, working the Plymouth mine (named for "the piety and principles of the old Plymouth colony") above Sacramento, where it seemed "he might increase his little fortune ten-fold." But the Plymouth failed, A. A. Bancroft became a Yakima Indian Agent at Fort Simcoe, and Hubert Howe Bancroft in San Francisco began his vast forty-volume history of the Pacific states. It was a long way from that Seek-No-Farther orchard.

One day in 1802 James Kilbourne, theologian, classi-
cist, and Episcopalian clergyman of Granby, Connecticut, and
husband of Lucy Fitch whose father had built the first of all
steamboats, closed his Greek and Latin texts and organized
forty people in a "Scioto Company" of his own. Going
ahead to locate a townsite in Ohio, he stopped at Pittsburgh
to buy "millstones, iron and other supplies" which he sent
down the river to the Scioto while he proceeded overland
with a blacksmith, a millwright, and a crew of laborers. He
planted his town of Worthington on the upper Scioto; it
flourished and Kilbourne became one of the leading citizens of the West. Besides being Rector of the church at Worthington, he founded Worthington Academy (his twelve children helped to fill its roster), served on the commission
which chose the site of Miami University, was a Colonel in
the Ohio militia, and superintended the surveying of Erie
County from the Maumee Rapids to Sandusky. In 1805 Albert
Gallatin, Secretary of the Treasury, appointed him Surveyor
of the Public Lands. He laid out fourteen Ohio towns,
founded the first newspaper in central Ohio, and served as
a member of Congress where he introduced the first Homestead bill. In 1812 with woolen factories in Worthington
and Steubenville he supplied uniforms for General Harrison's army—a business which left him penniless when the
war was over. He then founded the town of Bucyrus on the
Sandusky River, naming it for the founder of Persia's empire
with a prefix to suggest "beautiful," and wrote a luring
twenty-stanza poem to stimulate land sales.

> *I'll tell you how Bucyrus, now*
> *Just rising, like the star of morn,*
> *Surrounded stands by fertile lands,*
> *On clear Sandusky's rural bourn.*

> *Then here, my friends, your search may end,*
> *For here's a country to your mind,*
> *And here's a town your hopes may crown,*
> *As those who try it soon shall find.*

He lived to see Ohio become the foremost agricultural state in the Union, and he presided in 1840 over the noisy Whig Convention at Columbus which nominated William Henry Harrison for the presidency.

Samuel L. Mather, son of a stockholder in the Connecticut Land Company, came to Ohio to look at the family lands. He looked farther and saw the meaning of iron ore in upper Michigan—it was discovered by another Yankee, William Burt of Petersham, Massachusetts. Mather organized the Cleveland Iron Mining Company which brought the first ore cargo down the Lakes and began the Lake Erie iron and steel industry.

Benjamin Franklin Wade followed two brothers from Feeding Hills, Massachusetts, to Andover, Ohio. He became a farmer, canal-digger, woodcutter. One winter he read the Bible, from Genesis to Revelation, by the light of pine faggots in his wood-chopper's cabin. After another winter of reading law books he passed the bar examination and became a partner of Joshua Reed Giddings in a one-room office in the town of Jefferson. Thirty years later the two backwoods lawyers were giants in the United States Congress.

In tin trunks and saddlebags the settlers brought a few things—adze and ax, candle molds, garden seeds, orchard cuttings, a Bible, a dictionary, an *Emigrant's Guide*— but in their minds came all the Yankee interests, purposes, and capacities. Jonathan Goldsmith, architect and builder, left New Haven for the wild lands in 1811, settling in the village of Painesville. It was the right place for a builder. Lake County was prospering, and the log cabin years were already past. Soon Goldsmith's serene and sturdy Greek revival houses began to grace the streets of Painesville, Mentor and Willoughby. Lorenzo Dow, born two miles from the Nathan Hale house at Coventry, Connecticut, went west to save sinners from damnation. Wild and shaggy as a John the Baptist, he made twenty tours of the remote frontier, preaching where prayer and sermons had never been heard.

Fort Greene Ville (Greenville, Ohio)

Gallipolis when French settlers arrived in 1790

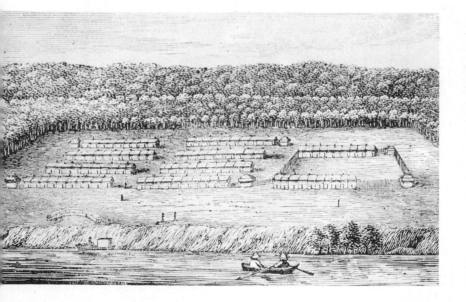

Frontier Farm

Anti-emigration cartoon

Martin Chuzzlewit inspects map of thriving City of Eden

What he and Mark Tapley found at Eden

ILLINOIS CENTRAL RAILROAD COMPAN[Y]

OFFER FOR SALE

ONE MILLION ACRES OF SUPERIOR FARMING LANDS,

IN FARMS OF

40, 80 & 160 acres and upwards at from $8 to $12 per acr[e]

THESE LANDS ARE

NOT SURPASSED BY ANY IN THE WORLD.

THEY LIE ALONG

THE WHOLE LINE OF THE CENTRAL ILLINOIS RAILROAD.

For Sale on LONG CREDIT, SHORT CREDIT and for CASH, they are situated near TOW[NS]
VILLAGES, SCHOOLS and CHURCHES.

The Illinois Central advertises for settlers

Prairie Scene, Indiana

Detroit, 1820. Showing first steamboat on the lakes, Walk-in-Water. Painted by Geo. Washington Whistler, Jas. A. Whistler's father

Hazel Grove Farm, Fulton County, Illinois, once wild prairie

Wisconsin Immigrant Farm: Dream and Reality

Fort Harmer

Whitewater Canal, showing Wm. Henry Harrison's "log cabin"

Miami and Erie Canal

Flatboat on the Ohio

Cincinnati in 1800

CINCINNATI-1800.

People called him "Crazy Dow," but they flocked through the woods to hear him, and they named their children for him months after he was gone. In thirty-eight years he traveled two hundred thousand miles, from the Mississippi to the Thames; before his death in 1834 he had introduced camp meetings into England. Jared Kirtland, son of a stockholder in the Connecticut Company, followed his father to Mahoning County. Already a distinguished naturalist and physician, he practiced medicine in the backwoods. Between calls he tramped the fields with his rangy, tireless stride, distributing improved seeds to pioneer farmers and studying the species of water mussels in Ohio's creeks. He served three terms in the state legislature, conducted the first geological survey of Ohio, and became a founder of Cleveland Medical College. The Ohio fever touched all kinds of men.

Oliver Phelps did not get rich with his Connecticut Land Company. Deep in debt after 1796, he went into hiding and lost his Western Reserve lands to the mortgage holders. He lived his last years in Canandaigua, New York, managing the remnant of his land in the Holland Purchase, a huge land speculation in western New York in which he had engaged in 1788 with one Nathaniel Gorham as his partner. Moses Cleaveland died in Connecticut in 1806. By then the town of Cleveland, ten years old, had not accumulated fifty people. But other settlements were thriving.

In 1808 Peter Chardon Brooks of Boston laid out the town of Chardon on a ridge in Ohio's most extensive maple forest; he saw it become the prosperous seat of Geauga County. In 1817 Heman Ely of West Springfield, Massachusetts, bought 12,000 acres at the falls of the Black River. He built a dam, a sawmill, a gristmill, and named his town for himself and his wife Maria. Soon Elyria was a busy village, with quarries, flour mills, a foundry, and the Lorain County Courthouse. Over in the Firelands Platt Benedict built a cabin in the wilderness and helped Surveyor Almon Ruggles lay out the town of Norwalk. In his absence Benedict's cabin burned, but he built another in the fall of 1817, and moved his family in. Next spring a dozen families settled there and Norwalk was made the seat of Huron County. In 1818 Zalmon Wildman of Danbury, Connecticut, laid out a town on Sandusky Bay. Ten years later mile-long lines of grain wagons brought corn and wheat to Sandusky's wharves; in one October day, 1828, two hundred and eighty-five wagons unloaded. Wildman's town became one of the great grain markets of the nation and the greatest fresh-water fishing port in the world. In 1818 Moses and Aaron Wilcox, twin brothers from North Killingworth, Connecticut, planted the town of Twinsburg, which soon became a center of learning. Under the Reverend Samuel Bissell the Twinsburg Institute had a staff of seven teachers and enrolled Indian and white students from many miles around.

While the Army of the Northwest marched toward Lake Erie in 1813, one of General Harrison's young officers took a special liking to a camp site in Sandusky County. Before breaking camp he drove a stake into the ground and made a little speech to his friends: "At this spot I shall build my future home, which shall be the nucleus of a thriving town." Eight years later he came back, scoured the woods for his weathered stake, and found smoke sifting up from a squatter's cabin. With a barrel of whisky he bought off the squatter and took possession. In time a crossroads settlement grew up on his land and the town of Clyde was plotted. A hundred years later Sherwood Anderson portrayed it as *Winesburg, Ohio.*

Settlement of the Firelands, the district assigned by Connecticut to its citizens whose property had been destroyed by British raids during the Revolution, lagged behind that of the Western Reserve. It lay farther in the west, and the Indian title to the tract was not extinguished until 1805 when on July 4th at Fort Industry the chiefs of seven tribes signed over lands totaling 1,030,000 acres for some

wagonload of horseshoes, scythes, saws, drawknives, grubbing hoes, harness, hammers, barrels of salt and iron nails.
And when cleared of Indian claim the Black Swamp still
impeded travel in the interior. But in time the speculators
found their way up the Maumee and laid out phantom
towns beside the river—sites like Austerlitz, Oregon, Manhattan, and Marengo, marked only by the circles of old Indian fires.

By that time settlement was pushing far beyond
Ohio. Indiana was the new Garden of America, with speculators roving the country looking for future townsites. In
1836 in his *New Guide for Emigrants to the West*, J. M.
Peck declared: "The importance of Indiana as a desirable
State for the attention of the emigrant to the West has been
too much overlooked. . . . Its soil is far superior to Ohio.
. . . Almost every part is easy of access, and in a few years
the liberal system of improvements, adopted and in progress, will make almost every county accessible to public
conveyances, and furnish abundant facilities to market."
The *Emigrant's Guide and Pocket Geography* reported a silver mine near Ouitenon on the Wabash and beds of iron
ore on the White River. "A large portion of Indiana is not
surpassed by any lands in the Union in point of fertility of
soil or beauty of situation." Population on the Wabash,
it reported, "increases with a rapidity unknown in the an-
nals of immigration."

By 1840 the Ohio fever had given way to the Michigan fever, the Illinois fever, and the lure of lands beyond
the Mississippi. In prosperous Cleveland, where a huge trade
was flowing from Lake Erie and the Ohio Canal, prosperous
Irad Kelley in his Euclid Avenue mansion at the sober age
of fifty-five got the California fever and went by way of
Panama to the Pacific. On a broad and empty harbor he
thought he saw a location that had promise for the future.
He bought a five-acre lot on the San Diego water front, thinking perhaps of his uncle, Joshua Stow, who took a chance

on empty land along the Cuyahoga. Back in Cleveland Irad
Kelley read about new countries and wild lands in South
America. At the age of eighty-four he packed his battered
trunk and started for Brazil. He died in New York, in 1875,
while waiting for the boat. His name came from the Old
Testament and it means "Seeker."

CHAPTER TEN

SHADOWS ON AN ISLAND

*

SQUATTERS came down the Ohio on rafts and shanty boats, bringing an ax and a musket, a grubbing hoe and a bag of seed corn. The settlers came in flatboats, with oxen and log chains, a brood sow and a crate of chickens. But Harman Blennerhassett came in a keelboat with his pretty wife and an English man-servant. He brought chests of books, chemical apparatus and musical instruments; he carried $150,000 in bank notes and letters of credit. He came in 1797 and he was gone ten years later. He stayed no longer than a squatter, and like a squatter he fled in secrecy and suspicion. But he left a ruined mansion for rivermen to wonder at and a memory for the valley people to make into a legend.

It was another Irishman, George Croghan, who first recorded "five very fine islands," a chain of wooded islands in the Ohio fourteen miles below the mouth of the Muskingum and the future site of Marietta. That was in 1765, when the Ohio country was a British domain and George Croghan, with posts among the Shawnees, Miamis and Wyandots, was its richest trader. Five years later George Washington passed down the river; he noted "a cluster of islands" below the mouth of the Muskingum. At low water they were a single island, screened with willows and sycamores, three and a half miles long, containing some five hundred acres—the largest island in the Ohio River. In 1780 it was claimed by an agent for an eastern warrant-holder. During the next twelve years it changed hands five times, and none of its owners ever saw their graceful island under the curving hills. In 1792 it was bought by Elijah Backus, a Marietta editor and lawyer; he had a man clear some timber and grow a crop of corn.

Five years later, in 1797, Harman Blennerhassett bought it for four thousand dollars and began to plan his mansion. Since then a series of owners have bought the land and filed their title, but it will always be "Blennerhassett Island."

Blennerhassett had more in common with the squatters than with the sober and hard-working settlers. He came to Ohio not for opportunity but for obscurity, and for the beauty and adventure of the wilderness. He called his island "Isle de Beau Pré," and he became involved in an adventure that made him a fugitive, hurrying on westward toward a wilder country.

In Ireland, at Conway Castle, Killorglin, and at the King's Inn Courts in Dublin, Harman Blennerhassett was a casual, cultivated and romantic-minded man. He must have read of the Ohio wilderness—"the fame of Ohio having gone into almost every nation upon earth"—and his romantic spirit would have warmed to its descriptions: "An immense forest, almost without bounds, swelling into stupendous mountains . . . covered with venerable trees hoary with age and torn with tempests . . . mighty rivers, raging in torrents or gliding in majestic silence. With her diversity of soils and climate, this magnificent region is calculated to become a rival to half the world in trade and riches." But what sent Blennerhassett to the wilderness was more than a dream of riches or a desire for adventure. It was scandal.

In Ireland, in the spring of 1796, Harman Blennerhassett called at a boarding school to escort his sister's daughter home for an Easter holiday. From that errand his whole life swung in a new direction. Blennerhassett was a bachelor of thirty-one; pretty Margaret Agnew was eighteen. They came home as man and wife. When the shocked family disinherited Margaret and ostracized them both, Blennerhassett sold his Irish estate and brought his bride to America. They could have stayed in New York, where they were entertained by the first families, but Blennerhassett feared that gossip would follow and find them across the Atlantic. The Ohio country offered adventure and romance; it also offered isolation. So he came down the Ohio to Marietta, and soon the tall, stooped Irish aristocrat took his vivacious wife to see Backus Island. They walked in its deep woods and watched the river gliding past its quiet shores. It was an enchanted place where the world would never find them. Soon Blennerhassett had a gang of workmen clearing his park, building his boat landings, bringing stone and timber from the Virginia hills. In 1800 he moved into his mansion.

It was an unexpected sight in that wild country. A broad opening in the woods led to a serene and gracious house, gleaming white against the forest trees, its two-story central unit flanked by curving wings. Ten windows looked across green terraces and colored gardens to the north point of the island where the river current parted. The south wing housed ten servants and the kitchen, cupboards, and

pantries; the north wing, fitted with bookshelves, desks
and tables, was Blennerhassett's study. To his stone landing
had come furnishings from Philadelphia, Baltimore and
London—silver, glass, linen, tapestries and carpets. A carriage drive curved from the boat landing to the mansion's
portico. Graveled paths led through the flower gardens. On
summer afternoons tea was served in grottoes banked with
English eglantine. All this in a country of log huts with
greased pigskin stretched across the windows.

While passing rivermen stared through the fringe of
trees, Blennerhassett strolled his grounds, a tall slow figure
in broadcloth coat, knee breeches and silver-buckled shoes,
peering near-sightedly at fine specimens of fruit and blossom. Margaret Blennerhassett cantered over the bridle
paths and sometimes rode her sorrel "Robin" fourteen
miles through the woods to Marietta, her Negro groom jogging along behind her. In a dress of scarlet broadcloth and
a white beaver hat flaunting an ostrich plume, she visited
her friends in Marietta. On the island she entertained with
musicals, readings and impromptu performances of Shake-
speare. On summer evenings they gathered their guests on
the terrace to look at stars through a portable telescope.

For a few seasons life was happy on the island. No
breath of scandal found their remote and beautiful retreat.
Blennerhassett read the Greek and Latin poets and experi-
mented with chemistry and electricity. From London he
imported Irish linen, pewter ware, slippers, velvet, fans,
putting them on sale in Marietta. He invested in ship-
building in the Muskingum boatyards. Margaret Blennerhassett had her French and Italian books, her stable of
horses, her rose garden. In this happy place two Blennerhassett sons learned to swim in the river and hunt in the
woods. Sometimes Blennerhassett took them digging for ar-
rowheads and pottery in a burial mound at the far end of
the island.

Up and down the Ohio people talked of the white
mansion and of its master strolling the garden paths and re-

peating the *Iliad* from memory. Friends came from Virginia for week-long house parties, and travelers, journeying west from Pittsburgh, were entertained in the Blennerhassett guest rooms.

On a cloudless May day in 1805 a visitor arrived in a houseboat—a notable visitor who was immediately at home in the Blennerhassett library and drawing room. A slight, quick man with small hands, graceful movements and a quiet and magnetic speech, he carried an indefinable importance with him. Something about him was dramatic and compelling. From the moment of his arrival the island was charged with a new vibration.

Aaron Burr, brilliant and ambitious, had left the East as a famous and an infamous man. A graduate of Princeton, he had studied theology and law in Connecticut, served brilliantly in Washington's army, become a political leader and a rival of Alexander Hamilton. In the presidential struggle of 1800 he tied in electoral votes with Jefferson. After a week of balloting the House of Representatives chose Jefferson as president, Burr becoming vice-president. His rivalry with Hamilton led to a duel at Weehawken, New Jersey; Hamilton fired into the air but Burr's bullet killed. Burr was charged with murder, his property was seized, the federalist newspapers hounded him. A few months later he went to the western country. Like Blennerhassett, he was a fugitive from his past, but he had a bolder project than a mansion in the wilderness.

At Pittsburgh Burr bought a commodious houseboat and set off toward the Mississippi, where, he let it be known, he had interest in a land speculation. Actually, he hoped to provoke a war with Spain along the lower Mississippi and in that crisis to seize control of Mexico. Journeying down the Ohio with these vast plans before him, he heard of the romantic Irishman who had built his island mansion below Marietta. Such a man must have money to invest in a bold enterprise and must have a mind for high adventure. So he stopped at the landing where the sycamore trees were green and the iris banks were bursting into color. Again Harman Blennerhassett's future swung in a new direction.

Three times Burr visited the island, between reconnaissance trips to the west. In the spring of 1806 he ascended the Wabash to Vincennes, capital of Indiana Territory, and called on Governor William Henry Harrison in his Grouseland mansion. Burr talked largely and vaguely about land projects up the Washita in the Arkansas country; Harrison listened with interest, knowing that men of bold designs could make fortunes and extend civilization in new territories. Burr went on to Louisiana, where he inflamed the minds of some wealthy and discontented Southerners. He went back East, raising more money for his undertaking. By the time of his third visit to the island, Burr and Blennerhassett were conspirators. Now Burr was ready to send an expedition down the river, and the romantic Irishman, sharing the vision of an empire from the Mississippi to the Rio Grande, wanted a full partnership in the adventure.

Blennerhassett's fortune had dwindled, and he feared that English travelers coming down the Ohio might bring word of his incestuous marriage; he was ready for a newer and more distant country. He mortgaged his mansion, sold his securities, and ordered a fleet of barges from a Marietta builder—fifteen craft for men and provisions; one for firearms, lead and powder; and a houseboat with glass windows, a fireplace, and a railed promenade for his own family. When word came, Blennerhassett was to bring this expedition down the Mississippi, where Burr with his forces would be waiting.

Burr counted on the isolation and the antifederalism of the frontier. But word found its way from town to town along the river and to settlements in the interior. The Ohio country buzzed with rumor and question. Why were fleets of barges assembling at Marietta and Louisville? Why did anonymous letters [written by Blennerhas-

sett] in a Marietta newspaper propose a division of the
eastern and western areas of the United States? What were
Burr's mysterious errands in the West? Word went back
over the mountains. President Jefferson declared that sedi-
tious plans were under way and alerted civil and military
officials. In the log capitol at Chillicothe Governor Tiffin informed the Ohio legislature of a plan to send an expedition
from Marietta to capture New Orleans and establish an independent rule on the lower Mississippi. The Ohio legislature gave the governor power to muster the state militia.
Burr had not looked for a test so early.

One of Blennerhassett's guests in happier days was
young Lewis Cass who brought his bride to the island for a
summer honeymoon. A native of Exeter, New Hampshire,
Cass had followed his father to Ohio and had read law in
Marietta in the offices of Return Jonathan Meigs and Mat-
thew Backus. He looked out of place at a book-strewn desk—
a stocky young man with unruly hair and powerful shoulders, always shifting in his chair, leafing through Blackstone's *Commentaries* and the *Crown Circuit Companion*
and jabbing penciled notes in his ledgers. He was happier
when he rode off to the circuit court, as prosecutor for Muskingum County, jogging over the woods trails, swimming
his horse across streams and rivers, spreading his blanket on
a settler's floor or making his camp under the forest trees.
In 1806 he was elected to the Ohio House of Representatives, though a year short of the qualifying age of twenty-
five. That summer he married a Virginia girl and they
spent a blissful week on Blennerhassett's island. They rode
horseback on the island trails and walked in the moonlit
gardens. While Elizabeth Cass drank tea with Margaret
Blennerhassett the two men discussed the future of the
western country—tall stooped Blennerhassett talking with a
far-away look in his dark eyes and his young friend thrash-
ing the air with big strong hands. Ten years later Cass
would be governor of Michigan Territory; fifteen years
later he would be exploring the lonely shores of Lake Su-

perior and searching the Minnesota wilderness for the source of the Mississippi. Six months after their island honeymoon Cass wrote from Chillicothe to his bride: ". . . We have engaged in business, which is very important to Mr. Blennerhassett, and as you will be somewhat anxious I will relate it to you. The plan of Col. Burr is finally and completely developed. We have received a private communication from the governor informing us, that Mr. Burr's plan is to collect about 1300 men, to rendezvous at the mouth of red river and to proceed from there to Orleans, to attack the city, to seize upon the bank and treasury, and upon the artillery and to form an independent government under the protection of Spain. . . . We have passed a law, which I drafted, empowering the governor to stop the boats now building, and all others provided for that purpose, and seize all persons concerned. This letter will be carried by a messenger dispatched by the Governor to arrest Mr. Blennerhassett and stop his boats."

Meanwhile Blennerhassett had a band of men on the island grinding corn meal and packing it in barrels. At Marietta pork, flour, bacon and whisky were already loaded on the barges. Burr gathered recruits from Pennsylvania and from the frontier towns of Chillicothe, Cincinnati, Lexington, bringing them to Blennerhassett's island. During the short days of December, 1806, the island swarmed with activity. In the outbuildings the recruits traded ideas about lands in the Southwest, lands glamorized by distance and danger, while in the drawing room Burr talked of being Emperor of Mexico and sending Blennerhassett as his ambassador to England. On a black December night Burr and his party pushed off in a keelboat. Blennerhassett would bring the barges to a rendezvous on the lower Mississippi.

Then came word of crisis; the Ohio militia had seized the expedition's fleet at Marietta. At this news some of Blennerhassett's men forgot the promised lands on the Washita and went back to their small Ohio clearings. But a troop of hot-headed young recruits went to Marietta to defy the state militia. After a confused tussle on the river bank they cut the moorings of one barge and ran it down the black river. On the island Blennerhassett was waiting; he had heard of the militiamen's threat to kill him. He climbed aboard, waved farewell to his wife and children (they would follow later) and was on his way to join Burr on the Mississippi.

Next morning Margaret Blennerhassett took her children to Marietta where the family boat was waiting. She found the town full of armed men and a military detail patrolling the boatyard. There was nothing to do but return to the island. She came home to a shambles. A troop of militiamen had taken possession. After rifling the wine cellar they had a drunken field day, smashing mirrors and furniture, shooting out the chandeliers, cutting the draperies to ribbons with bayonets and hunting knives. She packed her children's clothing and boarded a boat that had come down from Pittsburgh with some of Burr's belated followers. It was just a week before Christmas. She looked back where the gray hills closed the island from her sight. Over the water came the long sad call of a boatman's horn and then the oarsman's voice:

> —*All the way to Shawneetown,*
> *A long time ago.*

Blennerhassett, hurrying down the river in those gray December days, had good luck—for a little while. Troops riding across country to head him off arrived at Point Pleasant ahead of him and primed their rifles. But the chill weather called for a double ration of whisky, and that put them to sleep. Blennerhassett's boat rounded the Point unchallenged. Three days before Christmas he met Burr at the mouth of the Cumberland, near the western tip of Kentucky. Together they pushed on down the Mississippi. A month later Margaret Blennerhassett and her sons joined the conspirators at Bayou Pierre, Louisiana.

For two touchy weeks they eluded pursuit, but eventually Federal troops captured them in Mississippi Territory. Then began the slow return journey up the river, with not an empire but a court trial at the end. After a prolonged hearing at Richmond (the charge of treason was based on Burr's preparations in Virginia) presided over by Chief Justice John Marshall, Burr and Blennerhassett were discharged for lack of material evidence.

Burr's failure strengthened the bonds of Ohio with the Union. The western country was cut off from the East by a wall of mountains, and many frontiersmen felt remote from the federal government. Their destiny pointed toward the Mississippi and their trade must flow to the Gulf of Mexico. Burr had counted on that feeling in the West. But at the crucial moment, when the expedition was about to be sprung, young Lewis Cass offered in the Ohio House of Representatives a resolution affirming Ohio's loyalty to the federal administration. It was gratefully received by President Jefferson, and that commitment spread a spirit of national unity throughout the frontier.

In the spring of 1807 a crest of high water came down the Ohio. It swept over Blennerhassett's island, filling the mansion with muddy waters, drowning the gardens, littering the lawns with silt and debris. The Blennerhassetts came back for a last melancholy look, but there was nothing to return to. Everything movable had been carried off, and the island was in possession of a mortgage-holder. They went down the river again, not to an empire but to a cotton farm, *La Cache,* The Hiding Place. When the cotton market collapsed, Blennerhassett tried another venture, in a law office in Montreal. That failed too. At last he went back to an older island, the green isle of Guernsey off the south coast of England. There he died in 1831.

The house on Blennerhassett's island stood empty for four years, but on Christmas eve in 1811 it took fire, perhaps from the camp of a hunter or a flatboatman. That winter night a glare lit up the river banks and danced on the black water. On Christmas day there were only the charred foundation stones—which still mark the site of the romantic and unhappy mansion. In years afterward it became the subject of four novels, a poem, some idyllic paintings, and an opera, and of a legend that will outlast them all.

Twelve years after it was built the mansion was gone and the island was empty. Past the lifeless shores came squatters with their grubbing hoes and seed corn, settlers with land warrants in their pockets and a team of oxen tied to the rail. And across the water came the keelboat song—

Hard upon the beech oar!
She moves too slow
All the way to Shawneetown,
A long time ago.

CHAPTER ELEVEN

"HERE ARE GOOD
OPPORTUNITIES"

Here, whatever their original, whether English, Scotch, Irish,
German, or French—all are Americans: and of all the impu-
tations on the American character, jealousy of strangers is
surely the most absurd and groundless.

—MORRIS BIRKBECK: *Notes on a Journey to America*

IN 1802 the French naturalist François André Michaux
journeyed down the Ohio, his sharp right eye (the left
one had been shot out by a rifle bullet in his youth) sort-
ing out timber on the shore—willow, sycamore, swamp oak,
cottonwood, an occasional persimmon or pawpaw tree in the
underforest—and his notebook filling with observations of
the new country. On river landings, in farm clearings, in
blacksmith shops and taverns he heard the repeated greet-
ing: " 'What part of the world do you come from?'—as if
those immense and fertile regions were to be the asylum
common to all the inhabitants of the globe."

There was just one Blennerhassett spending an Irish

fortune in the wilderness, but multitudes left the Old
World's poverty and oppression for the opportunity and independence of the frontier. They sang old Welsh hymns in
new log meeting houses, they baked German cakes in Ohio
cabins, they argued Irish politics in construction shanties
beside the western turnpikes and canals. John Pope made an
early journey down the Ohio in a keelboat named the
Smokehouse; taking turns at the long steering oar were a
Kentuckian, a Virginian, a German, a Welshman, and a
man born at sea.

On Monday, August 3rd, 1795, the great treaty was
signed at Greene Ville. That evening Wayne ordered a
generous ration of whisky for the tribesmen, and the next
morning began the distribution of treaty goods. On that
day, August 4th, four thousand miles from Greenville Creek
six persons left Glamorgan, Wales, for the port of Bristol.
Aboard the ship *Maria* they carried a chest of bread, oat-
meal, cheese and salted meat, enough for an eight-weeks
journey. The fare ran low, for the *Maria* was thirteen weeks
on the stormy Atlantic. After gray wastes of water the busy
streets of Philadelphia looked good to the Welsh travelers,
but their destination was the West.

In a four-horse wagon they toiled over the Pennsylvania mountains. Four of them stopped in western Pennsylvania, but the other two, Ezekiel Hughes and Edward
Bebb, took a flatboat down the Ohio. From Cincinnati they
struck inland, looking shrewdly at land along the Great
Miami. The best locations in the Symmes Purchase, between
the two Miamis, were already taken, and public land west
of the Miami was not yet surveyed. But they had a look at
that country, picturing a Welsh settlement—roads, fields,
houses, barns, mills, shops, schools, churches—of the future.
Back in Cincinnati they worked as tradesmen, put away
their money, and waited for the public land to go on sale.
Up the Great Miami and the Whitewater government surveyors ran the section lines. In Congress Hall at Philadelphia lean young William Henry Harrison argued for his

Public Land Bill: *"Resolved,* That all townships directed to be sold . . . shall be divided into half sections, containing . . . 320 acres each," and that land could be claimed by a down-payment of one twentieth of the purchase price. Harrison did not know that Ezekiel Hughes and Edward Bebb had come four thousand miles to claim wild land, but he might have been describing them when he spoke of men in the Ohio country, men restless and resolute, with little money for investment but with purpose, hope and energy, waiting for a land law that would open the gates of the public domain.

When federal land went on sale at the Cincinnati Land Office in April, 1801, the Welshmen were among the first in line. Ezekiel Hughes bought two sections in Hamilton County and Bebb bought a half section on the Dry Fork of the Whitewater.

Edward Bebb's purchase was the first sale of land in Morgan township, near the southwest corner of Ohio, but he was not the first man there. When he pushed through the deer brush on Dry Fork he found smoke sifting up from a clearing and a squatter standing in a cabin door. His name was Aaron Cherry and he had raised two crops of corn. When the Welshman offered to pay him for clearing and breaking the land, Cherry remarked: "This is the thirteenth time I have squatted, and the first time I was ever offered any pay for my improvements." The squatter moved on to a fourteenth location, where his sons became notorious horse thieves. Having secured his claim and put some seed corn in the ground, Edward Bebb walked back to Ebensburg, Pennsylvania, married a young Welsh widow there and brought her to his Ohio homestead. Their son, born in 1802 and the first child born in Morgan township, was Governor of Ohio forty-four years later. In that year of 1802 Morgan Gwilym, having worked in the iron furnaces of Pennsylvania to get money for his purchase, bought a half section on Paddy's Run in Morgan township and began clearing forest. In 1804 he brought the first two-horse wagon into that district.

It was a good location—rolling land with fertile flats and prime hill timber—twenty miles up the Miami valley from Cincinnati. Soon there was a thriving Welsh settlement at Paddy's Run (named for an Irish Indian fighter who fell in a creek and all but drowned.) They raised fine corn and wheat and drove hundreds of hogs over the hills to the slaughter pens at Cincinnati. They made rich cheese and butter, packing it on horses over the old Miami trail; for years "Paddy's Run butter" was a favorite in Cincinnati's lower market. Though Ohio was not as healthful as mountainous old Wales, they survived the annual spells of "shakes" and fever. The summer of 1811 brought an amazing comet in the southern sky; then came a "cold plague" with prolonged sickness and ruinous hailstorms. That winter an earthquake terrified the district. But the devout Welshmen thanked Providence for their remaining blessings, and the next year they raised a company of volunteers to march under William Henry Harrison against the British at Detroit.

The Welsh were sturdy, sober, orderly people. Soon they had a church society at Paddy's Run, with prayer and preaching in a wagon-maker's shop. In fine weather they moved outside, singing their hymns in a grove of sugar maples; eventually a brick meeting house dominated the grove. Twenty years before Ohio established public schools there was a free school at Paddy's Run, the teacher boarding around and receiving an additional seventy-five cents per week. They organized a pioneer circulating library, selling sixty-five shares at three dollars and keeping the books at the grist mill on Dry Fork. In his saddlebags a man brought home from the mill a dusty book or two—Plutarch's *Lives*, Rollin's *Ancient History*, Johnson's *Lives of the Poets*, Butler's *Analogy*, Blair's *Lectures*, *The Lewis and Clark Expedition*—a fare as solid and wholesome as his bag of fresh-ground meal. When the Paddy's Run school dis-

trict was organized in 1826, its first teacher was William
Bebb, future governor of Ohio. Bebb's next school was at
North Bend, where he taught the younger children of William Henry Harrison. Back at Paddy's Run, on the farm
where his father had ousted a squatter twenty-seven years
before, he opened a boarding school for boys. His graduates
went on to Cincinnati College and to Miami University up
the valley. Though Paddy's Run remained an obscure village it produced 250 college graduates in the next hundred
years. Education flourished like corn and pumpkins in the
Ohio country.

From Paddy's Run other Welsh settlements were
planted on the frontier, and a steady flow of Welsh migration kept them growing. In 1803 a band from Wales settled
the Welsh Hills in Licking County, in central Ohio. They
cleared wild land and grew crops of corn and hay that
sounded incredible to their kinsmen on the rocky slopes
of Carmarthen and Montgomeryshire. In 1804 began a populous Welsh settlement at Radnor, a day's wagon-journey
north of Columbus. In the summer of 1811 six families
from South Wales, journeying down the Ohio on their way
to Paddy's Run, moored their keelboat at the Gallipolis
landing and spent the night ashore. Next morning their
boats were gone, and so they learned about pirates on the
river. The stranded Welshmen looked around; it was a hill
country, densely wooded, with seams of coal and iron glinting in the brushy cliffs. They decided to stay. Their town of
Jackson became a center of Welsh settlement, which spilled
over into neighboring counties. By 1840 Jackson was known
for its annual song festival; the old Welsh hymns and folk
songs had come to the Ohio hills. Another Welsh colony
spread over the rich flat lands of Putnam and Van Wert
counties, two days' travel north of Greenville; here the Reverend Benjamin Chidlaw, a visitor from Paddy's Run,
counted a hundred haystacks, of two to three tons each, in
a single meadow.

In the 1830's young Welshmen working on the big

ditch of the Miami and Erie Canal used their wages to buy land. Word went back to Wales: "Here are good opportunities for buying land to hold until the price increases." It was hardly believed in Glamorgan, Carmarthen and Brecknock that some Welsh farmers in Van Wert County held domains of 800, 1200, even 1600 acres. But a luring "America poem" was familiar in taverns and market places from Swansea to Carnarvan:

> *I will travel—I will sail over*
> *The salt sea—on an adventure;*
> *I'll warrant against disappointment*
> *I shall find there ample work*
> *And excellent Money.*

Foreign travelers on the frontier inevitably compared the lot of farmers in the Old World and the New. John Melish, geographer, merchant, textile manufacturer in Glasgow and importer in Philadelphia, took a long look at frontier life in 1809-11 and declared that farmers could not too highly prize the blessings they enjoyed in America:

"There [in Scotland] a farmer pays from seven to twenty-eight dollars per acre, yearly, for the *use* of his farm. . . . If he improve the farm, the improvements are for another, not for him; and at the end of the lease, if another is willing to give one shilling more than him, or if the proprietor has a favourite, or wishes to turn two or more farms into one, or has taken umbrage at his politics, or his religion, or anything else regarding him or his family, he will not get a renewal of the lease. Many a family have I known that has been ruined in this way. . . . Nor is there any remedy; the lands are nearly all entailed on the great families, and the lords of the soil are the lords of the laws; they can bind the poor farmer *in all cases whatsoever*.

"Compare this with the situation of an American farmer. He cultivates his own soil, or if he has none, he can procure it in sufficient quantity for 200 or 300 dollars. If he has no money he can get credit, and all that is necessary to redeem his credit is to put forth his hand and be industrious. He can stand erect on the middle of his farm and say, 'This ground is mine: from the highest canopy of heaven down to the lowest depths, I can claim all that I can get possession of within these bounds, fowls of the air, fish of the sea, and all that pass through the same.' And, having a full share of consequence in the political scale, his equal rights are granted to him. None dare encroach upon him: he can sit under his own vine, and under his own fig tree, and none to make him afraid."

A few years later another Scotsman, James Flint of Edinburgh, observed that 2050 immigrants arrived in New York harbor in a single week of August, 1818, many of them bound for the frontier. Flint made a thorough tour of the Ohio valley and, besides the Virginians, Yankees, Pennsylvanians, the English, Irish, Welsh and Germans, he found some of his own hardy countrymen settled there. Near the Ohio, twelve miles northeast of the busy port of Madison, Indiana, he visited a colony of Scots. Though living on second-rate land, they were a cheerful, industrious, and thriving settlement. He cited a blacksmith from Edinburgh who had come to this place with his family a year before. "He has purchased four hundred eighty acres of land, built two log houses and a small stable, cleared and inclosed about twenty-two acres, which is nearly all under crop; deadened the timber of about eighty acres more; and planted an orchard. In addition to these improvements . . . he has a horse, a cow, a few hogs, some poultry. I inquired if he felt himself happy in a strange land; he replied, that he would not return to Scotland though the property of which he formerly rented a part were given to him for nothing."

One traveler in the western country in 1825-26 signed the registers of frontier inns with a name that spilled over onto a second line—Bernhard Karl, Duke of Saxe-Weimar-Eisenach. He toured the Ohio valley looking for a

place to settle; since the Battle of Waterloo he had no career in Germany. The Grand Duke liked the New World,
particularly the frontier country, but he could not fix on
any one location. Eventually he went back across the Atlantic, becoming a commander in the army of the Nether-
lands. Meanwhile thousands of his countrymen found places
to their liking in the Ohio country. They settled the towns
of Bremen, Berlin, New Salem, New Lisbon. They formed
colonies in Cincinnati, Fort Wayne, Indianapolis, Terre
Haute. In the 1840s they pushed on to Chicago, to Peoria
and Pekin on the Illinois River, to Quincy, Alton and St.
Louis on the Mississippi.

At the old port of Bremen on the Weser and at Le
Havre, their chief points of departure, when asked what
they expected to find in America, the German emigrants
had a ready response. *"Kein König dort,"* they said
promptly—"No king there." They might have added,
"acres." In "America letters" and emigrant books they had
read that one day's labor in the New World would buy an
acre of farm land. They had heard of peaches and apples
rotting in Ohio orchards, of potatoes left in the ground, of
grain—enough to keep a parish—ungleaned in the fields, of
white bread, roast meat, and pastry, like a feast of Christmas, on the table every day. In 1836 Goethe wrote in a
poem: *"America, Du hast es besser"* (literally: "America,
you have it better.") Hundreds of families from Bavaria,
Saxony, Württemberg, and Hesse had found it so, and thousands more were coming.

In Cincinnati the Germans settled the colonies of
"Wooden Shoe Hollow" and "Over the Rhine" between the
canal and the highlands. They manufactured stoves and
musical instruments, they kept jewelry stores and breweries,
they tended gardens and vineyards. From Cincinnati a German colonizing committee led newcomers to likely locations in the interior. At New Bremen, twenty miles north
of historic Greenville, the German colony began with ten
acres, each settler receiving a lot 66 by 300 feet. But they

soon added more. In 1835 the men tramped off to Indiana to work on the Wabash and Erie Canal, leaving their women to tend the little farms. When they returned they had money to buy new acres and to enlarge their herds and flocks. Wherever German farmers settled, they built barns and granaries that dwarfed their houses. Their pastures were filled with fine hogs and cattle, no grain went ungleaned in their fields. They filled their barns with hay and their bins with wheat and corn and barley. They looked scornfully across their ordered fields to the slack farmhouses where their neighbors sat whittling on the doorstep or spitting into the fire.

Tight, coherent colonies of Germans grew up in the cities and along the canals that offered employment to young men and a way to market for farm produce. They organized singing and gymnastic societies and shooting associations. They established their own churches and their own press. In Cincinnati the weekly *Die Ohio Chronik* was begun in 1826 and the famous *Cincinnati Volksblatt* ten years later. The influential *Anzeiger des Westens* was launched in St. Louis in 1835.

In cold January weather of 1846 a young Connecticut Yankee came west not to take up land but to record frontier history. Henry Howe of New Haven, son of the publisher of Webster's Dictionary, had already spent years tramping through New York, New Jersey, and Virginia, compiling "Historical Collections" with his older friend John W. Barber. Now, not quite thirty years old, he came out to Ohio, a lean long-striding man with scarlet leggings, a baggy coat, and a knapsack on his shoulders, to begin a historical collection of his own. Walking, riding, traveling in stage coach and farm wagon, zigzagging from one county seat to another, he filled his notebook with anecdotes of old settlers, local legends and traditions, and drawings of town squares and country landscapes. In sixteen months he visited seventy-nine Ohio counties. He was endlessly curious, his dark eyes roving like a hunter's as he walked. And he was always collecting—sitting on a snow bank to sketch a town in the valley, knocking at a farmhouse door to find what kind of people lived there, or stopping a villager in the middle of Main Street to ask his life story. In Cincinnati in 1847 he published his *Historical Collections of Ohio*. What he had seen of Ohio satisfied him. He settled in Cincinnati for the rest of his life.

Henry Howe had an eye for the variety of the new country. "In traveling through the west, one often meets with scenes that remind him of another land." One such scene was in northwestern Columbiana County, a sheep-raising region above the up-curving Ohio River near the Pennsylvania border. Here, amid the wide sheep pastures a colony of German Swiss had built clay cottages framed in timber. A long sloping roof with a deep overhang, a wooden stairway climbing to a balcony, hop vines trained against the sunny southern wall—this was Bavaria come to Ohio. "Hard by," observed Howe, after sketching the picturesque cottage with a fat pig feeding in the foreground, "stands the abandoned log dwelling of the emigrant—deserted for one more congenial with his early predilections."

Christmas on the frontier was a noisy, rowdy holiday, a mingled Fourth of July and Hallowe'en, until the Germans made it over. At Wooster, forty miles south of Cleveland, a German immigrant, August Imgard, remembering the Christmas festival in Bavaria, cut down a young spruce tree on Christmas Run (named for John Christmas, one of the original trustees of the town) and brought it into his cabin. He strung the branches with colored paper and crowned it with a metal star hammered out by the Wooster blacksmith. That first Christmas tree was followed by others, in the Ohio country and throughout America. Around the tree the Germans sang traditional songs, from the kitchen came the spicy smell of Christmas baking. Church bells rang in the snowy air and Christmas Eve became the Holy Night.

The German immigrants, Henry Howe declared, did

not easily give up the attachment to their fatherland, and
so they settled in communities of their own. But they were
in a country without bounds or barriers, a land of open hori-
zons, and the restless frontier air blew through their ordered settlements. Young German workmen struck out for
themselves, and by 1840 German families were found in
every district of the new country. When John L. Peyton, a
young lawyer from Virginia, traveled over a jolting "cor-
deroy" road in northwestern Ohio in 1848, he passed two
days in Sandusky, waiting for the steamer to Detroit. He
found Sandusky a comfortless place, though the busy harbor
made it clear that "she only awaited her share of the immense bodies emigrating west, to become a place of no
small consequence." While walking through the town Peyton met a tall young German, Otto Paul, a native of Dres-
den, who was suffering from chills and fever. After a fit of
shaking the young immigrant told his story. He had first settled in Pennsylvania and had come on west to Ohio, believing from what he had heard that it was the true *El
Dorado*. Now he had the ague for his pains. But the western
fever, as well as malaria, had claimed him; he had no
thought of going back across the mountains. He meant to
go farther west, to some good location on the Mississippi or beyond, where he would "squat" as a frontiersman,
hunter and farmer. He even praised the Black Swamp country below Sandusky, unhealthy as it was. "You will not find
precious stones or metals here," he told the Virginia lawyer, "but innumerable dangers, discomforts and toil; but
these are inseparable from a new country, and if surmounted by industry any man can accumulate a fortune."
A love of travel and adventure, he said, had led him from
Saxony to Pennsylvania, and from Pennsylvania to Ohio.
Next spring his wife and children from Pennsylvania and a
brother from Saxony would join him at Sandusky, and they
would proceed together to the West. "The history of this
young man," Peyton concluded, "is that of thousands of

others who have sought homes in the western prairies of America."

In the peat bogs and potato fields of Ireland the going wage was sixpence a day, and Irish workmen lived on potatoes, milk and fish. Small wonder that news of cheap land and high wages in America went through Ireland like a sea wind. In the summer of 1817 the English colonizer Morris Birkbeck stopped at a farmhouse outside St. Clairsville, Ohio, across the river from Wheeling, and talked to an Irish settler. "He came to this place fourteen years ago, before an ax had been lifted, except to make a blaze road . . . which passed over the spot where the town now stands. A free and independent American, and a warm politician, he now discusses the interests of the state as one concerned in its prosperity:—and so he is, for he owns one hundred and eighteen acres of excellent land, and has twenty descendents. . . . He still inhabits a *cabin,* but it is not an *Irish* cabin."

When canal bosses offered thirty cents a day, plus board, lodging and whisky, the Erie Canal was "a capital road from Cork to Utica." By 1818 three thousand Irishmen were toiling on the Big Ditch across New York state. When that job was done, in 1825, Irish gangs moved on to Licking Summit, Ohio, where the Ohio Canal was begun in the same year, and to Middletown, in the Miami valley, where work commenced on the Miami and Erie Canal. So the road from Cork led on into the west, from Cleveland to Portsmouth on the Ohio, and from Cincinnati to Toledo. Other canals followed, linking the Wabash with Lake Erie and the Illinois with Lake Michigan. As soon as the canals were finished, survey crews were running lines for the western railroads. There was no lay-off for the brawny Irish shovelmen.

They toiled in summer's heat and winter's cold. They slapped at clouds of mosquitoes and fought off "canal fever" with a daily dose of whisky and a double dose on Sunday. Some died of malaria, and some from powder blasts and the kick of mules. Others died of political warfare brought to the Ohio country from the Old Sod; in every canal camp the "Irish war" smoldered—the men of Cork against the northern men of Ulster. But the Irish kept coming. In the 1820s the wharves of Cork and Belfast swarmed with men and families bound for the American frontier. They manned the "public improvements" of the new country, felling timber, digging waterways, grading roadbeds. In 1840 the commissioners of the Wabash and Erie Canal offered land, up to 160 acres, on easy terms, to canal workmen. The Irish settled on farms and towns along the traveled ways. The road from Cork led to hundreds of towns and cities between the Ohio River and the lakes.

Two expansive Irishmen had come before them into the western country—George Croghan with his great warehouses in Pennsylvania and his pack-horse trains crossing the mountains, and Harman Blennerhassett with his island mansion on the Ohio. Most of those who followed began with nothing. But by 1850 Irish settlers were sending a million dollars a year to friends and families on the Old Sod, and many were tucking tickets for America into their letters to Wicklow and Wexford and County Clare.

CHAPTER TWELVE

THE ENGLISH PRAIRIE

THE PIANKESHAW tract, two million acres extending west from the lower Wabash, relinquished on a December day in 1805 when Harrison signed a treaty with some shabby chiefs, went on sale in 1814. The war in the West was over and surveyors had run their lines through the empty prairie. A land office was opened at the old Ohio River landing of Shawneetown and Illinois began to boom; a population of 15,000 in all the Illinois country, in 1815, grew to 40,000 three years later. The first land rush came to the southern counties, facing the Ohio and the Mississippi, and the most noted settlement was the English colony, on Boltenhouse Prairie, between Bon Pas Creek and the Little Wabash. This was the heart of the Piankeshaw tract.

Writing to England from "English Prairie, Illinois" in November of 1817, Morris Birkbeck said, "I have not for a moment felt despondency, scarcely discouragement, in this happy country, this land of hope! . . . We shall have some English friends next summer; and a welcome they shall experience. But if not one had the resolution to follow the track we have smoothed before them, we should never wish to retrace it." He had been in the United States just seven months, but he was a confirmed American.

The dream of an English colony under the arching sky of the frontier West was shared by two idealistic men, Morris Birkbeck and George Flower. In England Birkbeck farmed a 1500-acre estate of rolling fields and meadows in the heart of Surrey. He was a good man with sheep and cattle; more than that, he was well read in history, science and philosophy. Liberal in politics and religion, he was irked by a government that denied the vote of landless men and by a church that took a tithe from every field and flock in the parish. Flower was the son of a prosperous brewer and gentleman farmer of Hertford; his father found time to write pamphlets calling for political and economic reform, and George Flower was impatient with the old staid ways of Hertford. In 1814, when the Piankeshaw tract was opened on the Wabash, the two Englishmen were tramping through France together; Birkbeck, short, spare, wiry, stretching his legs to match the long loose stride of his younger friend, the two exchanging ideas of education and religion, of morality and justice, and agreeing that the common man had little chance to better his condition in the Old World. Perhaps it was on the roads of Normandy that they first talked of a colony of English yeomen and artisans in the free air and on the free earth of America.

Two years later Flower came to America and set out for a look at new country. He traveled as far west as Illinois and Tennessee. In the spring of 1817 Birkbeck with his seven children (his wife was buried in England) arrived in Virginia on the good ship *America*. Flower met them, and the old friends set out for the frontier. There was one other member of the party. Miss Eliza Julia Andrews, a friend of both the Birkbeck and Flower families in England, had joined the venture at the urging of Birkbeck's older daughters. On the American journey both men fell in love with her—perhaps the prospect of an English settlement put them in a domestic frame of mind. She declined their proposals, for the time, and the colonizers moved on—by stage coach over the Pennsylvania mountains and down to the busy town of Pittsburgh, the gateway to the West.

They had decided to proceed on horseback, getting a close look at the land and the settlements. Pittsburgh was a cheap market for horses, as many travelers at that point quit their horses to take passage on the river. "The mode of selling is by auction," Birkbeck explained. "The auctioneer rides the animal through the streets, proclaiming with a loud voice, the biddings that are made as he passes along, and when they reach the desired point, or when nobody bids more, he closes the bargain." The English party bought good hackneys at fifty dollars each and with saddlebags and blankets they set out, nine in file. As they neared the Ohio border the bubbling Birkbeck pronounced it "a delightful region:—healthy, fertile, romantic. . . . Land is worth from twenty to thirty dollars an acre. An advance of a thousand per cent in about ten years!" On the roads in the fine June weather they found a stream of hopeful land-seekers. "Old America seems to be breaking up and moving westward," Birkbeck exulted. At St. Clairsville, just beyond the Ohio River, he counted the wagons passing through—fourteen yesterday, thirteen today—not forgetting that "myriads take their course down the Ohio."

The English colonizers wanted a large tract of unentered land, fertile, pleasant, accessible, at government prices. They found it, after passing through the settled counties of southern Ohio and rough districts of southern Indiana, in the southwest corner of Illinois, between Bon Pas Creek and the Little Wabash. George Flower described it: "A few steps more and a beautiful prairie suddenly opened to our view. At first, we only received the impressions of its general beauty. With longer gaze, all its distinctive features were revealed, lying in profound repose under the warm light of an afternoon's summer sun. Its indented and irregular outline of wood, its varied surface interspersed with clumps of oaks of centuries' growth, its tall grass, with seed stalks from six to ten feet high, like tall and slender weeds waving in a gentle breeze, the whole presenting a magnificence of park-scenery, complete from the hand of Nature. . . . From beneath the broken shade of the wood, with our arms raised above our brows, we gazed long and steadily, drinking in the beauties of the scene, which had been so long the object of our search."

Many settlers shrank from the open prairie, believing that the absence of trees indicated a sterile soil, but these English pilgrims were charmed with the open airy land. They were on the edge of the great Illinois grasslands, where "groves" were islands in the endless plain. Its fertility shouted from the wind-rippled bluestem and the rank bull-grass, the cinquefoil, Indian grass and steepling reed-grass. Pea vines tangled in the prairie swales and over the long swells tall beard-grass mingled with waving stems of cup plant, ox-eyes, blazing star, and the purple spread of iron-weed. "We are so taken with the prairies," Birkbeck wrote, "that no timbered land can satisfy our present views."

While Flower started back to England to raise money and recruit colonists, Birkbeck rode fifty miles south, over marsh and prairie, to a storied landing on the Ohio. Shawneetown was pitched like a camp on the shelf of land under the steep hills that frame the river. Keelboats and flatboats lined the riverbank; men sweated under boxes and bales, they rolled barrels down sagging gangways. Salt, gunpowder, pork, flour, whisky passed over the landing. Trappers and traders, squatters and speculators passed through the dusty street. Birkbeck saw signs of the latest flood that had washed away fences, shacks and woodsheds and left a layer of silt that smoked up under the roofs of mules and horses. Here, at the gateway to the Wabash valley, in a bare slab building on the dusty street, the United States land office allotted acres in the wilderness. Birkbeck had business there.

That night, writing up his notes in a Shawneetown tavern, with boatmen's voices drifting up from the landing and the mile-wide river murmuring under the summer stars, he could not hide his satisfaction. "I have just constituted myself a land-owner by paying seven hundred and twenty dollars, as one fourth of the purchase money of fourteen hundred and forty acres: this, with a similar purchase made by Mr. Flower, is part of a beautiful and rich prairie, about six miles distant from the Big, and the same from the Little Wabash. The land is rich natural meadow boundened by timbered land, within reach of two navigable rivers, and may be rendered immediately productive at a small expense."

Next spring George Flower returned from England with fifty-one colonists. They rocked over the greening prairie with wagon loads of plows, harrows, spades, hoes, scythes and mattocks; they had bulging bags of seed grain and burlaped orchard cuttings. Behind the wagons straggled hogs and cattle. That summer Birkbeck entered more sections of prairie, totaling 26,400 acres, and other colonists followed the rutted road from Shawneetown. By harvest time the solitary prairie that Flower had described a year before held two hundred settlers. One evening that winter a group of colonists met in Flower's cabin to choose a site for their central village. Their discussion outlasted the daylight and the sinking fire in the chimney. Stretching out on the floor, pulling blankets around them, they talked in darkness. They decided on a village site, a tract of high wooded ground surrounded by prairie, but still there was the question of its name. "At last," wrote Flower, "we did what almost all emigrants do, pitched on a name that had its association with the land of our birth. Albion was then and there located, built, and peopled in imagination. We dropped off, one by one, to sleep, to confirm in dreams the wanderings of our wakeful fancies."

A year later the town of Albion grew up at the edge of the prairie. On the beautiful south prairie George Flower built a mansion for his father, who sold his English estates and came to Illinois in 1818. In the following spring Richard Flower settled in Park House, at the edge of growing Albion. It was a noted residence, with plastered and papered walls, handsome stone hearths, imported rugs and furniture.

But the colony's best advertisement was the writing of Morris Birkbeck. His *Notes on a Journey in America from the Coast of Virginia to the Territory of Illinois* went through eleven editions in Philadelphia, London, Dublin and Cork between 1817 and 1819, with a German translation published in 1818. Seven English editions of his *Letters from Illinois* appeared in 1818, with French and German editions in the following year. No settlement in America was so widely known. And the colonists came, down the polished Ohio with the shores half-real in the changing light, past Marietta, Gallipolis, Maysville, Cincinnati, Louisville, to the Shawneetown landing. Then in wagon, on horseback and afoot they crossed the Wabash lowlands to the prairie that Birkbeck had described as offering "all that nature has decreed for the comfort of man."

Within two years the English settlement was the success story of the West. "No man since Columbus has done so much toward peopling America as Mr. Birkbeck," a traveler wrote, "and if all could have settled in Illinois whom he had tempted to cross the Atlantic and the mountains, it had now been the most populous state in the Union." Inevitably this luring colony was criticized by English writers of more cautious views. H. B. Fearon, countering Birkbeck's glowing reports, declared that all but the poorest Englishmen would do better to remain in their own country; he found opportunity for unskilled laborers in the United States but described the American farmer's life as one of toil, hardship, and scanty reward. Adlard Welby, traveling with a man-servant in a private carriage through the western country, found frontier settlers crude, brutish, ignorant and filthy, and pictured the English prairie as a remote and desolate settlement. He stated that Birkbeck must settle with his conscience "for bringing people so far by his misrepresentations to hopeless banishment." William Faux, riding through the Wabash valley from Vincennes, saw nothing but "sad neglected farms, and indolent, dirty, sickly, wild-looking inhabitants. . . . Here is nothing clean but wild beasts and birds, nothing industrious generally, except pigs." Life in the backwoods, he told his English readers, caused people to lose all self-respect. Faux had a taste for violence. He told how three Illinois travelers on the road from Vincennes to St. Louis were murdered, "two being shot and two having their throats cut, one of whom recovered sufficiently to tell his tale." At Albion he found ragged English settlers living in wretched one-room cabins, and he spoke of the two villages of Albion and Wanborough as "abodes of contention, party spirit, speculation, and feuds." The sharpest critic of the English colony was William Cobbett, then farming on Long Island and suspected of being in the pay of Eastern landholders who wanted to discourage the rush of emigration to the West. "Porcupine Cobbett," who had not been west of the Alleghenies, wrote that he would sooner join the fraternity of gypsies in this country than the settlement at Illinois. He branded the English colony as unfruitful, ungodly, unhealthy.

Birkbeck and Flower had ready answers. The prairie settlement had a busy gristmill, a distillery, a brewery; it had flourishing flocks of hogs, cattle and sheep. Flower confidently described the "hopes of future harvests, arising from the rich abundance of the present," and told of Englishmen who came to examine "this land of evil report" and promptly sent for their families. As to religion, a regular congregation assembled each Sunday in an Albion cabin where a Unitarian service was conducted, while two miles away Birkbeck officiated at another log meeting house, reading the Church of England service. On the score of health, the charges against the English settlement and the replies of the colonizers made national news. On April 15th, 1820 *Niles' Register* reported:

> The country inhabited by Mr. Birkbeck and his associates has been represented as very unhealthy—perhaps, with the view of preventing other emigrants from joining them. To correct such impressions [we have] the following report from the practicing physician there.

> The population of the English settlement is about four hundred—that of the surrounding country is computed at three times that number. During the first twelve months from October 1818 to the end of September 1819 only one natural death occurred—an infant six months old. In July a boy died in consequence of drinking whisky, unknown to his parents—aged eight years. In September 1819 three [elderly persons] died. . . . One man since deceased of the typhus—induced by excessive and continued intemperance. Thus *six* persons died out of a population of four hundred in the space of 16 months,—up to February 1920, or a ratio, *per annum,* of one in 94. In Berlin the rate is 1 in 26, in Paris 1 in 45, in Vienna 1 in 19, in London 1 in 21, in the country round Shrewsbury, England, 1 in 33.

This report disposed of the charge that the English prairie was a sickly place. But it was strangely unhealthy for the friendship of the two high-minded colonizers. On Flower's return from England in 1818, the two old friends did not speak to each other; from that time all their communication was through intermediaries. Birkbeck established his town of Wanborough, named from his former home in Surrey, and he seems to have stayed on his side of the prairie. There was prolonged gossip about the quarrel and a general agreement that it was rooted in the two men's rivalry in love. The

English woman who had accompanied them west in 1817 had declined proposals from both, but in Vincennes, near the end of their journey, she was married to Flower, in Birkbeck's presence. In his long winter on the prairie Birkbeck may have brooded on his injured feelings. However it was, Birkbeck and Flower never shared their hopes and plans again.

Though Wanborough languished and the English settlers tended to side with Flower, Morris Birkbeck had a busy and productive life. In all seasons he rode horseback to new communities and townsites, giving advice on the breeding of sheep and cattle. Wherever men gathered to talk about frontier politics and prairie farming, there was a familiar figure—a spare little Englishman with restless hands, a windburned face, a bald head fringed with rumpled hair. Long after he was gone men remembered his reedy voice arguing about slavery and blooded cattle. He was the first president of the Illinois Agricultural Society and a leader in scientific farming. Writing in newspapers under the name "Jonathan Freeman" he united anti-slavery sentiment in Illinois. When Robert Owen came from Scotland to the Wabash in 1825 with his dream of a socialistic community at New Harmony, he and Birkbeck became enthusiastic friends. By the light of a hickory fire in a drafty cabin they talked of human justice, equality and brotherhood, and pictured the new society that would flourish on the prairie. In Robert Owen, Birkbeck found a friend to take George Flower's place. But it was his last friendship and soon ended. Returning from a visit to New Harmony after a June cloudburst, swimming his horse across the swollen Fox River, the ardent little Englishman was drowned. He had written on a summer day eight years before: "As to traveling in the backwoods of America, I think there is none so agreeable. . . . Some difficulties occur from ferries, awkward fords, and rude bridges, with occasional swamps; but such is the sagacity and sure-footedness of the horses, that accidents happen very rarely."

George Flower saw the wilderness grow settled, tamed

and fruitful. Illinois was an empty landscape when he found it, but the prairie state had sent a president to the war-troubled capitol when he died. Both Flower and his wife died on the same winter day in 1862. They were buried together on the English prairie.

By 1825 vast areas that William Henry Harrison had secured by Indian treaty twenty years earlier were marked with roads and sprinkled with new townsites. The editor of *The Western Emporium* at Centerville, Indiana, counted 120 wagons loaded with families, trunks, and tools passing west in fifteen days. Other streams of movers were creaking through Brookville, Lawrenceburg, and Rushville. This was the same unresting movement that had brought the first men over the mountains after the Ordinance of 1787. It had a tidal power and rhythm, advancing, subsiding, pushing again into new leagues of wilderness. Ohio was only the first "fabled region." As the great migration broke across the first frontier, other lands glowed with the light of promise. A westering people pushed through the woods and over the prairies; there would be no stopping till they saw the white surf crashing on the coast of Oregon. Wars and depressions could slacken the tide, but nothing could stop it. In the 1830s land sales in the National Land Office swelled from two million acres in 1831 to four million in 1833, to twelve million in 1835, to twenty million in 1836, and dropped to five million in the panic year of 1837. But even in that dark year Samuel Augustus Mitchell of Philadelphia published a book with a title page like a broadside and an anthology:

ILLINOIS IN 1837
A SKETCH
Descriptive of the
Situations, Boundaries, Face of the Country
Prominent Districts
Prairies, Rivers, Minerals, Animals,
AGRICULTURAL PRODUCTIONS

Public Lands, Plans of Internal Improvement,
Manufactures etc.
of the
STATE OF ILLINOIS
also,
SUGGESTION TO EMIGRANTS
Sketches of the Counties, Cities, and Principal Towns
in the State
together with
A Letter on the Cultivation of the Prairies
by the Hon. H. L. Ellsworth
to which are annexed
The Letters from a Rambler in the West

—— It is a goodly sight to see
What heaven hath done for this delicious land!
What fruits of fragrance blush on every tree!
What goodly prospects o'er the hills expand!
. . . .
The vine on high, the willow branch below
Mixed in one mighty scene, with varied beauty glow.
Childe Harold's Pilgrimage

Twenty-five years before this alluring publication the
pioneer settlers of Amesville, Ohio, had added a copy of
Lord Byron's early poems to their "Coonskin Library." Now
Byron was dead of a swamp fever on the far shores of
Greece, and his lines on the landscape of Portugal were
luring settlers to Illinois.

In 1837, with black panic in the eastern states, a
traveler in frontier Springfield, not yet made the Illinois capital, reported: "Our far west is improving rapidly, astonish-
ingly. It is five years since I visited it, and the changes
within that period are like the works of enchantment. Flourishing towns have grown up, farms have been opened, and
comfortable dwellings, fine barns and all appurtenances,
steam mills and manufacturing establishments erected in a

country in which the hardy pioneer had at that time sprinkled a few log cabins. . . . The state of Illinois has probably the finest body of fertile land of any state in the Union, and the opportunities for speculation are numerous. Property will continue to advance, admirable farms and town-lots may be purchased with a certainty of realizing large profits. The country here is beautiful—equal in native attractions, though not in classic recollections, to the scenes I visited and admired in Italy. The vale of Arno is not more beautiful than the valley of the Sangamon, with its lovely groves, murmuring brooks and flowery meads—

> *Oh Italy, sweet clime of song, where oft*
> *The bard hath sung thy beauties, matchless deemed,*
> *Thou hast a rival in this western land."*

In this panic summer of 1837 Daniel Webster, burned darker than ever by the western sun and snorting with his annual hay fever, made a trip to the frontier. He came down the Ohio to Cincinnati and stopped at North Bend to visit William Henry Harrison; the lean, lined Westerner and the burly Yankee admired the sweep of the river from Harrison's veranda and talked about developments in the western country. Webster went on to the Mississippi, and north to Chicago where ten miles out on the prairie he was met by a long escort of carriages. Excited by the sweeping landscape, Webster bought a thousand acres in Sangamon County and planted a townsite named Salisbury for his birthplace in New Hampshire; he also bought six hundred acres near the branches of the Rock River in northwestern Illinois. The land rush had swept to the Mississippi.

The most celebrated of the English travelers in the yeasty West was Charles Dickens, who marked his thirtieth birthday in the United States. He was welcomed to Boston by Longfellow, Dana and Bancroft; to New York by Irving and Bryant; and to Washington by President Tyler. He traveled down the Ohio and up the Mississippi; from

Cincinnati he crossed Ohio to Cleveland, sailed to Niagara, and took his departure from Montreal. When he said that he might write a book on his observations in the United States, American readers could hardly wait. The *American Notes*, appearing later in 1842, sold 50,000 copies in two days in New York and 3,000 in fifteen minutes in Philadelphia. Americans resented his harsh criticism of their crassness and crudeness, but they read *American Notes*, and two years later they read his diatribe on the American frontier in *Martin Chuzzlewit*.

Dickens had traveled the water routes that brought multitudes to the frontier, going west on a river packet and returning on a lake steamer. He saw bustling settlements and empty townsites, he talked with speculators, land-jobbers and eager emigrants. Back in London, in his cheerful study on Devonshire Terrace, he wrote the story of an English emigrant, Martin Chuzzlewit, and a sorry tale it was.

Undaunted by the "melancholy crowd of immigrants" that he saw in New York, credulous Martin and his friend Mark Tapley went west to seek their fortunes on the frontier. Arrived at a makeshift town on the Ohio, they found the land office of the Eden settlement.

"It was a small place . . . but why may not a whole territory be bargained for in a shed? It was but a temporary office too; for the Edeners were 'going' to build a superb establishment for the transaction of their business, and had already got so far as to mark out the site. Which is a great way in America. The office-door was wide open, and in the doorway was the agent: no doubt a tremendous fellow to get through his work, for he seemed to have no arrears, but was swinging backwards and forwards in a rocking chair, with one of his legs planted high up against the door-post, and the other doubled up under him, as if he were hatching his foot.

"He was a gaunt man in a huge straw hat, and a coat of green stuff. The weather being hot, he had no cravat, and wore his shirt collar wide open; so that every time he spoke

something was seen to twitch and jerk up in his throat, like
the little hammers in a harpsichord when the notes are
struck. Perhaps it was the Truth feebly endeavoring to leap
to his lips. If so, it never reached them.

"Two grey eyes lurked deep within this agent's head,
but one of them had no sight in it, and stood stock still.
With that side of his face he seemed to listen to what the
other side was doing. Thus each profile had a distinct expression; and when the movable side was most in action, the
rigid one was in its coldest state of watchfulness. It was like
turning the man inside out, to pass to that view of his
features in his liveliest mood, and see how calculating and
intent they were.

"Each long black hair upon his head hung down as
straight as any plummet line; but rumpled tufts were on the
arches of his eyes, as if the crow whose foot was deeply
printed in the corners had pecked and torn them in a savage
recognition of his kindred nature as a bird of prey."

This grotesque figure agreed, somewhat reluctantly, to
let the English visitors inside the office, where Martin found
himself gazing at the great plan of the city of Eden, a
pictorial map which covered an entire wall of the room.

"There were banks, churches, cathedrals, market-
places, factories, hotels, stores, mansions, wharves; an exchange, a theater; public buildings of all kinds, down to the
office of the Eden Stinger, a daily journal; all faithfully de-
picted in the view before them."

Though he didn't wish to sell lots to any- and everybody but was reserving them for "Aristocrats of Natur'," the
agent at last agreed to take the Englishmen's money. When
he had paid a hundred and fifty dollars for a house and lot
of fifty acres on the handsome waterfront, Martin felt the
glow of a landed proprietor in the thriving city of Eden,
and he was immediately congratulated by the land-jobber.
"You air now, sir, a denizen of the most powerful and
highly civilized do-minion that has ever graced the world; a
do-minion, sir, where man is bound to man in one vast

bond of equal love and truth. May you, sir, be worthy of your a-dopted country!"

On the next steamboat Martin and his partner took passage for Eden. After a tedious journey down river they looked eagerly at the approach to the city.

"A flat morass, bestrewn with fallen timber; a marsh on which the good growth of the earth seemed to have been wrecked and cast away, that from its decomposing ashes vile and ugly things might arise; where the very trees took the aspect of huge weeds, begotten of the slime from which they sprung, by the hot sun that burnt them up; where fatal maladies, seeking whom they might infect, came forth at night in misty shapes, and creeping out upon the water, hunted them like spectres until day; where even the blessed sun, shining down upon festering elements of curruption and disease, became a horror; this was the realm of Hope through which they moved.

"At last they stopped. At Eden too. The waters of the Deluge might have left it but a week before: so choked with slime and matted growth was the hideous swamp which bore that name.

"There being no depth of water close in shore, they landed from the vessel's boat, with all their goods beside them. There were a few log-houses visible among the dark trees: the best a cow-shed or a rude stable. But for the wharves, the market-place, the public buildings!

" 'Here comes an Edener,' said Mark. 'He'll get us help to carry these things up. Keep a good heart, sir. Hallo there!' "

They found the Edeners all suffering from chills and fever, but one ragged fellow guided them to their house—"a miserable cabin, rudely constructed of the trunks of trees; the door of which had either fallen down or been carried away long ago; and which was consequently open to the wild landscape and the dark night."

Next day the two newcomers had a look at the city proper. "There were not above a score of cabins in the

whole; half of these appeared untenanted; all were rotten
and decayed. The most tottering, abject, and forlorn among
them was called, with great propriety, the Bank, and National Credit Office. It had some feeble props about it, but
was settling deep down in the mud, past all recovery.

"Here and there an effort had been made to clear the
land, and something like a field had been marked out, where,
among the stumps and ashes of burnt trees, a scanty crop of
Indian corn was growing. In some quarters, a snake or zigzag
fence had been begun, but in no instance had it been completed; and the fallen logs, half hidden in the soil, lay
mouldering away. Three or four meager dogs, wasted and
vexed with hunger; some long-legged pigs, wandering away
into the woods in search of food; some children, nearly
naked, gazing at him from the huts; were all the living
things he saw."

At last—but not till Dickens had painted the whole
dismal picture of the desolate place and its sickly people—
Martin Chuzzlewit began to shudder with fever and decided to sell his share of Eden. There were no purchasers.
" 'Nobody but corpses to buy 'em,' said Mark Tapley, shaking his head with a rueful air, 'and pigs.' " When a steamer
came up the river, they boarded it gratefully. As paddles
churned the muddy water they looked at their receding
home in the land of promise: "The log-house, with the open
door, and drooping trees about it; the stagnant morning
mist, and red sun, dimly seen beyond; the vapour rising up
from land and river; the quick stream making the loath-
some banks it washed more flat and dull."

It was a wiser pair of travelers who stood at the rail
of a ship outbound from New York harbor, her sturdy bow-
sprit pointing true to England. In that grateful hour it occurred to Mark Tapley how he would paint the American
eagle—" 'like a Bat, for its short-sightedness; like a Bantam,
for its bragging; like a Magpie, for its honesty; like a Peacock
for its vanity; like a Ostrich, for its putting its head in the
mud, and thinking nobody sees it—'

" 'And like a Phoenix, for its power of springing up from the ashes of its faults and vices, and soaring up anew into the sky,' said Martin. 'Well, Mark. Let us hope so.' "

There was an actual Eden Township in Licking County in central Ohio. There were two Eden post offices, in Ohio and Indiana; there was an Edenton in Ohio, an Edenburg in Indiana. (The last was visited in 1831 by wiry little Anne Royal, the free-swinging journalist in a poke bonnet and balloon-sleeve dress; she wrote: "As to soil and water, Indiana and Illinois are worth the whole United States.") There was an Edenville in lower Michigan. Ohio had an actual Felicity, and Indiana a Paragon. These all were crossroads settlements muddy in winter, dusty in summer, where people shook with ague every fall. But only Charles Dickens saw the sorry Eden of Chuzzlewit's misadventure. On his way back from the West H. B. Fearon saw one abject traveler returning from the land of promise—one Martin Chuzzlewit. But he saw thousands, some from the New World and some from the Old, pressing on toward the Miami, the Wabash, and the Illinois.

The six Welsh immigrants of 1795 had swelled to a multitude from many nations. Let Morgan Gwilym of Paddy's Run speak for all who stayed. Twenty-three years after he had walked over the Welsh mountains to the port of Bristol, fourteen years after he brought the first wagon up the Dry Fork of the Whitewater near the Ohio-Indiana border, he wrote to his brother in Glamorgan, Wales: "I was verry sorry to hear that my native country is in such a deplorable situation when we here enjoy peace and plenty. . . . We have done very well in this country. Have a fine farm which would sell for about 6,000 Dollars and every other thing in proportion. . . . Thank God no orthodoxy, no tithes, no high church, no king but good and wholesome laws."

PART IV

CABIN IN THE CLEARING

CHAPTER THIRTEEN

MAD ANN AND THE MADONNA

Thirteen years I was a virgin,
Two years I was a wife;
One year I was a mother,
The next year took my life.

—EPITAPH ON A FRONTIER GRAVESTONE

T HE WEST was a man's world. Its records tell of hunters, traders, soldiers, surveyors, speculators, squatters,
settlers, with more mention of Indian squaws than of white
women. But there are two heroines in Ohio country legend—
a light-foot girl and a fierce old woman—who brought gunpowder to besieged men. Betty Zane, a slip of a girl just
turned sixteen, ran out of a log stockade where Wheeling
now stands, filled her apron with gunpowder, and raced
through a rain of arrows to the fort; now her stone monument stands at Martin's Ferry where U.S. 40 crosses the
Ohio to the site of vanished Fort Henry of Betty's day. Ann
Bailey, seventy-five years old by one account, rode a hundred

miles through hostile country with a bag of powder over her saddlebow. She had no monument except the stubborn legend of her life.

On December 3rd, 1825, the *Free Press* at Gallipolis printed a column headed "Longevity." It began: "Died in Harrison Township, Gallia County, Ohio, on Tuesday, November 22, 1825, the celebrated Ann Bailey. From the best account we have she must have been at least 125 years old. According to her own story her father was a soldier in Queen Anne's wars; that on getting a furlough to go home, he found his wife with a fine daughter in her arms, whom he called Ann, after the Queen as a token of respect. In 1714 she went from Liverpool to London on a visit to her brother—while there she saw Lord Lovett beheaded. She came to the United States the year after Braddock's defeat, aged then forty-six years. Her husband was killed at the battle of Point Pleasant in 1774; after that, to avenge his death, she joined the garrison, under the command of Col. Wm. Clendenin, where she remained until the final departure of the Indians from the country."

Another account says that she was born in Liverpool in 1742, came to America at nineteen, and lived on the Virginia and Ohio frontiers to the age of eighty-three.

Mad Ann the soldiers and settlers called her. To the Indians she was the White Squaw of the Kanawha; they thought her insane and in their belief she lived under the protection of the Great Spirit. Throughout the Kanawha valley, after Lord Dunmore's war, she might appear day or night at the lonely stations, a short, burly woman in a camp-stained petticoat over buckskin breeches. She rode a powerful black horse named Liverpool, with a rifle on her shoulder and a hatchet in her belt. She drank and swore like a man, she hunted bear and deer and panthers, but she had a woman's ready tongue. Warming her huge blackened hands and spitting tobacco at the fire, she was a living story book to river squatters and mountaineers. She had seen the royal carriage of Queen Anne, the grim chambers of the Tower of London and the glittering ax-blade of the executioner. While a schoolgirl in London she was kidnapped, carried aboard a ship for America, and sold in Virginia as an indentured servant. She came west to Pennsylvania and married there; with her husband she hunted and camped in the wild valleys of Gauley River and the Greenbrier. When her husband lay dead at Point Pleasant she began a career as scout and Indian fighter. Her big black Liverpool outran many a band of Mingoes and Shawnees, but once, riding into an impassable thicket, she had to hide like a fox, leaving her horse to the Indians. For an hour the Shawnees sat on a sycamore log, gnawing dried venison while the black horse browsed around them. When they were gone the White Squaw crept out of the hollow log. That night she stole upon the Shawnee camp, caught her horse, cried out a cockney oath and galloped away.

After sixteen years of widowed life she married trooper John Bailey and went to live at Fort Clendenin on the Kanawha. There Bailey was murdered, and after a few more roving years Mad Ann settled on the Ohio near Gallipolis, building a hut of fence rails with a single window. She hunted in the hills and fished from a dugout in the river. She cooked her game, slept on the floor, and occasionally tramped in to Gallipolis, a powerful squat figure wearing a hunting jacket over a greasy petticoat, with a rifle over her shoulder and a shot pouch swinging at her side. Gallipolis shopkeepers treated her to whisky and filled her game bag with gifts. On a gray November day in 1825, when the Ohio country was growing tame and mild, a hunter found her dead in her fence-rail cabin in the hills.

By the time Mad Ann died, thousands of women had crossed the mountains, coming with hope and fear to the unknown West. Their monument can be seen in the old Illinois Statehouse grounds in the time-worn town of Vandalia. Beside the hurrying traffic of U.S. 40 (the old National Road) stands a pioneer woman with a child clinging to her skirts and an infant in her arms. She is frankly ideal-ized, a woman confident and strong, facing the West and the future—the Madonna of the Trail.

Put beside the Madonna on that long road to the wilderness some actual women—wives of squatters, ax-men, immigrants, mothers whose children would die of fever and be stolen by the Indians, women who did not know where they were going and hardly knew why. At the side of a mountain road in Pennsylvania a ragged woman bends over a whimpering child; around her press other children, silent with hunger and cold. They have huddled here all night while the father walked ahead to bring back food and medicine. The Scottish traveler John Melish, who found this family on the road in the spring of 1811, wrote in his journal: "We could hardly refrain from tears of sympathy, and Mr. Strong said it brought the circumstance of his own emigration fresh to his mind, during which 'the old woman shed many a salt tear.'" On a freezing winter morning in 1817 another English traveler, Henry B. Fearon, crossing Dry Ridge above Bedford, Pennsylvania, found a woman warming herself on a smoking poplar log. They were thirty-two days on the road from New Jersey; the wagon had broken down the day before and her husband had dragged it back somewhere to a blacksmith. All night she had fed the fire with sticks and huddled on the smoldering log, "Oh! Sir," she told the Englishman, "I wish to God we had never left home." Judge Wilkeson, a circuit rider of the first Ohio courts, remembered his own family's journey: "We were provided with three horses, on one of which my mother rode carrying her infant with all the table furniture and utensils." James Flint of Edinburgh found a family of twelve trudging over the Alleghenies. "The eldest of the progeny had the youngest on his back; and the father pushed a wheelbarrow containing the moveables of the family. A little farther we passed a young woman carrying a suckling child, and leading a very little one by the hand. . . . The Canterbury Pilgrims," he concluded, "were not so diversified nor so inter-

esting as these." Neither, he should have said, were they on
so long, arduous and uncertain a journey.

In the travel literature are other glimpses of women,
more cheerful and expectant. See two girls, Cynthia Rouse
and Sally Devol, bound down river to Marietta; on the flatboat they climb to the seats of the family wagons and chat-
ter back and forth while the wooded hills drift by. In 1788
in the raw new settlement of Marietta, Minerva Tupper,
waiting for wash-water to heat outside the cabin door, wrote
her first letter home to Chesterfield, Massachusetts: " . . .
We find the Country much more delightsome than we had
any idea of." In 1795 the new wife of John Cleves Symmes,
the former Susanna Livingston of New York City, arrived
at North Bend and began planning a spacious house above
the Ohio. While men with teams and log chains dragged the
building timbers, Susanna Symmes marked out a garden and
a courtyard fit for a country estate. On a thousand land
claims other women were marking out the garden and picturing the house that would stand in a sunlit clearing.

On a rutted, stump-filled street in a crude new settlement stood the little building that had lured settlers to the
wilderness. The land office was a square, bare room with a
rough table and an open ledger beside the surveyor's plots of
the public lands. Steubenville, Marietta, Chillicothe, Cincinnati had the first offices; as new land districts were created,
offices were opened at Zanesville, Vincennes, Shawneetown,
Kaskaskia. By 1820 they had reached to Detroit and St.
Louis. In all these places a familiar ritual was repeated, day
after day, season after season, year after year, till the public
lands were private homesteads and the wilderness was gone.
A woman sits with her children in the loaded wagon, peering through the doorway where her husband bends over the
district maps. At last he counts out eighty dollars, signs his
name in the ledger or makes his mark, and sees the decisive
"A. P., *advance paid,*" marked upon the general plan. When

he comes out, squinting in broad sunlight, he has a certifi-
cate which he can exchange for a deed of entry when he has
completed the three-hundred-twenty-dollar payment for his
quarter section. Now the wagon leaves the straggling town.
It creaks through the woods, rocking over roots and stumps,
swaying past the blazed trees. At the end of the day a new
family arrives on their land. The long journey is ended.

Out come ax and rifle, skillet, kettle and blankets.
Smoke sifts up from a supper fire. The ax swings in under-
brush and the slanting sunlight finds a tiny opening between
big butts of oak and beech and walnut. That night the
woman sleeps in the wagon bed while the man rolls up in a
blanket on his land. It has been a silent land for three hundred centuries—ever since the great ice blanket, two miles
deep, retreated northward, pulled a few wagon-lengths a day
by the relentless power of climate. But now the silence is
ended. Thud, thud, thud, the ax is never still. With a swish
of air and a cushioned thunder a big oak crashes down. Thud,
thud, thud. The ax is gnawing at the forest.

If the season was late, with colored leaves falling and
frost crisping them underfoot, the whole family turned to,
making a pole-shed or "half-faced camp" for the first winter.
It could be built quickly, since it had neither door, window,
nor chimney. With two growing trees for corner posts, pole
walls were raised on three sides and a roof of poles was
covered with bark and branches. In the open side, faced
south and away from the weather, a log fire would burn all
winter. In the far corners blankets were spread on beds of
rustling leaves. The rifle kept the pot full of game—squirrels, pigeons, turkeys, raccoon, deer meat. They lived like
Indians that winter, but a woman kept her picture of a snug
cabin with cupboard shelves, a warm stove chimney, and a
clean-swept puncheon floor.

Girdled trees made a deadening around the first rude
cabin and spring sunlight struck through bare branches
where a man chopped noiselessly through leaf mould and
dropped Indian corn into the gashed ground. Then the ax

thudded again at the base of trees. From the cabin doorway a man looked small against the forest. He stood there like the little men of that strange land of Lilliput, ticking away at a towering tulip tree. One great trunk and its lofty branches dwarfed him—a single tree. And the woods were beyond all numbering; they stretched on and on, dense, dark and dismaying, county after county cast in a timeless twilight. The forest was old, powerful and endless, and it was a man's folly to raise his tiny ax against it. Now for a moment the silence came back, the gloom and silence of the whole Black Forest, while a whetstone whispered on the ax-blade. Then it swung again, white chips snowing on the dark ground. It was biting in.

The trees were a wary and stubborn enemy; beeches leafed out even after girdling and, from the roots of the thorny locust new shoots bristled overnight. Yet the woods were man's bounty, too. They gave walls for his dwelling, fire for his warmth, light in his darkness. They made his benches and tables, his wagon-spokes, his plow handles. They provided a fence to keep the deer out of his cornfield and his cattle from the woods. They even gave him an ax-helve for his naked blade; he used a piece of the forest to bring the forest down. *Thud, thud, thud.* It was the sound that a woman worked by, sifting wood ash to make soap, boiling oak bark to tan buckskins, while a man swung a four-inch blade on a hickory handle, hacking away at the endless woods.

Look at their place five years later. An open field smooth as a barn floor, flooded with sunlight, ribboned with young blades of corn. A fence of straight-split hackberry and black walnut, eight poles high, to keep the hogs and cattle out. A log house, solid and tightly-chinked, with woodsmoke feathering from a cat-and-clay chimney. Inside, a clean puncheon floor, a bluestone hearth with the logs smoldering, a pantry shelf along the wall, spinning wheels beside the fire—a big wheel for wool and a little wheel for flax—clumps of herbs hanging from the rafters, boneset for fever, pennyroyal to purify the blood, ginseng for tonic, sassafras for supper tea. Around the room are beds, tables, benches, stools, all made from the vanished trees. Outside, at the edge of the field, soft smoke columns go up to the Ohio sky. Brush and branches burn with a crackling blaze, the big logs smolder night and day. Beyond the field rise the dark walls of the woods, but the wind brings the tang of other burnings. Other families are pushing back the wilderness. It was a deep, strong, dark country but now a woman is churning in the doorway while she rocks a cradle with her foot—

> *One in a bush, two in a log,*
> *One in a bush and two in a log,*
> *Run here, Sal, what a big groundhog—*

and across the clearing comes the *thud, thud, thud.* The ax would change it all.

In 1819 William Cobbett contrasted the neat farms of England with the tangled landscape of rural America. American farmers, he said, knew nothing about banking, hedging, and other details of "miniature cultivation" which every English farmer understood. "They have no idea of the use of a *billhook,* which is so adroitly used in the coppices of Hampshire and Sussex. An *ax* is their tool, and with that tool, at *cutting down* trees or cutting *them up,* they will do *ten times* as much in a day as any other man that I ever saw. Set one of these men upon a wood of timber trees, and his slaughter will astonish you." Here was a true glimpse of western character and of a man's task in wild country.

A man worked in the woods and fields, he drove hogs to market and packed grain to the mill, he went hunting for bear, deer and turkey. But a woman's life was bounded by the clearing. She planted potatoes, pumpkin, squash, beans, beets and turnips in the garden; she made soap and candles in the dooryard; she spun flax and wool beside the hearth. She cooked and washed and sewed for a circle of children. Her task was endless. Wrote William Faux: "Soap, candles, sugar, cotton, leather and woollen clothes, of a good quality, are here all made from the land, but not without the most formidable, unremitting labor on the part of the females." A man could be lazy—"Armstrong, a hunter farmer, this day shot four deer, while he is still too idle to inclose his cornfield, which is devoured by cattle and horses, save when a boy watches to keep them off"—but his wife never got away from the spinning wheel and the cooking fire. The woman who picked up her knitting to do a few rounds while neighbors gathered for her husband's funeral was merely following the industrious habit of her life.

Many frontier settlers were satisfied when they had a roof, no matter how leaky, over their children's heads. Twenty miles from Princeton, Indiana, Faux found the Ferrel family, ten of them, crowded into a ten-by-fifteen foot cabin floored with earth. On one side of the narrow room stood two beds, where all ten managed to sleep. On the other side a dining board rested on two blocks of wood. In wet weather a board was clapped over the chimney ("which I can reach with my hand") and the family huddled in smoke. Settler Ferrel had moved eight times on the frontier. Now he had this elegant house with a stump-filled field around it. Proudly he rubbed his rough hands together— "This is all I had to begin with."

Morris Birkbeck found frontier people fond of the word "elegant," observing that *an elegant improvement* is a cabin of rude logs, and a few acres with trees cut down to the height of three feet, and surrounded by a worm-fence, or zig-zag railing. You hear of an *elegant* mill, an *elegant* orchard, an *elegant* tanyard, etc., and familiarly of *elegant* roads,—meaning such as you may pass without extreme peril." On a trip through the Wabash bottoms, Birkbeck arrived one evening at a squatter's cabin in a ragged clearing. It was the third dwelling this man had built within twelve months ("To move," said another squatter, "all I hafen to do is put out the fire an' call the dog") and he might have a fourth before winter. His wife, surrounded by children, made the visitors welcome, clearing a place for their blankets on the floor, which she assured them was "too damp for fleas." Birkbeck described the cabin—"formed of round logs, with apertures of three or four inches between: no chimney, but large intervals between the "clapboards" for the escape of smoke. "The roof was, however, a more effectual covering than we have generally experienced, as it protected us very tolerably from a drenching night. Two bedsteads of unhewn logs, and cleft boards laid across;—two chairs, one of them without a bottom, and a low stool, were all the furniture required by this numerous family. A string of buffalo hide, stretched across the hovel, was a wardrobe for their rags; and their utensils, consisting of a large iron pot, some baskets, the effective rifle and two that were superannuated, stood about in corners, and the fiddle, which was only silent when they were asleep, hung by them."

The literature of the western country shows many women left alone, or with their children, to deal with wolves, bears, Indians, or to endure cold and darkness, while the head of the household was off on some roving errand or fortune. "Oh, you had to be a stout body to be a woman way back here, for this was way up west in the Ohio wilderness," said Conrad Richter's Sayward Luckett—whose father had gone off with a rifle on his shoulder to see the Mississippi, whose brother strode off toward the Great Lakes, whose little sister wandered down the deer trail and was never seen again. There were many women like Sayward Luckett who faced the wilderness alone.

The first white household to winter in the Western Reserve, it is recorded, was the family of James Kingsbury, who, four years later, became the Reserve's first judge, in the wilderness near Conneaut Creek. But James Kingsbury left for New Hampshire before the winter winds swept over Lake Erie. Coming back in late December, he found New Connecticut buried in wastes of snow. When his horse died of exposure, after breaking through the ice on Elk Creek, Kingsbury struggled through drifts of snow with twenty pounds of flour on his back. He reached the cabin on Christmas Eve. He found his wife in bed, with a hungry child beside her and a new-born infant starving in her arms. The baby died soon after, and James Kingsbury hacked out a grave in the frozen woods. After weeks of fever and delirium his wife grew stronger. When the surveying crew arrived at the end of May, 1797, the Kingsburys went on to Cleveland with them.

In the backwoods above Marietta, Henry Howe heard the blithe story of a Yankee settler in Washington County who built himself a half-faced camp on sixty acres, two and a half miles from any house or road. "I soon (like Adam) saw the necessity of a help-mate, and persuaded a young woman to tie her destiny to mine. I built a log house twenty feet square—quite aristocratic in those days—and moved into it. I was fortunate enough to possess a jack-knife: with that I made a wooden knife and two wooden forks, which answered admirably for us to eat with. A bedstead was wanted; I took two round poles for the posts, inserted a pole in them for a side-rail, and two other poles were inserted for the end pieces, the ends of which were put in the logs of the house—some puncheons were then split and laid from the side-rail to the crevice between the logs of the house, which formed a substantial bed-cord, on which we laid our straw bed—the only bed we had—on which we slept as soundly and woke as happy as Albert and Victoria.

"In process of time, a yard-and-a-half of calico was wanted; I started on foot through the woods ten miles to Marietta to procure it; but, alas! when I arrived there I found that, in the absence of both money and credit, the calico was not to be obtained. The dilemma was a serious one, and how to escape I could not devise; but I had no sooner informed my wife of my failure, than she suggested that I had a pair of thin pantaloons, which I could very well spare, that would make quite a decent frock; the pants were cut up, the frock made, and in due time the child was dressed.

"The long winter evenings were rather tedious, and in order to make them pass more smoothly, by great exertion I purchased a share in the Belpre library, six miles distant. From this I promised myself much entertainment, but another obstacle presented itself—I had no candles; however, the woods afforded plenty of pine knots—with these I made torches by which I could read, though I nearly spoiled my eyes. Many a night have I passed in this manner till twelve or one o'clock reading to my wife, while she was hatchelling, carding or spinning. Time rolled on, the payments for my land became due, and money, at that time in Ohio, was a cash article; however, I did not despair. I bought a few steers; some I bartered for, and others I got on credit—my credit having somewhat improved since the calico expedition —slung a knapsack on my back and started alone with my cattle for Romney, on the Potomac, where I sold them, then travelled on to Litchfield, Connecticut, paid for my land and had just $1 left to bear my expenses home, six hundred miles distant. Before I returned I worked and procured fifty cents in cash; with this and my dollar I commenced my journey homeward. I laid out my dollar for cheap haircombs, and these, with a little Yankee pleasantry, kept me very comfortably at the private houses where I stopped till I got to Oswego, on the Susquehanna, where I had a power of attorney to collect some money for a neighbor in Ohio."

The records of the Ashtabula Historical Society contain the tale, considerably stranger than fiction, of Salmon Sweatland who went off before breakfast one windy morning in September, 1817, to hunt deer. It was his custom to let his dogs drive the game into Lake Erie and to take after them in a cottonwood canoe. On this morning he threw his rifle into the dugout, pushed into the water, and paddled after a swimming buck. A strong south wind carried him out of the cove and soon he was less concerned with hunting than with keeping afloat. A quarter of a mile out the wind shot him past the bobbing deer. When he tried to turn back his paddle was useless in the angry water. Soon mounting waves hid the land from sight.

From the shore his wife watched Salmon Sweatland disappear over the tossing lake. She roused a couple of neighbors who launched a light boat from the mouth of Conneaut Creek and pulled into the heaving water. They met an exhausted deer struggling toward the land, but they saw nothing else. Back ashore, leaning against the wind and drenched with spray, they watched for a sign of Salmon Sweatland or his canoe. They pushed out again, farther this time, until their boat tossed like a chip. It seemed impossible that a canoe could survive that sea. They fought their way back, giving up their neighbor for lost.

Out in Lake Erie, glimpsing a gray line of land when the canoe rose on a wave, Sweatland kept his craft afloat, waiting for the wind to change. If it swung to the north it would blow him back to Ohio, if it died he would paddle home—Lake Erie kicked up suddenly, and as quickly it could grow calm again. But now the wind howled on, a gray scud of clouds racing over the broken water. Twice he saw schooners, their sails close-hauled and topmasts pitching, but the wind tore his cry away and his waving paddle was not answered. A mounting wave gave him a last glimpse of shore; he saw his tiny cabin with the fields around it. Then a fury of wind all but swamped him. He pulled off a shoe and began bailing out water. When darkness came he fixed his hope on reaching the shore of Canada, fifty miles from home.

All night the craft rocked and rolled and pitched, and the blown spray lashed him. At last the sky cleared, giving him a course to follow; he kept his bow pointed toward the cold north star. The wind went down at daybreak and the morning light showed a long line of land over the heaving water. Two hours later he steered for the shelter of Long Point. A cross-sea nearly swamped him, but his tired arms kept the paddle thrusting. It was midday when he felt the beach grate under his canoe. He stumbled through knee-deep surf and sank down on the sand.

The Canada coast was lifeless, without a habitation for forty miles. It was a slow journey—a man ragged, hungry and exhausted dragging along the empty shore, finding some berries and shellfish, sleeping half-buried in the sand. He came on the remains of a beached schooner, but there was no food in the wreckage. He kept on. A week after he had gone hunting from Conneaut Creek he stumbled into a Canadian settlement where he was given food and clothing.

With his Canadian friends he pulled back alongshore in a boat and salvaged the cargo of the wrecked schooner. There was money in his pocket when Salmon Sweatland tramped on to Buffalo. He bought a suit of clothes, ate a hearty dinner, and took passage on the Schooner *Traveler*. When the *Traveler* arrived at Conneaut Creek guns were fired from the deck and the crew cheered Sweatland's return from his hunting. "On landing," the account concludes, "he found his funeral services had been preached, and he had the rare privilege of seeing his own *widow* clothed in the habilaments of mourning."

A "settler" was often roving and restless, but once she had set up her spinning wheel, churn, and cradle, a woman was there to stay. "At one of these lone dwellings," Birkbeck reports, "we found a neat, respectable-looking female spinning under the little piazza at one side of the cabin, which shaded her from the sun: her husband was absent on business, which would detain him some weeks: she had no family, and no companion but her husband's faithful dog, which usually attended him in his bear hunting in the winter: she was quite overcome with *lone* she said, and hoped we would tie our horses in the wood, and sit awhile with her, during the heat of the day. We did so, and she rewarded us with a basin of coffee. Her husband was kind and good to her, and never left her without necessity, but a true lover of bear hunting; which he pursued alone, taking only his dog with him, though it is common for hunters to go in parties to attack this dangerous animal. He had killed a great number last winter; five, I think, in one week. The cabin of this hunter was neatly arranged, and the garden well stocked."

The loneliness of their lives made frontier women welcome any visitor—a passing hunter, a neighbor on the way to the distant mill, the circuit rider with Bible and hymn book in his saddlebags, the peddler with his wagon full of wonders and his speech full of news of other places. It made them cherish neighbors, even the *idea* of neighbors who lived miles away and were seen only at an infrequent house-raising, log-rolling or camp meeting. In the Wabash communities Birkbeck found "such a genuine warmth of friendly feeling, a disposition to promote the happiness of each other, that the man who is lonely among them is not formed for society. . . . There is a great amount of social feeling, much real society in new countries, compared with the number of inhabitants. Their importance to each other . . . creates kind sentiments. They have fellow feeling in hope and fear, in difficulty and success, and they make ten-fold more of each other than the crowded inhabitants of popular countries." Even the caustic William Faux observed: "Humanity and hospitality seem national in the west."

Every cabin had a cradle, hollowed like a tiny dugout from a poplar or cottonwood log, and the cradle was seldom empty. Children came in the clearings almost as regularly as the seasons. "I cannot enumerate all the productions of this fine country," wrote Elias Fordham, Morris Birkbeck's colleague and friend. "Man is the only growth that's wanted here: and that want will soon be supplied. Every log cabin is swarming with half-naked children. Boys of eighteen build huts, marry, and raise hogs and children at about the same expense." Large families were an advantage in new lands; girls soon learned to help with primitive housekeeping and boys went to the woods and fields with their fathers. One day on his prairie farm beyond the Wabash, James Lemon was breaking a piece of stubble ground, his small son puffing beside him with a pitchfork—the boy's job was to rake accumulated stubble from the plowshare. At noon farmer Lemon pulled the harness off his sweating horse, hung it on the plowhandle, and went to the cabin for dinner. The boy, tired of raking stubble, hid the horse collar, thinking he would get a rest while his father plaited a new collar of corn husk and straw. But when the farmer came back there was no rest. He pulled off his buckskin breeches, stuffed the legs with straw, straddled them over the horse's neck and took up plowing—"as bare-legged as he came into the world." The boy puffed after him, stabbing a pitchfork at the matted plowshare.

Ten, twelve, fifteen children were common in frontier families, though not all of them survived. With the perils of cholera infantum, summer complaint, croup, epidemic fevers, the mysterious milk sickness, many infants died in the first year, and many others did not live through the dreaded "second summer." It was a rare and fortunate family that did not have a little graveyard in the fence corner under a spreading oak or sycamore.

There were few widows in the western country, for in the clearings and on the prairie farms a woman's life was likely to be shorter than a man's. Many a settler buried a wife at the fence corner and looked for another woman to tend his fire. Some men married and buried two wives and stood a fair chance of outliving a third. The headstones in old cemeteries of the Ohio country tell of countless wives and mothers who did not live to their fortieth year. Mad Ann Bailey in her fence-pole cabin in the hills had outlasted two husbands and she would leave a legend of "Longevity." But the Madonna of the Trail is a young woman who will never see her grandchildren playing on the floor.

CHAPTER FOURTEEN

NEWS FROM HEAVEN

ON A soft spring day in Richland County, Ohio, in the pioneer town of Mansfield, a circuit rider tied his horse to a sapling and began preaching to the village loafers. As he warmed to his subject, men gathered under the new-leafed trees. He pointed a bony finger at Williams' Tavern, calling God's attention to all who frolicked in dens of sloth and drunkenness. He waved a hand past the log courthouse and over the wooded hills, condemning all claim-jumpers, land-grabbers and townsite speculators. Men came west to claim God's green earth, he declared, and in their greed and grasping they lost their immortal souls. Where, he demanded, is the barefoot Christian, traveling to Heaven?

Something rustled in a thicket. Behind a maple log two bare feet waved in the air and a voice cried "Here he is!"

Up jumped a half-clothed man, brown almost as a Delaware. He had hollow cheeks, bright and kindly eyes, a ragged beard, dark hair falling to his shoulders. He wore a shirt of tow-cloth and tattered trousers beaded with beggar's lice and cockle burrs. He carried a tin mush pot in his hand and a deerhide pack on his shoulder.

No one in Mansfield was surprised to see this scarecrow jump up from a thicket on the public square. He was likely to turn up anywhere, from Pittsburgh to the Wabash, just arrived from the Scioto or the Sandusky and on his way to somewhere else. He knew the roads to the scattered towns —Steubenville, Zanesville, Mount Vernon, Coshocton, Ashland, Mansfield; and the trails to the wild and silent places —the great woods of White Woman Creek, the dark gorges of the Cuyahoga, the wild green ridges of the Whitewater and the dim wastes of the Black Swamp. Indians had shared their fire with him on winter days, and lonely settlers had welcomed him to their clearings. And while he roamed the Ohio country, the story of his wanderings had crossed the Atlantic.

In Manchester, England, in January, 1817, the report of the Swedenborg Society included an item from the American wilderness.

"There is in the western country a very extraordinary missionary of the New Jerusalem. A man has appeared who seems to be almost independent of corporal wants and sufferings. He goes barefooted, can sleep anywhere, in house or out of house, and live upon the coarsest and most scanty fare. He has actually thawed the ice with his bare feet.

"He procures what books he can of the New Church; travels into the remote settlements, and lends them wherever he can find readers, and sometimes divides a book into two or three parts for more extensive distribution and usefulness. This man for years past has been in the employment of bringing into cultivation, in numberless places in the wilderness, small patches (two or three acres) of ground, and then sowing apple seeds and rearing nurseries.

"These become valuable as the settlements approximate, and the profits of the whole are intended for the purpose of enabling him to print all the writings of Emanuel Swedenborg, and distribute them through the western settlements of the United States."

His name was Jonathan Chapman and he had come from Leominster, Massachusetts, where as a boy he had wandered the fields in search of birds and flowers. He arrived in the West in 1800, with a sack of apple seeds on his shoulder. In the autumn of 1801 he floated down the Ohio with two canoes lashed together and loaded to their gunwales with apple pumice from Pennsylvania cider mills. He was not a land-seeker but a wanderer who started apple orchards in the harsh wild country and talked to people of the road to heaven. "Have you heard the doctrine of Swedenborg, my friend? It is a simple gospel—the oneness of all things, the kinship of all men, the nearness of God." For forty years he roamed the western country with a sack of rustling apple seeds or a bundle of seedlings. Wherever he went he was welcome, and the settlers gave him a name and kept it warm in their memory.

"Thanks to Johnny Appleseed we found an orchard in our meadow."

"He ran all night, thirty-five miles from Mansfield to Mount Vernon, to warn us when the Indians were coming."

"He had a horse with an apple twig in its bridle and nobody—not even the Indians or the horse thieves—ever touched that animal. But Johnny gave him away to a family moving west that had lost a horse in high water at Third Crossing."

He had a few huts of his own, lean-to shelters of poles and bark and a bed of leaves beside his scattered nurseries. But his home was everywhere: at twilight he might cross the clearing and stand at a settler's door. "How is it with you, friend? How is the orchard bearing?" In his deerhide sack he carried gifts—a pinch of tea for a woman who had never forgot the taste of it, a few beads or a bit of ribbon for a child, a bright feather he had found on the trail. He had things to tell about—a blacksmith building a shop at the crossroads, a new family settled above the fork, surveyors running lines in the new purchase, a miller ready for grist on the Auglaize. When the meal was eaten and the fire glowed on the hearth he brought out the gospel tracts, reading a passage to them, tearing out a page or two to leave till he came again. He mingled talk of heaven with talk of apple trees. "There is no luck more bitter than poor seed, but one as bitter—the planting of plump, dark seed in soil that fails. Look to your seed, my friends. Look to your seed and remember your soil." He slept on the floor in the doorway, and in the morning he was gone.

As shrewd as any land-jobber, Johnny Appleseed knew where the settlements would come. At first he planted orchards along the Hocking, the Tuscarawas, and the Waldhoning. Then he moved on to the Scioto and the Olentangy. When work began on the Ohio and Miami Canal, in 1825, he was roaming Shelby, Auglaize and Defiance counties—his trees were bearing when the canal towns grew. Then on to the Illinois country, following the portage from the Maumee to the Kankakee, tramping the Des Plaines prairie where surveyors were laying out new townsites. He went on, some say, to the rich Des Moines valley in Iowa before he turned back, in 1845, to Indiana. The towns were settled then, the Indians were gone. His old apple trees were dying beside the rivers, and he had work to do.

> *Washington buried in Virginia,*
> *Jackson buried in Tennessee,*
> *Young Lincoln, brooding in Illinois;*
> *And Johnny Appleseed, priestly and free,*
> *Knotted and gnarled, past seventy years,*
> *Still planted on in the woods alone.*

He died in a friendly farmhouse two miles from old Fort Wayne, having taken a chill while driving cattle out of his nursery on the St. Joseph. He was buried on the first day of spring under the budding apple trees.

Jonathan Chapman's life was over, but Johnny Appleseed became immortal in the folk-memory. In poems and stories, in tales and traditions, people kept him wandering the western country. In legend his trails grew longer, his orchards multiplied, his path joined that of all the folk-heroes of the frontier. He had gone bird-hunting, the folklore said, with Jean James Audubon and campaigning with George Rogers Clark. He knew George Washington, Simon Kenton, and Daniel Boone. He tramped the prairies with long-striding Abe Lincoln. When William Henry Harrison marched his troops up the Wabash, Johnny Appleseed was his intermediary with the Indians, slipping into the Shawnee town in the rainy November night; while the battle raged Johnny tended the wounded on the banks of Tippecanoe Creek. Before the British attack on Fort Stephenson, Johnny Appleseed stole through the woods to give young Major Croghan warning; then he was on his way again. He had a sweetheart in Kentucky, pink and white as an appleblow, who died on the eve of their wedding in old Owensboro; by her grave he set out an orchard, spacing the trees to spell APPLE BLOSSOM. Johnny wandered Missouri as a fiddler and ballad-singer; there he married a brown-skinned Osage maiden and saved the French refugees from capture by the Indians. In the woods of Ohio he befriended the "Lost Dauphin," son of Louis XVI and Marie Antoinette—the half-legendary Eleazer Williams who followed the hunting camps of the Indians. According to this story, ragged Johnny Appleseed wandered the trails with the exiled Prince. The Indians thought them touched in the head because, unlike the race of white men, they carried no firearms for killing and swung no ax against the forest.

But the legends are not so enduring as the simple

man himself, planting apple trees and talking of the road to
heaven, scattering seeds of healing herbs—catnip and fennel,
hoarhound and pennyroyal—to serve the settlements of the
future. So he is best remembered, a barefoot man, ragged in
the twilight, slipping his deerhide sack from his shoulder,
his voice like wood doves at evening: "Peace to you, friend.
I come with news from heaven."

     A sterner gospel came over the forest trails with the
circuit riders. Theirs is a rugged story, of men who smelled
of woodsmoke and saddle leather and talked of the power of
the Holy Ghost. They ranged over a huge dark country,
bringing word of God to lonely and brutish people. Sometimes they lost their way, often they met hostility and re-
sentment, in house meeting or camp meeting they might be
jeered by rowdies and ruffians. But they kept on with their
journey. They followed settlement to the farthest claims,
threading forests, splashing through rivers, reading the Bible to a half-wild household by firelight, organizing congregations—Presbyterian, Baptist, Methodist—in the wilderness. They went out with Bible and hymn book in their
saddlebags, arms and head through a blanket for a greatcoat,
with a schedule of preaching in squatters' camps and stump-
filled clearings and a roster of church members where no
church bell had ever rung.

     People in savage country took savage ways; it was the
circuit riders' task to call them back to kinship with man
and God. Their records are of men on an unending journey:
"I rode . . . I traveled . . . I pressed on . . . I traversed
. . . I kept on my way." Said William Henry Harrison who
sometimes met a mud-splashed missionary on a distant trail,
"They lived as though they had taken the vows of poverty
upon them, and had to face the dangers and difficulties that
beset their path alone and unattended." Surveyors entered
the wilderness in crews, soldiers with an army; even the
remotest settler had his wife and children. But the circuit
rider is the lone figure of the frontier, riding through swamp

and forest, in sun and snow and rain, brooding on a text for his next preaching. He knew hunger, weariness and cold, but there was a grim glory in his calling.

"Yesterday I traveled upward of thirty miles in mud and water, being wet all day without; yet heaven was within. Glory to God! I had three tempters to encounter, the devil, the mosquitoes and my horse; and my wet clothes were my element, and God my comforter and victory my white horse."

Here is one of them, who can stand for many, the Reverend Henry Smith on his circuit in the wild Scioto country that Nathaniel Massie's men were then surveying: "Lewis Hunt a young man traveled Miami circuit in 1799; but we had heard that he was broken down, and I was sent to take his place. On the 15th of September I set out, in company with brother Francis M'Cormick, to meet brother Hunt, on Mad river. We met him at brother Hamer's, and found him so far recovered as to be able to go on in his work. My instructions were, that if he should be able to continue in the work, to go up the Scioto, and form a circuit there. We consulted our friends, and formed a plan, uniting Scioto to Miami, making a six weeks' circuit. This plan was, however, abandoned, on account of the great distance between the two circuits, and the dismal swamp we would have to pass through every round. . . .

"Monday, 23d. I was unwell, but rode about ten miles toward my new field of labor, and lodged with a poor but pious Methodist family.

"Tuesday, 24th. I pursued my journey up the Ohio river, and put up with James Sargent, an old Methodist friend from Maryland, who received and treated me with all the kindness of an old Maryland Methodist. Here I left two appointments for my next round.

"Wednesday, 25th. I still pursued my course up the Ohio river, but had a very intricate path, and, indeed, sometimes none at all; but by the good hand of the Lord upon me, the evening brought me to the house of a kind

Presbyterian family. We spent the evening in conversation on religious subjects. The old gentleman asked me to pray with them in the evening, and again in the morning, and pressingly invited me to call again whenever I came that way. I thanked them for their hospitality, but never had another opportunity of calling upon them.

"Thursday, 26th. I left this kind family at the mouth of Red Oak, and started for Eagle creek, and began to inquire for Methodists, but could hear of none. I took up Eagle creek, and being directed to a family where I could get some information, I rode up to the house, and asked the good man of the house if he could tell me where any of the people called Methodists lived. He said he could give me no information. But his wife formerly belonged to the society, and invited me to alight and come in. I did so; and while my horse was eating, I told them who I was, and my business. I entered into conversation about spiritual things, and requested the man to call his family together, and I prayed with and for them, and was much drawn out. I gave them a short exhortation, and left them all in tears. I rode about eight or nine miles, and inquired for Methodists again, and was directed to a poor man's cabin. I found him and his wife Jane in the cornfield. I called to him, and inquired if he could tell me where I could find any of the people called Methodists. He leaped over the fence, ran to me, and took me by the hand with all the cordiality of a true Irishman. I told him my name and business, and he received me with every expression of joy, called to Jane, and conducted me in triumph to the cabin. Jane came out of the field in cornfield habiliments, it is true; but she soon washed and changed her dress, and appeared to make me as welcome to their cabin as her husband. Such a reception was worth a day's ride. If I was but poorly qualified for a missionary in every other respect, I was not in one thing; for I had long since conquered my foolish prejudice and delicacy about eating, drinking and lodging. I could submit to any kind of inconvenience where I had an opportunity of doing good, for I thought myself honored in being permitted to labor in any part of the Lord's vineyard. My call was among the poor, and among them I could feel myself at home. Jane gave me something to eat, and we ate our morsel with gladness, and talked about Jesus. In time of family prayer the melting power of God came down and filled the place with glory. The merciful people had taken their poor horse in with them the previous winter, and of course it could not be very agreeable; but poor Jane brought out of her chest as clean white sheets as ever came from Ireland, and spread them on my bed, and I slept sweetly, and arose refreshed. Here I was informed there were four or five Methodist families still higher up the creek, who had formed themselves into a society, and met on Sundays for prayer and class meeting.

"Friday, 27th. I rode to old brother John Foster's, and the dear family received me with open arms, and sent out word to their neighbors, and I preached on Saturday the 28th, to about eighteen or twenty persons with a degree of life, and the word seemed to find way to their hearts.

"Sunday, 29th. I preached at Peter Rankin's, four miles down the creek, to a small but very attentive congregation—this was the place where the small society met—and the poor starving sheep fed freely upon the word of life.

"Monday, 30th. I rode to a brother Wormsley's on Ohio Brush creek. With this family I had been acquainted in Kentucky, and we had an unexpected but joyful meeting. In family worship the Lord was present in power, the dear family were melted into tears, and the room appeared to be filled with glory and with God. We sang and talked about Jesus, and shouted aloud for joy. And who would not shout for such an unexpected, but seasonable visitation of mercy? Word was sent out, and preaching appointed at William Bushill's. . . .

"Wednesday, October 1st. I rode to Joseph Moore's, Scioto Brush creek. Here I found a considerable society already organized by brother Moore. Here I had some success, and the society increased, so that on the sixth of August, 1800, we proposed building a meeting-house; for no private house would hold our week-day congregation. But we met with some opposition, for some wanted a free house. But as no one seemed to care for their souls but the Methodists, it appeared to me like foolishness to build a house for other denominations, before they came and wanted a house. We, however, succeeded in building a small log-house, but then large enough for the neighborhood, the first Methodist meeting-house on the circuit, and perhaps the first in the North-Western territory. I did not stop to preach here on my first visit, but left an appointment for my next, and pressed onward toward Pee Pee, on the Scioto.

"Friday morning, 4th.   I rode through a heavy rain to Pee Pee, and called at the house of Snowden Sargent, a kind-hearted old Methodist from Maryland. I was wet, hungry, and brought plenty of company with me, from a bear-skin, my bed the night before. I introduced myself, and met with a cordial reception by a very kind family."

When the circuit rider was to preach in a settler's cabin, word went to the neighbors for miles around. Families came through the woods. While women laid the babies on a blanket in the loft, the men listened hungrily to the preacher's news about a gristmill on the river, a trader at the crossroad, and a new settlement beginning above the fork. When the room was full the preacher lined out a hymn—

On Jordan's stormy banks I stand—

the people singing it after him, a line at a time, and then the whole stanza together. After two hymns came the prayer, roaring down God's wrath on guilty sinners and pleading for God's mercy to people in a wilderness. Another hymn, then the sermon. It might be two hours long, but backwoods people did not complain. They were starved for the sound of a new voice and for any thoughts beyond their stump-filled clearings. The preacher chose sturdy texts: *Except ye repent, ye shall likewise perish. . . . Thou wilt show me the path of life. . . . I have fought the good fight. . . . Remember now thy Creator in the days of thy youth.* After the sermon they sang the Doxology. New converts became church members, the next preaching date was settled, neighbors arranged to meet for psalm-singing and Bible-reading till the preacher came again. They went home singing:

> *On the other side of Jordan,*
> *In the sweet fields of Eden,*
> *Where the tree of life is blooming—*

Meanwhile the preacher was on his way, fighting clouds of mosquitoes and thinking about another people who wandered in the desert while seeking a promised land. While his horse drank at the crossing he took the Bible out of his saddlebag and found a new text for the next meeting: *And the land shall yield her fruit and ye shall eat your fill and dwell therein in safety. . . . The land shall not be sold forever, for the land is mine and ye are strangers and sojourners with me.*

"I will here say," wrote the Reverend Henry Smith when church spires were lifting where he had preached from wagon beds and walnut stumps, "that those were the happiest days of my life—log cabins to preach in, puncheon floors to sleep on, long rides, corn bread and milk to eat, a constant succession of kind friends to make welcome, and the love of God in the soul."

Of all the long laborious circuits, the longest was traveled by that strange and hairy itinerant, Lorenzo Dow. With sermons, tracts, and bottled medicine, "Crazy Dow" ranged from Connecticut to Mississippi, from Georgia to Wisconsin, with tours of England and Ireland between long seasons on the American frontier. Millions of people saw him preaching to a multitude from a camp-meeting platform or to a family from a sycamore stump, and none forgot his gaunt and swaying figure, his wind-blown beard, his rasping voice and hypnotic eye. This hairy pilgrim took the whole frontier for his parish. He rode through the forest wheezing with asthma, toes poking through his broken moccasins, flaying a bony horse with a tattered umbrella. He pushed west, through Ohio, Indiana, Illinois; he circled south through Tennessee, Mississippi, and Georgia. He harried the ungodly in New England and then turned west again.

In 1801 he passed like an apparition through the dark Ohio country. That was his first visit and it left a legend and an agitation. He came again and again, for thirty years, a man out of the Old Testament, gaunt and mud-stained, proclaiming doom and glory. "In the year 1819," recalled an Indiana judge, years afterward, "I was one of a congregation assembled in the woods back of Rising Sun, anxiously awaiting the arrival of Lorenzo Dow. Time passed away, we had all become impatient, when in the distance we saw him approaching at a rapid rate through the trees on his pacing pony. He rode up to the log on which I was sitting, threw the reins over the neck of the pony and stepped upon the log, took off his hat, his hair parted in the middle of his head, and flowing on either side to his shoulders, his beard resting on his breast. In a minute at the top of his voice he said, *'Behold, I come quickly, and my reward is with me.* My subject is repentance. We sing, "While the lamp holds out to burn, the vilest sinner may return." That idea has done much harm and should be received with many grains of allowance. There are cases when it would be easier for a camel to go through the eye of a needle than for a man to repent unto salvation. Let me illustrate. Do you suppose that the man among you who went out last fall to kill his deer and bear for winter meat, and instead killed his neighbor's hogs, salted them down and is now living on the meat, can repent while it is unpaid for? I tell you nay. Except he restores a just compensation his attempt at repentance will be the basest Hy-

pocrisy. Except ye repent truly, ye shall all likewise perish.'
He preached some thirty minutes. Down he stepped,
mounted his pony, and in a few minutes was moving on
through the woods at a rapid pace to meet another appointment."

Always ill, frail, exhausted, Lorenzo Dow burned with
a quenchless vitality. Coarse, crude, unkempt, he was also
a man of mysterious and hypnotic power. He could clown in
the pulpit, shaking his hearers with laughter; he could silence rowdies and prostrate whole congregations. Reading his
text from the open Bible—*I can do all things*—he remon-
strated with St. Paul. "No, Paul," wagging his long beard
over the Epistle to the Philippians and cutting the air with
a bony finger, "No, Paul. You are mistaken for once, and
I'll bet you five dollars on it." He took a bank note from his
ragged pocket, holding it over the open page. Then he read
the rest of the text—"through Christ which strengtheneth
me." He crammed the money back into his pocket. "Ah,
Paul, that's a very different matter. The bet's off." Once in
the south he found on the meeting grounds a Negro boy
with a tin trumpet, and hired him to climb a tree above
the congregation. In his sermon he described Gabriel's
trumpet sounding the dread hour of judgment. "Then suppose, my dying friends, suppose this should be the very
hour! Suppose at this moment you should hear the sound of
Gabriel's trumpet!" He gave the hidden boy a sign and the
trumpet blasted from above. With cries of fear and pleas for
mercy the congregation writhed on the ground.

To travelers on the road Dow gave out his schedule
of preaching, and crowds gathered at the appointed time and
place. He posted notices in town taverns and on the village
pump; in the country he sent a messenger galloping from
one farm to another to herald the coming of Lorenzo Dow.
Often he preached five times a day. He wore out scores
of horses, flogging them through rain and sun, through bot-
tomless mud and drifting snow. Once, concluding a sermon with a wheezing prayer of exhortation, he cried *Amen!*,

seized his mud-splashed hat, leaped through the meeting-house window, landed on his horse and pounded away to the next preaching.

He looked like a hermit just down from the hills, but whether he spoke from a pulpit or a woodpile he had the common touch. In a moment that rasping voice could catch the curious and hold the vulgar. His sermons were gamy as smoked sausage, full of salt and pepper. Hear him warning the backwoodsmen against "Falling from Grace," his text a scrap torn from the first verse of the second chapter of Hebrews:—*lest we should let them slip.* "Now, my brethren," cries the spectral preacher, "let me take a case, and a very likely one to happen. Nay, I'm not at all sure that it hain't happened, and not a hundred miles off. Well, here is Major Smith, who becomes converted. He joins the church, and is safe as a codfish, pickled, packed, and in port. Of course his calling and election are sure. He can't let 'em slip. He can't fall from grace—not he! Don't be too sarten of that, my brethren! Don't be too sure, Major!

"I say nothing agin the character of Major Smith, mind you. He is a very fair sort of man, as the world goes. Nevertheless they du say that he is in the habit of taking now and then a glass or two more than was good for him. He was fond of a warm gin toddy, especially of a cold day, for he was subject to wind on the stomach; and then, in order to settle his toddy, he would take a glass of flip, and then to settle his flip, he'd take a glass of toddy, agin. These he usually took in the arternoon and at Northrup's tavern.

"But, as I say, one day the major was converted, and taken into church, and so he must reform. He must give up toddy and flip, and Northrup's tavern. And he has gin them all up—for he is parfeckly sincere—mind you. Well, some weeks later, on the arternoon of a cold blustering day in December, he happens to be passing by Northrup's tavern. Just at that time, as the devil will have it—for the devil is always looking out for a chance—his old friend and bottle companion, Nate Seymour, comes to the door, and sees the major. Well, the latter rides up, and they shake hands, and talk over the news, and finally Nate says, 'Won't you come in for a minute, Major?'

"Now, as I tell you, it's a cold winter's day, and the major says he'll jest get down and warm his fingers. He won't drink anything of course, but he thinks it best not to break all at once with his old friends, for they may say he's proud. Perhaps he'll have a chance to say a word in season to some one. So he goes in, and as it happens Nate jest then puts the redhot poker into a mug of flip. How it bubbles and simmers and foams! What a nice odor it does send forth into the room! And jest then the landlord grates in a little nutmeg. What a pleasant sound is that to poor, shivering human nater, on a cold day in December!

"Well, Nate takes it and hands it to the major. The major says to himself, 'I'll just put it to my lips, so as not to seem frumptious and unreasonable, but I won't drink any.' So he takes it, and it feels mighty warm and nice to his cold fingers. He looks at it; its fumes rise to his nostrils; he remembers the joys of other days; he puts it to his lips!

"Well, and what then? Oh nothing, my brethren —only I tell you, that elect or no elect, that is a very slippery spot for the major!"

In one of his widely circulated tracts Dow quoted:

> Man *wants* but little *here*,
> *Nor* wants that little *long*.

But in 1816 far out on the northwestern frontier he bought 46,000 acres to establish a colony where true democracy and religion might flourish. On the upper Mississippi where the river widens to form spacious Lake Pepin, he marked out the central square and laid off the streets of "Loren, or the City of Peace." This was to be the capital of his new society of brotherhood and justice; in the wilderness beside the great river would rise the golden city. Soon he acquired a second domain, 77,000 acres bordering the Chippewa River, naming it Beulah Ethiopia because it was to be an asylum for redeemed Negroes. A third tract of 70,000 acres he called "The Cosmopolite's Mount Sinai Domain." Other purchases increased his colony to 452,000 acres, for which the ragged evangelist paid some ninety thousand dollars. Where did that fortune come from? From his land dealings in New England, from gifts that poured in from his converts, but chiefly from the sale of his printed discourses—on theology, history, marriage, the Popish plot, and the vicissitudes of his own career. These writings were peddled from door to door in a dozen states and sold in shops all over the country.

The huge domain on the upper Mississippi was purchased from Benjamin Munn of Philadelphia, who had bought the land from the heirs of Jonathan Carver. In 1767, in a torch-lit ceremony in an echoing cave under the bluffs of the Mississippi, two Sioux chiefs had granted that Yankee shoemaker and explorer a huge sweep of land along the river. But Dow could not begin settlement of the territory until the federal government ratified the Indian cession; and though the cession was not doubted, the government was not ready to evacuate Indians and protect colonists in that far country. So Preacher Dow sold his empire for a few hundred dollars and took to the road again. He mended his fortune by selling Lorenzo Dow's Family Medicine, compounded of Epsom Salts, tincture of Bloodroot, Nitre Salts, and sulphuric acid, all dissolved in boiling water and stirred with a wooden paddle.

Laced in a leather jacket to hold himself upright and gasping out his sermons, Dow kept on the road—to New England, to Pittsburgh, to Indiana, to Tennessee, to Virginia—with thousands crowding into every meeting place. Frontier settlers named their children for him, bought his tracts on heaven, hell, marriage, Masonry, and popery, and swilled down countless bottles of Lorenzo Dow's Family Medicine—"a sincere attempt to relieve the sufferings of mankind . . . with a peculiar quality to remove obstructions in the stomach and bowels, and in carrying off bad humours

. . . and efficacious in all those disorders called Bilious and affections of the liver, exceeding common credibility."

In 1832, emaciated and spectral and still casting his shadowy spell, Lorenzo Dow was presented to Andrew Jackson in the White House; he gave the President a cryptic warning about impending death. Two years later, in December 1833, he was in Washington again, apparently to inform the President of a Papist conspiracy. There the gaunt and restless prophet died—murmuring about his spavined horse and a preaching appointment ahead of him.

Lorenzo Dow was called the "inventor of the camp meeting," but he had not yet arrived in the West when the first frenzied crowds pressed around rude pulpits in the wilderness. In the 1790s the great revival in the East swept westward, and immediately the camp meeting became a frontier institution. The first great forest meeting was the work of a Presbyterian, though the later camp meetings were dominated by Methodists and Baptists—sects which asserted a democratic religious individualism and which did not shrink from the crudeness and harshness of the frontier.

At Cane Ridge, Kentucky, in the rich bluegrass district of Bourbon County, stood the Cane Ridge Meeting House, built in 1791 by a company of Presbyterians from North Carolina. Its pastor, the Reverend Robert W. Finley, moved north to pioneer Chillicothe, Ohio, in 1796, and so he missed the great revival that swept Kentucky like a storm wind. In the spring of 1800 Finley's successor at Cane Ridge, the Reverend Barton W. Stone, went to Logan county to hear the fiery McGee brothers, one a Presbyterian and the other a Methodist, preach from the same pulpit. This experiment in inter-denominationalism attracted a crowd that overflowed the meeting house and filled the woods for acres around it. Log platforms were raised in the forest, and preaching went on day and night. In August 1801, back at Cane Ridge, Stone held a "General Camp Meeting" that has been remembered for a hundred and fifty years. Whole counties poured in to the Cane Ridge campground. Twenty thousand people, many of them from north of the Ohio, set up tents and pole-sheds in the woods. For three weeks a relay of twenty preachers prayed, preached, and exhorted from log platforms under the trees. At night, in the light of flaring torches, five men preached from five pulpits, their voices rising and falling while a multitude sang, sobbed, and shouted. At the height of the frenzy thousands danced and jerked among the tree trunks and hundreds fell entranced and exhausted to the ground.

The western country, the huge, harsh, violent and somber country, had found a religious institution that would endure for forty years. Frontier people rarely saw new faces or heard new voices. They were far from the mill, the market or any public meetingplace. They lived darkly in the forest; they struggled with the earth and the seasons. The gloom of the great forest pressed around their clearings. Their emotions were walled in silence and solitude—until camp meeting time. Then, in the great crowd frenzy, pent-up feelings broke free. Wonder and dread, ecstasy and anguish, pain and love and glory shook them in the forest.

In the early 1800s the camp meeting spread through Ohio—up the Hocking, the Scioto, the Miami, across the Western Reserve. Families traveled twenty, fifty, a hundred miles to the great gatherings. It was "roasting-ear time," the end of summer. Weather was warm and dry; there was a break in the farm tasks, wheat already harvested and corn not yet ripe for husking. Along the road signs pointed the way to the assembly and listed the camp meeting rules. As they approached the meeting ground the road was worn deep with travel and the weeds hung white with dust. Then through the woods, still miles away, came a sound like a great wind rising and falling. The fervor reached out to the newcomers. They whipped up the tired horses, anxious now to be swept out of themselves, to be seized and shaken by the Pentecostal power.

Soon they found a thinned-out forest and hundreds of horses tethered among the trees. Amid acres of wagons, carts, traps, buckboards, they pulled the sweated harness off the team. They hurried on, the great sound enveloping them now, past rows of tents, smoldering fires, signs and numbers posted on the trees. They pushed through the restless fringes of the crowd and saw, over a multitude of heads, the preacher swaying on the raised platform. Already their voices were joining the great chorus, *Glory! Glory! Glory!* that answered the preacher's cry.

For five days the settlers forgot their silent clearings. Each sunrise a trumpet aroused the camp for a daybreak prayer service. Fires were kindled, breakfast eaten, the horses watered and tethered freshly, then the trumpet announced the first preaching. Services were held all day—at eight o'clock, at eleven, at three, at dusk; between preaching sessions people gathered in breathless tents to pray with the mourners. Most powerful and impressive was the night service. By the flickering light of campfires and torches people crowded into the assembly. Heaven and hell were in the preacher's words, and waves of wailing, weeping and singing swept the crowd. Torches shook in the night wind, from the restless shadows the preacher pleaded for penitence and surrender. Something primitive and powerful invaded the close-pressed crowd. They began jerking, laughing, crying. They leaped up ecstatic and fell rigid to the ground. The fallen were carried into the "glory pen," a straw-strewn enclosure beneath the preaching platform, and the shouting rolled over them like a rising tide. After the first seasons, whisky shops were outlawed from the meeting grounds, but rowdies and ruffians remained. At night they came galloping through the woods, leaped off their horses and began roaring at the preachers and preying on the crowd. Fistfights raged in the shadows, girls and women were led off to the woods, horse-thieves and wagon-thieves went to work while the preacher held the people under the torch-lit spell.

At the end of five days the family cooked their last

breakfast, heard the last sermon, loaded their wagon and rocked away. Back to loneliness and silence, back to monotony and toil. But they carried with them the remembered excitement and they hummed above the knocking wheels:

There is rest for the weary,
There is rest for the weary,
There is rest for the weary,
And we'll rest there too.

Every traveler to the western country heard of the great frenzy of the camp meetings, and most visitors wanted to see that spectacle for themselves. Their accounts of the forest revivals make up some arresting chapters of frontier literature. James Flint, Mrs. Trollope and Frederick Marryat all gave startled accounts of camp meetings in the Ohio country.

Captain Marryat, a sharp-eyed and far-ranging English traveler who had seen "men under almost every variety of government, religion, and climate," was astonished by his first visit to a forest meeting in 1837.

"I was informed that a camp-meeting was to be held about seven miles from Cincinnati, and anxious to verify the accounts I had heard of them, I availed myself of this opportunity of deciding for myself." After passing through a huge encampment and joining in a service of singing, prayer, and preaching, the Englishman looked into a tent in a railed space near the pulpit. "It was open at the end, and, being full of straw, I concluded it was used as a sleeping-place for those who had not provided themselves with separate accommodation. About an hour after the service was over, perceiving many people directing their steps toward it, I followed them. On one side of the tent were about twenty females, mostly young, squatted down on the straw; on the other a few men; in the centre was a long form, against which were some other men kneeling, with their faces covered with their hands, as if occupied in prayer. Gradually the numbers increased, girl after girl dropped down upon the straw on the one side, and men on the other. At last an elderly man gave out a hymn, which was sung with peculiar energy; then another knelt down in the centre, and commenced a prayer, shutting his eyes (as I observed most clergymen in the United States do when they pray) and raising his hands above his head; then another burst out into prayer, and another followed him; then their voices became all confused together; and then were heard the more silvery tones of woman's supplications. As the din increased so did their enthusiasm; handkerchiefs were raised to bright eyes, and sobs were intermingled with prayers and ejaculations. It became a scene of Babel; more than twenty men and women were crying out at the highest pitch of their voices, and trying apparently to be heard above the others. Every minute the excitement increased. Some wrung their hands and called for mercy; some tore their hair; boys laid down crying bitterly, with their heads buried in the straw; there was sobbing almost to suffocation, and hysterics and deep agony. One young man clung to the form, crying, 'Satan tears at me but I would hold fast. Help—help, he drags me down!' It was a scene of horrible agony and despair; and, when it was at its height, one of the preachers came in, and raising his voice high above the tumult, entreated the Lord to receive into his fold those who now repented and would fain return. Another of the ministers knelt down by some young men, whose faces were covered up, and who appeared to be almost in a state of phrensy; and putting his hands upon them, poured forth an energetic prayer, well calculated to work upon their over excited feelings. Groans, ejaculations, broken sobs, frantic motions, and convulsions succeeded; some fell on their backs with their eyes closed, waving their hands with a slow motion, and crying out— 'Glory, glory, glory!' I quitted the spot, and hastened away into the forest, for the sight was too painful, too melancholy."

From Mrs. Trollope, shocked and fascinated by the

crudeness of the frontier life, came a vivid and gruesome
account of an Indiana camp meeting. "The prospect of passing a night in the back woods of Indiana was by no means
agreeable, but I screwed my courage to the proper pitch, and
set forth determined to see with my own eyes, and hear with
my own ears, what a camp-meeting really was. I had heard
it said that being at a camp-meeting was like standing at
the gate of heaven, and seeing it opening before you; I had
heard it said, that being at a camp-meeting was like finding
yourself within the gates of hell; in either case there must
be something to gratify curiosity, and compensate one for
the fatigue of a long rumbling ride and a sleepless night.

"We reached the ground about an hour before midnight, and the approach to it was highly picturesque. . . .
The first glance reminded me of Vauxhall, from the effect
of the lights among the trees, and the moving crowd below
them; but the second shewed a scene totally unlike any
thing I had ever witnessed. Four high frames, constructed in
the form of altars, were placed at the four corners of the enclosure; on these were supported layers of earth and sod, on
which burned immense fires of blazing pine-wood. On one
side a rude platform was erected to accommodate the
preachers, fifteen of whom attended this meeting, and with
very short intervals for necessary refreshment and private
devotion, preached in rotation, day and night, from Tuesday to Saturday. . . .

"At midnight a horn sounded through the camp,
which, we were told, was to call the people from private to
public worship; and we presently saw them flocking from
all sides to the front of the preachers' stand. Mrs. B. and I
contrived to place ourselves with our backs supported
against the lower part of this structure, and we were thus
enabled to witness the scene which followed without personal danger. There were about two thousand persons assembled.

"One of the preachers began in a low nasal tone, and,
like all other Methodist preachers, assured us of the enor-

mous depravity of man as he comes from the hands of his Maker, and of his perfect sanctification after he had wrestled sufficiently with the Lord to get hold of him, et cetera. The admiration of the crowd was evinced by almost constant cries of 'Amen! Amen!' 'Jesus! Jesus!' and the like. But this comparative tranquillity did not last long; the preacher told them that 'this night was the time fixed upon for anxious sinners to wrestle with the Lord'; that he and his brethren 'were at hand to help them,' and that such as needed their help were to come forward. . . . 'The pen' was the space immediately below the preachers' stand; we were therefore placed on the edge of it, and were enabled to see and hear all that took place in the very centre of this extraordinary exhibition.

"The crowd fell back at the mention of the pen, and for some minutes there was a vacant space before us. The preachers came down from their stand and placed themselves in the midst of it, beginning to sing a hymn, calling upon the penitents to come forth. As they sung they kept turning themselves round to every part of the crowd, and, by degrees, the voices of the whole multitude joined in chorus. This was the only moment at which I perceived any thing like the solemn and beautiful effect, which I had heard ascribed to this woodland worship. It is certain that the combined voices of such a multitude, heard at dead of night, from the depths of their eternal forests, the many fair young faces turned upward, and looking paler and lovelier as they met the moonbeams, the dark figures of the officials in the middle of the circle, the lurid glare thrown by the altar-fires on the woods beyond, did altogether produce a fine and solemn effect, that I shall not easily forget; but ere I had well enjoyed it, the scene changed, and sublimity gave place to horror and disgust. . . .

"Above a hundred persons . . . came forward, uttering howlings and groans, so terrible that I shall never cease to shudder when I recall them. They appeared to drag each other forward, and on the word being given, 'let us pray,' they all fell on their knees; but this posture was soon changed for others that permitted greater scope for the convulsive movements of their limbs; and they were soon all lying on the ground in an indescribable confusion of heads and legs. They threw about their limbs with such incessant and violent motion, that I was every instant expecting some serious accident to occur. . . . After the first wild burst that followed their prostration, the moanings, in many instances, became loudly articulate; and then I experienced a strange vibration between tragic and comic feeling. . . .

"The stunning noise was sometimes varied by the preachers beginning to sing; but the convulsive movements of the poor maniacs only became more violent. At length the atrocious wickedness of this horrible scene increased to a degree of grossness, that drove us from our station; we returned to the carriage at about three o'clock in the morning, and passed the remainder of the night in listening to the ever increasing tumult at the pen. To sleep was impossible. At day-break the horn again sounded, to send them to private devotion; and in about an hour afterwards I saw the whole camp as joyously and eagerly employed in preparing and devouring their most substantial breakfasts as if the night had been passed in dancing; and I marked many a fair but pale face, that I recognised as a demoniac of the night, simpering beside a swain, to whom she carefully administered hot coffee and eggs. The preaching saint and the howling sinner seemed alike to relish this mode of recruiting their strength.

"After enjoying abundance of strong tea, which proved a delightful restorative after a night so strangely spent, I wandered alone into the forest, and I never remember to have found perfect quiet more delightful."

At many camp meetings a ten-o'clock curfew brought an end to the excitement, and the grove grew quiet under the summer stars. But some gatherings, like that witnessed by Mrs. Trollope, kept up an all-night frenzy. Another night scene was described by the Scottish traveler James Flint. Although observing that "you can form no adequate idea of a camp meeting from any description which can be given of it," he proceeded to picture a great assembly leaping, jerking, swooning, shouting and sobbing beneath a log platform where a preacher cried "Glory! Glory! Glory!" The frenzy mounted as darkness came.

"About dusk I retired several hundred yards into the woods to enjoy the distant effect of the meeting. Female voices were mournfully predominant, and my imagination figured to me a multitude of mothers, widows, and sisters, giving the first vent to their grief, in bewailing the loss of a male population, by war, shipwreck, or some other catastrophe.

"It had been thought proper to place sentinels without the camp. Females were not allowed to pass out into the woods after dark. Spirituous liquors were not permitted to be sold in the neighbourhood.

"Large fires of timber were kindled, which cast a new lustre on every object. The white tents gleamed in the glare. Over them the dusky woods formed a most romantic gloom, only the tall trunks of the front rank were distinctly visible, and these seemed so many members of a lofty colonnade. The illuminated camp lay on a declivity, and exposed a scene that suggested to my mind the moonlight gambols of beings known to us only through the fictions of credulous ages. The greatest turmoil prevailed within the fence, where the inmates were leaping and hobbling together with upward looks and extended arms. Around this busy mass, the crowd formed a thicker ring than the famous Macedonian phalanx; and among them, a mixture of the exercised were interspersed. Most faces were turned inward to gaze on the grand exhibition, the rear ranks on tip-toe, to see over those in front of them, and not a few mounted on the log-seats, to have a more commanding view of the show. People were constantly passing out and into the ring in brisk motion, so that the white drapery of females, and the darker apparel of the men were alternately vanishing and reappearing in the most elegant confusion. The sublimity of the music served to give an enchanting effect to the whole. My mind involuntarily reverted to the leading feature of the tale of Alloway Kirk:

> Warlocks and witches in a dance;
> Where Tam o'Shanter
> ———— Stood like ane bewitch'd,
> And thought his very een enrich'd.

"Late in the evening a man detached himself from the crowd, walking rapidly backward and forward, and crying aloud. His vociferations were of this kind: 'I have been a great sinner, and was on the way to be damned; but am converted now, thank God—glory, glory!' He turned round on his heel occasionally, giving a loud whoop. A gentleman with whom I am well acquainted told me that he had a conversation with a female who had just recovered from the debility of the day. She could give no other account of her sensations than that she felt so good, that she could press her very enemy to her bosom.

"At half past two A.M. I got into a tent, stretched myself on the ground, and was soon lulled asleep by the music. About five I was awakened by the unceasing melody. At seven, preaching was resumed; and a lawyer residing in the neighbourhood gave a sermon of a legal character.

"At nine the meeting adjourned to breakfast. A multitude of small fires being previously struck up, an extensive cooking process commenced, and the smell of bacon tainted the air. I took this opportunity of reconnoitring the evacuated field. The little inclosure, so often mentioned, is by the religious called Altar, and some scoffers are wicked enough to call it Pen, from its similarity to the structures in which hogs are confined. Its area was covered with straw, in some parts more wetted than the litter of a stable. If it could be ascertained that all this moisture was from the tears of the penitent, the fact would be a surprising one. Waiving all inquiry into this phenomenon however, the incident now recorded may be held forth as a very suitable counterpart to a wonderful story recorded by the Methodistic oracle Lorenzo Dow, of a heavy shower drenching a neighborhood, while a small speck including a camp meeting was passed over and left entirely dry. In Lorenzo's case, the rain fell all around the camp, but in that noticed by me, the moisture was in the very centre."

Nothing was lenient, benign or gentle in the western country. The settlers endured hardship and isolation; their wary lives held dark and silent yearnings. Their religion was as crude and powerful as the wild dark land around them, as violent as the flooded rivers in the spring or the crashing cloudbursts of midsummer. Excesses flourished on the frontier. Drunkenness, gambling, feuding, violence of various kinds were natural reactions to a hard life in a hostile land; even the schoolmaster commonly kept a jug of whisky underneath his desk. The circuit riders strove against the forces of darkness and savagery, they fought a depravity that threatened to destroy all moral standards. As the first forty-eight men at Marietta held court without a case, going earnestly through that ceremony to remind themselves of their social and moral heritage, the mud-stained preachers called a frontier people back from brutishness to their inherited aspirations.

When life grew safer and softer in that country the forest frenzy passed and church bells rang soberly above the village streets. Three denominations spread through the settlements. The Presbyterians had a thoroughly schooled clergy, men who became leaders in civic and educational life in new communities. The Methodist itinerants, though less learned than the Presbyterians, carried tracts and pamphlets on their forest rounds, distributing a religious literature in a bookless country; later the Methodist leaders vigorously supported movements for public education. The Baptists were least burdened with learning. Most of their early preachers were farmers, untrained and unpaid, who on Sunday morning knocked the clods from their shoes and rode off to preach at the "corners." All these denominations took the crude frontier for their parish and lifted it slowly out of darkness.

The first churches, rude frame buildings with birds nesting in the wooden belfry, were a rallying point for moral standards. In their struggle against depravity the churchmen grew rigid and extreme, condemning drinking, dancing, card-playing, denouncing all worldly amusements. They fought the grog shop, the theater, the billiard hall and card room. Later the pendulum began to swing back, and the churches supported the Chautauqua movement which moved its big tents across the Middle West with a program of family entertainment laced with inspiration.

Along with spiritual comfort and moral discipline the frontier church provided the first and strongest social unit in new communities. The church bell had a friendly sound. As the camp meeting had drawn lonely people into a frenzy of shared emotions, the crossroads church was a place where people raised their voices together in song and prayer, where they christened their infants and buried their dead and shared their inmost feelings. In no older country with traditional institutions could the church have such a social role. The frontier meeting house was a place for tying the horses to the hitching rack and talking under the trees before the preaching began, for lingering, sometimes with a basket dinner, after the service was over. From the foundries of Cincinnati the pioneer railroads carried church bells all the way to the Mississippi, to the woods of Michigan and the islands in Lake Erie. The sound of the church bell meant praise and prayer; and it meant box socials, community suppers, Christmas and Easter entertainments, Sunday School parties, neighborhood picnics by the creek or on the hill.

It also meant learning. "Ye shall know the truth and the truth shall make you free" was a favorite text in the rough-hewn pulpits. In many districts land was provided for the support of schools, but a designated section did not automatically transform itself into a schoolhouse, a school board, a learned master and rows of children at their lessons. Neither did a college township convert itself into a college. The organizing of education, and its continued support, had to be the work of groups of people, and the first groups on the frontier were church congregations. They became the fathers of countless schools and the founders of colleges that sprang up in almost every other county in the Midwest. Long before a state university was chartered in Ohio (the Ohio State University was not established till 1870) the state was dotted with Presbyterian, Methodist, Baptist, Congregational and other sectarian colleges. The presidents and faculties of the early academies were ordained ministers, their trustees were churchmen, and church societies raised funds to keep their doors open to the young. William Holmes McGuffey, the schoolman who through his *Eclectic Readers* had the greatest influence on children in Midwestern schools, was an ordained Presbyterian minister as well as a college professor and a college president.

Inevitably the Bible had a central place in the college curriculum, along with the classics, mathematics and as much or as little science as would harmonize with the Book of Genesis. But a common reliance on the Bible left ample ground for doctrinal disputes between the sects and within them. In the fall of 1832 a famous preacher and educator left Boston for the West. The Rev. Lyman Beecher, with his brood of thirteen children, came to Cincinnati to take charge of the newly established Lane Theological Seminary. As a preacher he attacked drinking, duelling, infidelity, Romanism, and Unitarianism. As a reformer he pressed for the abolition of slavery and the colonization of American Negroes in Africa. As a theologian he embraced both the fore-ordination dogma of Old-School Presbyterianism and the New School's belief that man is accountable for his actions.

The West was a broad country, but not broad enough to accommodate Lyman Beecher's diverse beliefs. Soon after his arrival in Cincinnati he was charged with heresy, and his Seminary was accused of a reckless and violent brand of Abolitionism. Beecher faced two stormy trials and through his own nimble defense won his acquittal. Meanwhile the students at the Seminary debated the slavery question for nine successive nights, ending with a call for immediate emancipation; then to "elevate the colored population of the city" they visited in Negro homes, taught their children, and invited Negro visitors to Lane Seminary. This was too much for the Seminary trustees in a border city that had grown rich on trade with the South. When they ordered the Anti-Slavery Society at the Seminary disbanded, the entire Senior Class walked out. Along with a following of younger students they went north to Oberlin College, which became a center of Abolitionism.

From the start the western colleges were vigorously democratic. Cincinnati and Oxford, Ohio, became pioneer centers of education for women. Oberlin opened its doors equally wide to rich and poor, to male and female, to colored and white students. When Miami University announced the opening of a "Farmers' College" in 1829 its offering was not an Agricultural course but a three-year academic curriculum for farm boys. "Literary and scientific knowledge is no longer to be the exclusive property of a few professional men," the notice read. "It is to become the common property of the mass of the human family."

By the time of the Civil War Ohio led the nation in the number of its colleges, and Indiana and Illinois were not far behind. The flickering light of the camp meeting had become the steady lamp light in college halls across the Midwestern country.

CHAPTER FIFTEEN

MOONLIGHT ON THE WABASH

And here it is, in the heart of the United States and almost in the center of its unequaled internal navigation, that Power which governs and directs the universe and every action of man, has arranged circumstances which were far beyond my control, and permits me to commence a new empire of peace and good-will to men, founded on other principles and leading to other practices than those of present or past, and which principles in due season, and in the allotted time, will lead to that state of virtue, intelligence, enjoyment, and happiness which it has been foretold by the sages of the past would at some time become the lot of the human race.

—ROBERT OWEN

Indiana is a vast forest, larger than England, just penetrated in places by the backwood settlers.

—ELIAS PYM FORDHAM

THE WABASH is an empty river now, winding between rich fields of corn and wheat, and it is surprising to think of the trade it carried a century and a quarter ago—skiffs and dugouts, rafts and barges, side-wheelers and stern-wheelers. Ferries churned across the old fording-places. At a hundred scattered woodyards men ricked up fuel-wood to keep the funnels fuming. Around the bend came the *Florence,* the *Ploughboy,* the *Josephine,* the *Decatur,* the big, bright, tall-stacked *Belvidere,* and all the rest. In 1831 the New Harmony *Disseminator* reported sixty-three steamboat arrivals in a single month and stated that "seventeen hundred flatboats descended the Wabash this spring." Up the

275

river came people with plows, grubbing hoes, and axes, and also with dreams of a new society, with ideas of social perfection. European ideas these were, from the Old Testament and the Book of Revelation, and from the essays of Shaftesbury, Fourier, and Rousseau, but the Old World offered no fresh starting ground. So the visions of prophets and the dreams of reformers came to the Indiana wilderness.

Like foxtail, milkweed, and thistle, wandering ideas rode the winds of the West. Wherever they lodged, the earth was rich and ready; they put down roots and grew.

In 1831 prophet Joseph Smith led his Latter-day Saints from Palmyra, New York, to northern Ohio, where they built their big bare temple at Kirtland and began to bicker with the gentiles around them. According to Joseph Smith, the Christian church had lost its revelation and authority. There had been no communication with heaven for hundreds of years until the angel Nephi (later corrected to Moroni) brought him God's instruction to restore the true church on earth. A further revelation sent him to the Western Reserve, where there was room for the New Jerusalem to grow. Though their hope was in heaven, the Mormons had a lively interest in real estate. New converts were urged to buy land, and more land; the New Jerusalem, they were told, would extend from Kirtland township to the Pacific Ocean. In the resulting speculation land prices rose from a hundred to a thousand per cent, and the whole Western Reserve was swept by a land frenzy. "City lots" were sold on the lake shore all the way from Buffalo to Toledo; a grandiose Kirtland City was laid out with two hundred twenty-five blocks totaling forty-five hundred building lots—like a Florida promotion a hundred years later. But the gentiles grew more hostile, the real estate bubble burst, Joseph Smith received a new revelation and the Mormons packed their wagons and moved on to a promised land farther west.

In 1817 in the old province of Württemberg on the Danube a band of Separatists, who kept their children from the Lutheran schools and their young men from the German army, were ordered to dissolve their colony. Remembering how Lot in ancient times had fled from the evil of Sodom and found refuge at Zoar, they set out for America. In Philadelphia they found a Quaker merchant who owned fifty-five hundred acres on the Tuscarawas River in Ohio. He sold it to them for $16,500, on time, and so the Separatists built their town of Zoar in the woods of the Western Reserve. Together they cleared the forest, plowed the fields, planted crops, and brought their harvest to a common storehouse. The first years were a time of struggle in the wilderness, but in 1833 the Ohio Canal came through their lands. Work on the big ditch earned them money to complete their land payments, and the canal gave them a road to market. A flour mill and two iron furnaces were built beside the waterway and the Society operated four barges of its own. By 1840 Zoar was a neat and comfortable village among thrifty gardens and fragrant apple orchards. In the center of town a symbolic garden showed twelve paths to heaven crossed by walks that led to nowhere. The pious Zoarites raised fine fruit and flowers, made fine products of textiles, pottery, wood and metal, and followed the paths of salvation. But in time the colony grew lax and indolent, and the outside world lured the younger generation away. In 1898 the Society was disbanded, land and property being divided among the members and private granaries replacing the public storehouse. Then the symbolism of the garden was forgotten: the Tree of Life was just a blue-green spruce, the Hedge of Heaven was a circling arbor vitæ, the Trees of the Apostles were twelve dark junipers, and the Paths of Heaven were no different from the ways of the world.

In 1770 in the clammy Manchester jail under the smoky skies of the English midlands a 34-year-old woman sat brooding on "the root of human depravity and the cause of man's fall." Her meditations resulted in a dozen settlements on the American frontier.

Ann Lee—Mother Ann to the Shakers—was born in Toad Lane, Manchester, one of eight children of a pious and illiterate blacksmith. As a child she went to work in a cotton factory; she never learned to read and write. From early years she received heavenly visions and aspired to a life of perfect purity. Purity, it was revealed to her, meant denial of sex. But the pressures of the world outweighed her revelation, and she was early married to a young blacksmith, Abraham Stanley. Within a few years she bore four children, all of whom died in infancy. Perhaps that confirmed her conviction of the sin of sexual union. At twenty-two she joined the Shakers, a sect that had originated in seventeenth-century France among a group of peasants who claimed inspiration from the Holy Ghost. In the fervor of primitive faith they saw visions, they were shaken with ecstasy and frenzy, they foretold Christ's return to a pestilential earth. In England this doctrine won a few Quakers who developed a ritualistic dance, a form of worship expressed by body, mind and soul. So they became Shaking Quakers, or Shakers. With them Ann Lee took to the roads, preaching that Christ was about to come to earth again, this time as a woman; perhaps Ann Lee herself was the new incarnation. For "Sabbath-breaking" with the frenzied Shaker dance and the crying out in strange tongues, she was locked up in the Manchester jail. On her release Ann Lee imparted to her followers a new revelation—they could not follow Christ "while living in the works of natural generation"; they must become celibate. When she was examined by officials of the Church of England, Mother Ann spoke to them in seventy-two separate tongues and declared that the Millenium had begun. In confirmation of this belief she had a vision of a great tree whose leaves shone with flame-like splendor. A voice from the burning tree directed her to go to America and establish there the Church of Christ's Second Appearing.

In those years America was many things to England. To merchants and speculators the New World was trade, profit, riches; to landless peasants and jobless mechanics it was hope and opportunity; to religious zealots it was refuge and asylum, a promised land.

In August, 1774, when the first Continental Congress was assembling at Philadelphia, when Daniel Boone was warning land-lookers in Kentucky of attack by Ohio Indians, the ship *Mariah,* twelve weeks out of Liverpool, arrived in New York. Ashore came Mother Ann Lee with eight Shaker followers. While the rest went inland to work on American farms, Ann Lee stayed in New York, working as a laundress and taking care of her sick husband. In time he recovered and ran off with another woman. Mother Ann then joined her followers at Watervliet, New York. Despite persecution and imprisonment they won new converts, and when Mother Ann died in 1784 the Shaker doctrines were firmly planted in America.

In 1800 word came east of a great revival in the frontier settlements of Kentucky—a religious awakening that brought thousands of people to hear relays of preachers in the forest and that left throngs stricken by the power of the Holy Ghost. At news of the great revival the Shakers recalled some prophetic words of Mother Ann. Before her death she had pointed westward, saying: "The next great opening of the Gospel will be in the Southwest. It will be at a great distance, and there will be a great work of God." She turned to her followers. "You may live to see it. I shall not." Now, in the summer of 1800 three Shaker missionaries set out on foot for Kentucky to see if the great revival was the work foretold by Mother Ann. They found their trip worth while. The turbulent camp meeting crowds were ready to hear of Christ's second coming, and the Shakers had a welcome for all converts—"Indian, pioneer, or planter, ignorant Negro or Presbyterian divine." Soon five Shaker societies were established in Kentucky, Ohio, and Indiana.

The oldest and largest of the Shaker colonies was Union Village, on a high and fertile ridge four miles from Lebanon, Ohio, in the heart of the Miami valley. For more than a century—from 1805 to 1913—the village lived in self-sufficiency, with its big sturdy "halls," its weaving and woodworking shops, its three thousand acres of fields, orchards and pasture. These Shakers supplied grass seed for all southwestern Ohio—William Henry Harrison bought their seed to use on his North Bend farm. They developed the famed "Miami Valley hog," by importing fat China hogs to cross with the native "rail-splitters." They raised Merino sheep and Durham cattle. In 1826 Bernhard Karl, Duke of Saxe-Weimar-Eisenach, visited the community, where he found two ex-Presbyterian ministers and two Frenchmen, father and son, among the six hundred Shaker brethren. In 1842 Charles Dickens left the village in bad humor when he was told that the Shaker religious meetings were not open to the public. He summed up his observations in a grim statement: "We walked into a grim room, where several grim hats were hanging on grim pegs, and the time was grimly told by a grim clock which uttered each tick with a kind of struggle, as if it broke the grim silence reluctantly, and under protest."

The Shaker worship had previously been scoffed at by curious Lebanon gentiles who drove out on Sunday afternoons to watch the ritual dance on the lawn between the two big living halls. Five times in the early years of Union Village mounted gangs pounded out from Lebanon and jeered at the hymn-singing brethren. Now the Shakers are gone; their land is an Ohio state prison farm and the big brick and frame barracks strung out along a country road are a home for children and the aged. But it is still recalled that in the summer of 1820 two Shakers, obeying a vision from God, rode down Lebanon's dusty Main Street intoning a curse on the town. At the same time they gave blessings to the neighboring settlements of Cincinnati and Dayton. When the Shaker village disbanded, ninety-three years later, Lebanon was still a country town midway between the two cities of the Miami Valley.

The richest soil for Utopia was the Wabash bottoms, a valley of dreams for half a century when the West was young. Here came the Shakers in 1804, locating twelve miles north of Vincennes on two thousand fertile acres of Shaker

Prairie. Past their cornfields the Shawnee Prophet, Tecumseh's brother, came to the Vincennes Council in 1810, and a year later William Henry Harrison marched his men to Tippecanoe. But the Shakers had no part in frontier warfare. Steadily they grew in number, winning converts, taking in homeless widows and orphans. In 1820 they built their community house, with sixty windows and twenty-one fireplaces. The next year they raised a big square meeting house, with the men's benches on one side and the women's on the other. They operated a distillery, a sawmill and a gristmill. Every spring they loaded produce on Wabash flatboats, taking wheat, apples, potatoes all the way to New Orleans. In their common dining room stood two long tables. At a signal from a horn the brothers entered one door and the sisters another, marching to their separate tables. They knelt for silent prayer, rose in unison, sat at the tables and ate their meal in silence. Then they marched out to the shops and fields. In the evening they sang hymns—with pent-up power that carried for miles across the dark prairie—and marched to their sleeping quarters, men on one floor, women on another. On Sundays they held long services of worship, with prayer, reading, and preaching alternated with the ritual Shaker dance. Each brother was assigned to a sister who looked after his clothing, told him when he needed a new garment, and reproved him for any disorder. Men and women never met alone. So life went on, year after year, at Shakertown, while the Wabash wilderness became the busy Wabash valley, while young Abe Lincoln grew tall in Posey County, while canal boats came down from the Maumee, while Indiana volunteers marched off to the Civil War. At last, in the 1870's, the Shakers disbanded. Their religious and economic principles could not attract new converts, and their young people went to the world outside. Finally an epidemic of fever silenced the shops and left the fields unharvested. Nothing remains of Shakertown except a farmhouse in the midst of Shaker Prairie, built with brick from the old Meeting House.

Mrs. Trollope, more finicky than her countrymen who came down the river to farm the English Prairie, lamented the absence of German castles on the Ohio.—"Were there occasionally a ruined abbey, or a feudal castle, to mix the romance of real life with that of nature, the Ohio would be perfect." If she had sailed up the Wabash in the tall-stacked *Belvidere,* she would have found some Old World architecture. Over the neat and orderly village of Harmonie on a handsome bend forty miles above the river's mouth, rose a huge cruciform church with long aisles shadowed by oak and walnut colonnades. It had four entries, each one a hundred feet from the next. Twenty-eight columns of walnut, cherry and sassafras—great trunks from the Wabash forest—held up the upper story; the walnut pillars stood twenty-five feet high, the others twenty-one feet. This unlikely structure was built according to plans sent down from heaven during a thunderstorm, in black ink on a golden scroll. A settler who had brought his grain to the Harmonie mill went back to the English Prairie shaking his puzzled head. "I studies and I studies on it," he told George Flower.

When Mrs. Trollope admired the Ohio valley, in 1828, the builders of the strange temple were gone from the Wabash. They had come thirteen years before—eight hundred German peasants from the province of Württemberg. Under their leader and prophet, George Rapp, they had arrived in America in 1804, taking up five thousand acres in western Pennsylvania, living there in a "community of equality" (they owned all things in common, even clothing, except their chickens), renouncing marriage, working like ants in their fields, shops and mills. But the Pennsylvania land was not suited to vine and fruit culture, and they were twelve miles from navigation. In 1815 Father Rapp sold the community for a hundred thousand dollars and the whole village moved down the Ohio in a fleet of flatboats. The men wore coarse blue blouses and flat black hats, the women pale blue jackets, dark skirts and skull caps or straw bonnets. A band played from one of the boats and among their seedlings, tools, implements and livestock the Rappites sang the old German hymns. They came with music down the river.

At Harmonie, forty winding miles up the Wabash and forty-five miles below Vincennes, they soon brought order to the wilderness. By 1820 they had three thousand acres of corn, wheat and barley. They had a brickyard, a tannery, a distillery, a woolen factory. Though expecting the Millennium, they built houses that still stand today—solid dwellings of stone, brick and clapboard, and a granary as massive as a fortress. Over the town rose the great temple, where Father Rapp preached to his sober followers. He foretold the end of the world—God would sent a poisonous dew upon the earth and a conflagration would sweep the land. The Rappites had that to think about on Sunday, as they ate their hearty dinner. On Monday they drove heaping harvest wagons to their five-floored granary with its four-foot walls of brick and stone. Signposts in the village streets showed the entrance to underground passages where they could hide like Indiana groundhogs when the poisonous dew and the purging fire came down.

Harmonie was a triumph of discipline and order. At daybreak the herdsman blew a long-throated horn and fat milch cows marched out of their stable, two by two it was said, to the lush pastures. The chief herdsman, who bore the name Gabriel, drove a wagon known as Noah's Ark, painted in the old Württemberg style with scrolls of flowers and German script assuring the Rappites that they were the heirs of salvation. While a band played vigorous hymn music the colonists marched to work, two by two, to the wheat harvest, the apple picking, the hat shop, the tanning works, and the distillery. They worked twelve hours a day, with time out for four huge meals. Sunset brought a religious service, with Father Rapp, tall, snowy-bearded, white hair falling to his shoulders, standing God-like in the pulpit. He was a good blacksmith, a good miller, a good sheep-shearer and hog-breeder, a good judge of horse flesh. He knew how to drain the bottom fields and he also conversed with angels—he imparted these revelations while the sun set over the wheat. There was band music in the twilight, and at nine o'clock the church bell rang the end of another earthly day. The Rappites went to their separate beds and the watchmen took up their rounds, walking all night in the starlit village streets.

The Rappites did not go beyond their lands, marked with white flags to show the boundaries of the colony. But their neighbors came to Harmonie—to get a horse shod, to buy clear Rappite whisky, to wonder at the huge granary, the flatboat loads of apples, the great columned church. In a big barn they stared at a threshing machine powered by four matched teams of horses, and at a winnowing machine that magically separated grain from the chaff. They looked in at the ringing blacksmith shop, the cooper shop, the huge vats of the dye works and the tannery, the spinning and carding mills. From fifty miles around settlers came to shop in the Rappite store, its shelves laden with goods bearing the "rose" trademark—the golden rose of Micah—hats, shoes, cotton and woolen cloths, flannel and linsey, whisky, wine and oil —along with foreign goods freighted by Rappite wagons from the wharves of Shawneetown.

Free-thinking Morris Birkbeck could not condone Rappite theology, but he admired the colony's production. "It furnishes from its store many objects of great value, not so well supplied elsewhere, and it is a market for all spare produce." Birkbeck was sorely puzzled that ignorance should be so productive. "At this our third visit, Harmony becomes more enigmatical. This day, being Sunday, afforded us an opportunity of seeing grouped and in their best attire, a large part of the members of this wonderful community. It was evening when we arrived, and we saw no human creature about the streets:—we had even to call the landlord of the inn out of church to take care of our horses. The cows were waiting round the little dwellings, to supply the inhabitants with their evening meal. Soon the entire body of people, which is about seven hundred, poured out of the church, and exhibited so much health, peace, and neatness in their persons, that we could not but exclaim, surely the institutions which produce so much happiness must have more of good than of evil in them; and here I rest, not lowered in my abhorrence of the hypocrisy, if it be such, which governs the ignorant by nursing them in superstition; but incline in charity to believe that the leaders are sincere. Certain it is that living in such plenty, and a total abstraction of care about the future provision for a family, it must be some overbearing thralldom that prevents an increase of their numbers by the natural laws of population."

The spiritual care of the Rappites was in the hands of venerable George Rapp, the material in the strong hands of his adopted son, Frederick. Father Rapp, huge, kindly and strong-willed, kept his people pious, orderly and expecting the end of the world. But while awaiting earth's holocaust the Rappites prospered, and this was the achievement of stalwart Frederick Rapp. He organized the work, kept the records, supervised the trade. With low-cost labor and superior goods he attracted trade to Harmonie from all the Wabash valley. After the harvest, when frontier roads were smooth and dry, he sent Rappite teamsters, with matched horses and heaped wagons, to storekeepers distant as the Mississippi.

While the Rappites marched to the fields, the church, the mills, to meals and to bed, the West was heaving with change. *Nile's Register* for November 30, 1816 described every ferry on the rivers as "daily occupied in passing families, carriages, wagons, negroes, carts, &c., &c." Fifty wagons a day crossed the Muskingum at Zanesville. Forty-two thousand people came into Indiana in the year 1816. One of the farmers who arrived that year, "because of the difficulty of land titles in Kentucky," was Tom Lincoln, who selected a quarter section sixteen miles north of the Ohio and marked its corners with brush heaps: that fall his seven-year-old son Abe helped to build their half-faced cabin. The Indiana population was doubled, to 150,000, between 1815 and 1820. In 1820 came the new federal land act, reducing the price of public land from $2 to $1.25 an acre and allowing the sale of eighty-acre tracts. Now a settler need not go in debt for more land than he could farm or pay for.

While the Harmonie colonists remained inside their boundary flags, Frederick Rapp represented them in public affairs. He signed the bills of lading at Shawneetown and checked cargoes at the village landing. He served on the commission, meeting during twenty hot June days of 1816 under the great elm at Corydon, that framed the Indiana constitution. He sat with the committee, in May of 1820, that removed the capital from Corydon. (William Henry Harrison had first owned the site of that settlement and had named the village for the young shepherd in his favorite song, "The Pastoral Elegy.") He helped to coin the hybrid name "Indianapolis" for a future capital in the huge New Purchase of central Indiana. Frederick Rapp from godly Harmonie met soldiers, peddlers, gamblers, politicians, merchants, steamboat captains, homeless Indian chiefs, claim-jumpers, wildcat bankers. He saw the disorder and confusion, the scheming and grasping, the stretching and growing of the frontier West.

In 1824, when the state government was moved in four farm wagons to the brushy site of Indianapolis far up the dwindling waters of Fall Creek, Harmonie looked like the most permanent town in Indiana. But in that year an angel stood on the bank of the Wabash and instructed Father Rapp to take his people to a new place. Ten years the colonists had toiled and prayed and waited, and the end of the world had not come. Meanwhile they had prospered. When they had left Germany the Rappites' property could not have amounted to twenty-five dollars a person. Twenty years later their property was worth two thousand dollars for each man, woman and child—ten times the average wealth in America at that time. Their town had grown famous on the frontier, and across the Atlantic Lord Byron wrote, in *Don Juan*, about Father Rapp's colony—" 'tis said the sect is rich and godly." Godly they must be as long as George Rapp was their leader, and riches was a threat to godliness. So, it is supposed, Father Rapp decided that his people needed a new encounter with hardship. He put the sale of his town in the hands of Richard Flower, of the neighboring English Prairie; it was worth perhaps a million dollars, but he would sell it all, even the heaped granary and the cattle in the pastures, for a hundred and fifty thousand. Then, loading their seeds and seedlings, their tools and implements, and doubtless looking back at their pretty village as the hills closed in, the Rappites floated down the Wabash. They did not go west, with the current of America, but poled laboriously up the Ohio. They landed eighteen miles below Pittsburgh and began the task of clearing forest, building a new town, bringing new fields to harvest, while they waited for the earth's destruction.

To the English, American real estate was an old story. But it was news when Richard Flower of the Wabash prairies arrived in London in 1824 advertising a town for sale in the western wilderness. The town of Harmony, in Indiana, with two churches rising above streets of brick, stone and frame houses, with factories, a distillery, a tannery, a brewery, with a warehouse and a boat landing, with orchards, gardens, vineyards, with cattle in the fields and sheep in the meadow—a town and thirty thousand acres, one third of it under cultivation. Who would buy a town in the far West of America, a ghost town left by the hymn-singing followers of Father Rapp? It was an extraordinary piece of real estate, and there was in the town of Lanark, ten miles up the Clyde from Glasgow, an extraordinary man.

Robert Owen, born, prophetically, in Newtown, Montgomeryshire, Wales, in 1771, had been a scholar, a worker, a manager and owner of spinning factories. At seven he became assistant to his teacher, Mr. Thickness, in a Welsh village school, and he was in love with learning all his life. At the sturdy age of ten he went to London and became apprenticed to a draper in a shop above the Thames. At eighteen he was a factory manager in Manchester; there he saw how the industrial revolution had blighted the lives of English workmen. In 1800 when he took control of the New Lanark mills in Scotland he found a desolate town of fourteen hundred sullen and sodden families. Every morning in the murky dawn hundreds of pauper children filed with ragged men and women through the factory gates. Work was long, dangerous, deadening. Children were flogged for nodding at their benches. The men and women were ignorant, vicious and helpless, slaves to the factory and the company store. Few of them would reach the age of forty. Their lives were short, mean and brutish.

Robert Owen, a slight, soft-spoken man with a loose cape over his shoulders and steel spectacles sliding down his nose, did not look like a man to change the world, or even Lanark, Scotland. But his restless mind had shaped a world-changing theory of human nature and society. "Make a man happy and you make him virtuous—this is the whole of my system. I enlighten his mind and occupy his hands. . . . I require my people to labour only eight hours out of the twenty-four. Instruction and amusement diversify the intermediate hours. . . . All vice is the result of unhappiness: give a man a chance and he will prove a good citizen."

In a few years Lanark was a clean, busy, contented town. Dunghills and mudholes had vanished, the village streets were paved and flower gardens brightened the dooryards. Bathtubs were installed in the cottages and a sanitary committee made inspection every week. The work day was shortened (while it went up to fourteen, fifteen, sixteen hours in the English mills) and the pay increased. Children were in school, learning reading and writing, agriculture and mechanics. For the workers there were evenings of music and dancing, readings and lectures on human harmony and happiness. Though the Lanark mills, manned with capable and willing hands, made increasing profit, Owen's partners feared his ideas and tried to force him out. He turned to a group of wealthy Quakers in London and formed a new corporation, getting full control of the mills. When he returned to Lanark the villagers loosed the horses from his carriage and drew him through cheering streets to his house at Braxfield. So factory owners were regarded where machinery was used to benefit the workers. And so Robert Owen put his faith in the laboring class, dreaming, far beyond Lanark, of a cooperative commonwealth, a socialist society without rivalries and conflicts. He began a series of essays on human society and its prospects and conceived a model town in which all would share alike in ownership, work and welfare. While the Rappites, four thousand miles away on the Wabash waited the day of doom, Robert Owen pictured the beginning of a brave new world.

Then came Richard Flower with a town for sale in America, and Robert Owen promptly peopled that townsite with his dream of the new society. When Owen spoke of Harmony as the beginning of a New Moral World, a system of equality, cooperation and brotherhood, the salesman tried to caution him. It was a remote frontier country, Indiana, with three types of settlers: bushy hunters as wild as Indians, crude and often shiftless farmers, grasping merchants and mechanics—all restless and individual, each seeking his own fortune in his own way. Robert Owen, gazing into Utopian distances, was not dissuaded. He applauded the freedom and spontaneity of frontier life; he was ready to buy the Rappite town. Flower, remembering homesick people on the Wabash prairie, was amazed that a man could leave a prosperous situation, with every comfort and luxury, and take his family to the wilds of the far West. "He did not know," said Robert Dale Owen, the reformer's oldest son, "that my father's one ruling desire was for a vaster theater in which to try his plans of social reform."

In December, 1824, Owen came to America to inspect his property and to launch the New Moral World. That winter in the eastern cities he made public addresses on his plan for New Harmony. In Washington he spoke to an assembly of Congress, the Judges of the Supreme Court, President Adams and his cabinet. He explained the New Moral World as "a

new organization of society which would give a new existence to man by surrounding him with superior circumstances only." The society, open to all, would be cooperative,
its members owning all property in common and sharing
equally in work and its production. He believed this system
of social union would soon lead all people to abandon the
"miserable, anxious, individual system of opposition and
counteraction." In leaving the Old World this mild and gentle
man had left small conceptions; he now had a dream as
broad as the new lands of America and as bright as moonlight on the Wabash. New Harmony, he said, would be but
the first town organized on socialistic principles. The old Rappite village would serve as temporary quarters while his colonists should build a new community above the Wabash.
He had a model of his model town—a solid square of frame
and masonry, a thousand feet on each side, with temples of
culture rising at the corners. The "temples" would contain
lecture rooms, laboratories, ballrooms, concert rooms, committee and conversation rooms. Inside the enclosure was ample space for parks, gardens, shops and schools, an academy
and a university.

This was a heady prospect, and newspapers in Washington, Philadelphia, New York, Boston and Albany printed
the announcement of "a new society to be formed at Harmony in Indiana." Soon the plan was reported in papers
throughout the Ohio valley, and in London, Glasgow and
Dublin, for Robert Owen offered a welcome to "the industrious and well disposed of all nations." The luring West had
never offered so generous an invitation.

To take up the good life on the Wabash there came a
motley crowd of pilgrims. By midsummer nine hundred colonists had arrived—dispossessed squatters, unfrocked clergymen, mortgage-ridden farmers, ragged schoolmasters, blue-
nosed temperance men, fugitives from Old World politics
and persecution, the curious and the discontented, the lazy
and the fanatical. They came from every state in the Union
and from all the countries of northern Europe, in stovepipe

hats and coonskin caps, in frock coats, coarse woolen wadmal blouses, and shirts of greasy buckskin. Some carried books under their arms, some had speeches in manuscript, some bore rifles on their shoulders, and some brought a flute or a violin. New Harmony was an undiscriminating magnet.

When Robert Owen arrived in April he found several hundred of his people moving into the Rappite houses. He set up community kitchens and stocked the pantries. At the end of April he spoke to his community in the Hall of Harmony, as he had named the former Rappite church. "New Harmony, the future name of this place, is the but halfway house I could procure for those who are going to travel this extraordinary journey with me—and although it is not intended to be our permanent residence, I hope it will be found not a bad travelers' tavern, in which we shall remain only until we can change our old garments, and fully prepare ourselves for the new state of existence into which we hope to enter."

With this cheerful word he went back to London, while the colonists made a tentative organization of the community and the newly established *Gazette* began printing essays on Moral Responsibility and Human Happiness along with agricultural and scientific articles. New arrivals came in skiffs and flatboats, in carts and wagons, on horseback and muleback, and afoot. Women were assigned to the nursery, the gardens, the kitchens; men chose their work in the factories or the fields. Robert Dale Owen, who had stayed behind his father, tried manual work before he turned to teaching and editing the *Gazette*. A weekly recreation program was arranged—dancing on Tuesday, town meeting on Wednesday, concerts on Thursday, readings, lectures, discussions on the other evenings. When Owen returned to America, glad to breathe again the restless air of the New World, he lectured in the East on the New Moral World, inviting more recruits to New Harmony (though his son protested "We have no room for them") and advertising for carpenters, masons, mechanics (though young Owen informed him

"We have no lime, no rocks, no brick, no timber") to go immediately to the Wabash. Then he called on William Maclure in Philadelphia.

Maclure, scientist, philanthropist and educational reformer, had come to America from Scotland in 1763 to make a geological survey of the United States. Since then he had tramped from the St. Lawrence to the Gulf of Mexico and had crossed the Alleghenies more than fifty times. A restless, long-striding, free-thinking man, he had made a fortune in the Atlantic merchant trade. Now he was perennial President of the Philadelphia Academy of the Natural Sciences, a donor of libraries, a zealous supporter of the Pestalozzian theory of practical and utilitarian education. Catching Owen's ardor, Maclure agreed to take charge of education at New Harmony. He promptly contributed some thousands of dollars, shipped his library and scientific apparatus to the Wabash, and gathered a faculty for the school system. He meant to make that frontier settlement the center of learning in America. He was a bachelor, with warm friendships and enthusiasms. New Harmony became his child—for a little while.

Too impatient to await spring weather, Maclure ordered a keelboat built in Pittsburgh and set out with thirty scientists, philosophers and educators for the West. They crossed the Alleghenies in December, boarded the barge *Philanthropist*—the "Boatload of Knowledge"—and began a winter journey down the Ohio. Thirty miles below Pittsburgh, in the midst of the ice-clogged river, the *Philanthropist* came to rest. For a month the company of scholars stared out at the frozen river and the snowy hills. Robert Owen sat by the cabin fire jotting notes on the New Moral World, while Maclure paced the deck, recalling his journeys by foot over the mountains and into the West. Thomas Say, a Philadelphia Quaker and the foremost naturalist in America, was wondering about the hawks and the groundhogs, the crayfish and butterflies he would find on the Wabash. He had been in the field with Maclure, tramping the length of Florida with a specimen bag on his shoulder and exploring the islands off the Georgia coast. He had gone with Major Long to the Rocky Mountains, had climbed the granite ridges of the Continental Divide and gathered specimens at timber line. Now, with his quick face and dark side-whiskers, he walked in the winter wind, voices coming faintly to him from the women's cabin. A shy, reflective man, frail despite the ardors of his expeditions, speaking with a lisp, he was still, at thirty-eight, a bachelor. He did not know that his future wife was in that company of Philadelphia girls in charge of Madame Frategeot whom Maclure was bringing to New Harmony to give grace and refinement to the New Moral World. Charles Alexander Lesueur, naturalist and painter, weathered like an Indian, was a veteran of a four-year scientific voyage around the world; from that expedition in the corvette *Géographe* he had brought back to Paris a hundred thousand zoological specimens. Since then he had made field trips with Maclure in the West Indies and the American wilderness. Now he looked down the snow-veiled river, impatient to be on the trail again. In the West he would map the mounds of Indiana and classify the fishes in the Great Lakes, and in his New Harmony studio his fine pen would illustrate the six volumes of Say's great *American Conchology*.

The voices in the cabin were mingled—English, French and German, men and women, old and young. Gerard Troost, just turned fifty, a kindly, courteous, broadly learned man from Herzogenbusch, was the foremost authority of his generation on fossil crinoids. The chemist and pharmacist Speakman had closed his shop in Philadelphia, a famous gathering place of doctors, herbalists, bird-watchers, collectors of mosses, sedges, and fungi. The English artist and engraver John Chappelsmith looked lost in the frozen Ohio. With him was his tall, spare wife, an enthusiastic student of entomology and an intense lecturer on mud-daubers, wasps and spiders; no doubt she wondered what winged life would hatch from the banks of the Wabash in the spring. Stedman Whitwell, a London architect with literary inclinations, had been enlisted to design the new community building—the hollow square that would house the New Harmony of the future. Two disciples of Pestalozzi's system of education according to nature, Phiquepal d'Arusmont and Madame Marie Louise Fratageot had been persuaded to leave their private schools in Philadelphia to shape society on the frontier.

Just three weeks before the *Philanthropist* froze in the river Mad Ann Bailey had died in her shanty in the frozen Ohio hills. Now came Madame Fratageot, stepping out on deck with bright eyes dancing and French curls edging her little Paris cap. After a breath of the bitter air she went back to the bevy of girls in the cabin. Beside the fire she began a bubbling discussion of the effect of music on the minds of small children, and on the perfectibility of all human nature. Disillusionment was in store for most of the girls in that circle, but one of them would find all her dreams fulfilled. Months after the voyage down river, charming Lucy Sistaire became the wife of slender Thomas Say. In the years ahead at New Harmony she would help him complete his monumental work on American entomology.

After a month the gray skies brightened with a warm south wind. The ice broke up and the *Philanthropist* moved on a crest of water between the winter hills. In mid-January the scholars trooped ashore at New Harmony and were led to their cottages, Maclure went to live in the house of Father Rapp, a brick mansion topped by two tall lightning rods, with its gardens sloping to the river. Robert Owen, abstemious in all but idealism (from childhood he had a delicate stomach and his later wealth brought him no taste for luxury), unpacked his bag in a room in the village tavern. Then he called the community together to form a permanent organization. He declared the principles of the New Moral World here and now beginning: equality of rights, a just sharing of duties, community of property, freedom of speech and action, sincerity in all proceedings, kindness in all actions, courtesy in all intercourse, order in all arrangements, the preservation of health, the acquisition of knowledge, and obedience to the laws of the country. The moon lay bright on the Wabash as the brave new world began.

It was spring, a green and golden season, and all the earth was new. Meadow larks sang from the fence rails, in the swamp red-wing blackbirds flashed the scarlet badge on their shoulders, new-born calves and colts tottered in the pasture, squirrels chattered from the young-leafed sycamores, rivers of pigeons shadowed the April sky, in the long fields the furrowed earth curled over from the plow.

Old Professor Joseph Neef arrived from Louisville— he had come from France to Philadelphia at the urging of Maclure; since then he had taught a Pestalozzian school in Kentucky. He rounded up the New Harmony children, leading them to study in the classroom and to work in the fields. Maclure set out exotic "Trees of the Golden Rain," imported from China, at the gateways of the Rappite houses—they are the "gate trees" which every June halo New Harmony with their long yellow tassels. The scientists lectured in the Hall of Harmony and tramped off to gather fossils, birds' nests, and fungi. The Women's Literary Club read Byron's poems. A Thespian Society put on French and English plays and gave the première production of Robert Dale Owen's romantic drama *Pocahontas*. Stedman Whitwell, who was drawing on paper the four-sided city of the future, turned from his temples of culture to devise a simplified plan of geography, naming cities by their location, with letters expressing latitude and longitude. New Harmony, at Latitude 38 degrees, 11 minutes North, and Longitude 87 degrees, 55 minutes West, became Ipba Veinul. New York came out as Otke Notive, London as Lafa Vovutu.

Reform, experiment and innovation came to that green valley like the urge of spring. Soon a new colony was formed, an offshoot society setting itself up on Owen's lands under the name Feiba Peveli. Frances Wright, the handsome and magnetic Englishwoman who came to America to improve the condition of Negroes, arrived at New Harmony and began lecturing on Women's Rights and the prospects of

American society. "There is something unspeakably sublime in the vast extent of earthly domain that here opens to the mind's eye; and truly sublime in its contemplation, when we consider the life and energy with which it is fast teeming. An industrious and enlightened people, laying in the wilderness the foundations of commonwealth after commonwealth, based on justice and the immutable rights of man!" Into the village strolled that scholar gypsy Constantine Samuel Raffinesque. He had collected plants, shells and fishes all the way from Turkey, where he was born in 1784, to the Mississippi. For a few weeks he traded specimens with the scientists and theories with the philosophers, then he was on his way again. Even the New Moral World could not hold him long.

Visitors came from near and far—for example, Morris Birkbeck from across the Wabash and Count Bernhard from across the Atlantic. Birkbeck, whose word for the superstitious Harmonie of Father Rapp was "enigmatical," did not record his view of the rational system which replaced it; on his return from a visit to Owen's village he was drowned in the flooded waters of Fox Creek. Count Bernhard, who arrived in New Harmony on the 15th of April, 1826, and stayed for a week, left a detailed account of his visit, showing that along with enthusiasts for the principles of liberty, equality and communion of property, Owen's colony had attracted "a number of vagabonds and lazy worthless persons from all parts of the world, that would willingly live well at public expense, who had drank away the little money, if they had brought any at all, at the tavern, and who would not work, but desired to say a great deal."

In the New Harmony tavern Count Bernhard found a man who was "well aware of the present disorder of the town" but expected things soon to be different. This chance acquaintance—"very plainly dressed, about fifty years of age, rather of low stature"—proved, to the visitor's astonishment, to be Robert Owen himself. He became the Count's guide—taking him first to the old Rappite church where in a clatter under the peaked roof boys were learning carpentry and cobbling, then to Father Rapp's huge temple, now the Community Hall, still bearing over its stone doorway a carved and gilded rose with the inscription from Micah: "Unto thee shall come the golden rose, the first dominion." The hall was now devoted to music, dancing and public discussion. Schoolrooms, a library and a museum were to be walled off in parts of the cruciform building.

In the town mansion Count Bernhard was entertained by William Maclure, who genially recalled his studies and travels and friends in Germany in years gone by. There, over the teacups, he met lean old Professor Neef who talked of emancipation of Negroes and the necessity of atheism, a young ex-clergyman from Philadelphia who talked about the failures of the church, and the elderly Warner Lewis from Virginia who on the strength of a remote kinship with George Washington had been elected secretary of the Community of Equality. From the conversation of these officials Count Bernhard gathered that members of the colony were fretting under the frugal life required of them until the Community was fully established. One disgruntled group, led by an Irishman with a tangled beard, was talking about a departure for Mexico where, if they had the needed money, they could set up a colony of their own. Meanwhile they grumbled over the food and lodging at New Harmony.

In the evening Count Bernhard heard a concert—five instruments and several vocalists—and a series of poetry readings which included Lord Byron's stanzas to his wife after their separation. Social dancing followed the program, though some shirt-sleeved men preferred to read newspapers which strewed the side-tables. Even in this slack scene Count Bernhard could not escape the theory of the New Society. "An elderly French lady, who presides over the department of young mothers, and the nursing of all the very small children, stuck by my side during a large portion of the evening, and tormented me with her philosophical views."

In the following days the German visitor was taken through the schools, laboratories, shops, forge, furnaces, and factories. He encountered a Russian woman, native of St. Petersburg and widow of an American merchant, who "being somewhat eccentric and sentimental, quickly became attached to Mr. Owen's system." But now she complained of the low society of New Harmony and the lamentable table Owen provided. She was on the point of joining the Shaker settlement sixty miles up the Wabash.

Count Bernhard visited two outlying communities—Number Two, peopled by backwoods families who remembering the frenzy of their camp meetings disliked the prosaic atheism of New Harmony; and Number Three, a colony of English farmers who had left the English Prairie after Birkbeck's death—though attracted to Owen's system they objected to the motley cosmopolitanism of his town. Further conversations with Robert Owen deepened the Count's wonder. "He looks forward to nothing less than to remodel the world entirely, to root out all crime, to abolish all punishments, to create similar views and similar wants, and in this manner to avoid all dissension and warfare."

On his third evening in the village the Count followed the crowd to the Hall of Learning and heard Mr. Owen describe steam navigation, its prospective extension, improvement and advantages. During the discourse he observed "some tatterdemalions stretched themselves on the platform close by Mr. Owen. The better educated members kept themselves together, and took no notice of the others." Later he joined a gathering restricted to "the young ladies and gentlemen of *quality*" and took his place in a new dance figure called the "New Social System." It was the only glint of humor he found in New Harmony.

Before his visit was over the Count met a hermit who lived in the side of an Indian mound eight miles from the village. He had come to the Wabash from afar. After an adventurous youth in the Württemberg cavalry and in the Greek War for Independence, he followed Father Rapp's Separatists to America. But he did not march to work and to prayer with the Rappites. For ten years he lived with his

horse in the forest. Just a week before this meeting with
Bernhard, the hermit's horse had died. Now he lived alone,
looking down the Wabash from the top of his mound and
shaking his head over the godless community of Robert
Owen.

At the end of his visit Count Bernhard, swaying away
in a stage coach, looked back with a dubious mind at the
quiet village between the hills and the river. It seemed
more a reformers' convention than a town. "I can hardly believe that this society will have a long duration." His departure from the New Moral World did not reassure him. On
the first hill the horse refused to pull the load, and the passengers plodded up the hill ahead of the empty carriage.
Half a mile farther on, the coach overturned. Some passengers went back to New Harmony but Bernhard tramped on
sixteen miles to Mount Vernon, "over a very hilly road, in
five hours."

A year later New Harmony was a dwindling, weed-
grown town. Barns were empty, shops silent. Cattle roamed
the fields, sheep and hogs wandered off through broken
fences. Three separate communities had withdrawn to the
edges of Owen's land and organized their own societies. The
Gazette cheerfully reported that the exodus was forming vital branches of the New Society, vigorous offshoots from the
parent tree. "All minds seem now to comprehend the true
grounds of future cooperation, and all hearts have united in
claiming the benefit of Robert Owen's experience and
knowledge in reducing to practice the principles which form
the basis of our association. General satisfaction and individual contentment have taken the place of suspense and un-
certainty." The *Gazette* then listed names appropriate for
similar communities: Lovedale, Peace Glen, Everblest, New
Duty, Glee, Philosophy, Lovely, Voltaire, Platonea, Elysium,
Socrates, Utopia, Confucia, Powhatan, Olympus.

That spring Robert Owen was back again, seeing his
community dissolve. On Sunday, May 26th, 1827, he gathered the remnant in the Community Hall and gave them his

farewell. Most of his fortune had been spent, his model town was still a dream on paper. He had fallen out with his associates; now he was bringing James Dorsey from Miami University to organize a school on tamer theories than those of Neef and Maclure. With Maclure he had begun a tangled financial controversy. But he was not discouraged. "Industry, economy, beauty, order, and good feeling are silently and gradually growing up around you, and the right spirit of the great system, not derived from enthusiasm or imagination, but from a real knowledge of your own nature, and of your true interest, is gaining ground among you, and cannot fail soon to become general." He regretted that he could not continue to provide the best advantages for the children of the town.—"But having expended a large capital in putting you into your present independent condition; having paid for the whole of the real and personal property that I purchased since I came to this country, and having discharged every other debt, I do not yet know whether my remaining income will enable me, with the prudence that is necessary in my situation, to undertake to clothe, feed, and educate all your children without cost, or with such aid from your surplus produce as you can spare without inconvenience. Relying, however, upon the faithful stewardship of the parties in whose hands the remaining property which I possess here has been entrusted, I shall appropriate three thousand dollars this year toward defraying the expenses of this all-important subject, the general direction of which I leave to Mr. Dorsey, late treasurer of Miami University, in whose steadfastness, integrity, ability, and disinterested devotion to the cause I have full confidence. . . . When I return I hope to find you progressing in harmony together."

So his last word was harmony, and he never returned. He lectured in the East, planned a new colony in Texas, went back to England, spent the remainder of his fortune to advance the Cooperative Movement, grew deaf and distant, and took up Spiritualism as happily as he had once embraced the New Moral World. Meanwhile "For Sale" signs appeared on his Wabash lands. Some farms went to industrious settlers, some fell into the hands of speculators. Like all the American West, New Harmony was not heaven, but it was attractive real estate.

The New Moral World dissolved like a summer cloud over the Wabash. Some of its leaders went far away. Madame Fratageot followed Maclure to Mexico where they both died. Robert Dale Owen and Frances Wright went to New York, campaigned for universal education and edited the *Free Enquirer*. But the pretty village, the massive church, the solid granary and some of the mental ardors remained. The scientists stayed on, free from social equality and their turn to labor in the corn rows. Around them was the wild and beautiful country, with its mysterious variety to be explored. Gerard Troost tramped off to collect fossils in the creek beds. Lesueur explored the mounds of Indiana and gathered fish and mollusks from the western rivers. Thomas Say tended his exotic garden and worked in his study on the great *American Conchology*. The old Rappite granary housed a famed museum, with specimens from the Mediterranean to the Mississippi. To the quiet town on the Wabash came scientists from across the Atlantic: the chemist Samuel Bolton, the paleobotanist Leo Lesquereux, the great Scotch geologist Sir Charles Lyell. Prince Maximilian von Neuwied brought his party of explorers; from a base in New Harmony they ranged the western country, collecting birds, reptiles, ferns, flowers and Indian artifacts. For seventeen years, under the leadership of David Dale Owen, the U. S. Geological Survey operated from headquarters in New Harmony. Meanwhile old Joseph Neef played with his grandchildren on the sunny doorstep, while James Dorsey managed Owen's lands and supervised the village school.

Robert Dale Owen, publishing a Socialist paper in New York, had not forgotten his holdings on the Wabash. In 1830 he wrote to Dorsey like any hopeful landlord. "Does the town improve. Do the lots rise in value? . . . It comforts my heart to think you have at last got rid of such a nest of bad ones, as those that have pestered us for the last three years." In 1832 he was with his father in London, editing a reform weekly, *The Crisis*. But his thoughts were back in Indiana. To James Dorsey he wrote of his intention "to make New Harmony my *permanent* residence. After having revisited Europe, I know of no place, take it all together, that I prefer to Harmony." If not the New Moral World, the valley of the Wabash could still haunt a man's memory.

Robert Dale Owen came back to New Harmony, served notably in the Indiana legislature and the United States Congress, where he championed women's rights, free and universal schools, abolition of slavery and the creating of the Smithsonian Institution. He saw Indiana fill up with sober people, while the frontier moved on across the Mississippi. The town on the Wabash did slowly improve, and the lots rose in value.

PART V

ONCE A WILDERNESS

CHAPTER SIXTEEN

PADDLE WHEELS SPLASHING

The Children of Israel could scarcely have presented a more
motley array of men and women, with their "kneading troughs"
on their backs and their "little ones," than were here assembled,
on their way to the land of promise. To judge by the tone of
general conversation, they meant, in their generation, to plough
the Mississippi valley from its head to its foot. There was not
an idea short of it. What a world of golden dreams was there.

—HENRY ROWE SCHOOLCRAFT

IN THE summer of 1809 a comfortable houseboat drifted
down the Ohio and the Mississippi carrying Nicholas
James Roosevelt and his bride, Lydia Latrobe, on a honeymoon. It was a long, leisurely journey, past the new settlements and the silent shores, under the hills of Ohio and Indiana and between the long green coasts of the lower river.
They passed floating gristmills using the river current to
grind the settlers' corn, floating tinsmiths mending pots and
pans and kettles in the river towns, floating-store boats ped-
dling salt, soap, sugar, calico and muslin at the landings.
They saw the heavy keelboats freighting tobacco, pork, apples, cheese and whisky. They counted scores of flatboats,

known in the western vernacular as "broadhorns," laden with settlers, oxen, wagons, plows and bags of seed grain. Occasionally they passed a raft, big as a pasture, with a tent at one end and a haycock at the other; in between there was room for horses, pigs, poultry, and sometimes a bright green parakeet or a wild bronze turkey settled down on that moving island to feed with the hens. They were on the great highway of the west, and wherever he stopped Nicholas Roosevelt mystified the settlers by promising to return in a steamboat.

Roosevelt was forty-one that summer, old for a bridegroom. He had been busy from his boyhood and had just got round to marriage. His youth in New York City was filled with ardor for machines and mechanics; he was excited by everything that moved on wheels. At fifteen, between chores on a farm up the Hudson, he built a model boat with paddle wheels turned by an axle cord attached to springs of hickory and whalebone. A few years later he was in Philadelphia designing steam engines. To that city from London came Benjamin Henry Latrobe in 1798, and soon he was commissioned to create a Philadelphia water system. Nicholas Roosevelt built steam engines for the water works, and so he became acquainted with Latrobe's daughter. But his first love was mechanics and for the next ten years he was absorbed in experimenting with boilers and steam propulsion at his foundry in Belleville, New Jersey, just outside of Newark.

Meanwhile Robert Fulton of Pennsylvania, after studying painting in London under Benjamin West, had gone on to Paris where he launched his first steamboat in the Seine. The French Government was not interested in the patent, but Robert Livingston, U.S. Minister to France, became Fulton's backer and partner. Fulton returned to the United States. In 1807 he launched his triumphant *Clermont* in the Hudson.

When Nicholas Roosevelt married Latrobe's daughter, he also entered a partnership with Livingston and Fulton who planned to introduce steam navigation on the western rivers. The wedding journey down the Ohio and the Mississippi was a business trip for Roosevelt. He was gauging river currents, studying channels and landings, collecting figures on the river settlements and the river trade, and sampling political sentiment along the frontier. His partners had a fourteen-year monopoly for steam navigation in the western country.

Before the *Clermont's* triumph on the Hudson—New York to Albany and back in sixty-two hours—the steamboat had been dreamed of in the West. In Lexington, Kentucky, in 1790, Edward West was busy making clocks, silverware and a cure for rheumatism—a set of iron bands to fit wrists and ankles and to draw out the ailment by metallic attraction. He also invented a machine for making iron nails; his nails helped build Pittsburgh, Cincinnati and Louisville. Then, thinking of all the flatboats and keelboats that went down the rivers and could not get back, he began work on a miniature steamboat. In 1793 he had it ready, and a crowd gathered on the banks of South Elkhorn Creek. The tiny boiler hissed and seethed, the paddle wheels threshed the water. The boat churned steadily across the creek. But Edward West had no money to build a boat of commercial size, and men in Lexington doubted such a craft could navigate rough water. No one else had caught the fervor of West's dream. His model was sent to Washington where it amused some Congressmen. It was destroyed when the British burned the public buildings in 1814.

Another dream came to a more painful end in Kentucky on a summer night in 1798. That was the end of the lonely, uphill life of John Fitch who had envisioned fleets of steamboats carrying the commerce of the West. As a farm boy in Windsor township, Connecticut, John Fitch was weak and undersized. His father and his brother scorned him for shirking heavy farm work and for reading geography, astronomy and mathematics. He left home at fifteen, worked as a store clerk, a sailor on a coasting vessel, a clock-maker in the town of Windsor. He had the misfortune to marry a nagging wife (he called her "turbulent") and he made a failure of a potash factory. He left his wife in 1769 and was managing a Trenton gun factory at the outbreak of the Revolution. During the war he sold beer and tobacco to the Continental Army and invested in Virginia land warrants. In 1780 he went west to locate and survey his claims in Kentucky. There he was captured by Indians, turned over to the British, held for a year in Canada. On being exchanged, he went to Bucks County, Pennsylvania, and organized a company to acquire lands in the Ohio country. Though his plans failed, he helped to fix the government land policy of a regular survey of the public domain into mile-square sections.

His slow journey down the Ohio must have planted in his restless mind the dream of a steamboat, and his long idleness as an Indian captive gave it time to grow. In 1785, penniless but excited, he began work on a forty-five-foot boat with twelve long paddles, like an Indian war canoe, driven by steam power. He organized a company in Philadelphia and launched his craft in the Delaware River in 1887. It worked. The next year he launched a sixty-foot boat propelled by a paddle wheel. It carried thirty passengers between Philadelphia and Burlington, New Jersey. The public showed no interest, but Fitch found new backers and built a third and larger boat in 1790. Then a fourth boat—the *Perseverance*—was wrecked by a storm before its completion at Philadelphia and he could raise no more money; to support himself he peddled a map he had drawn of the Ohio country during his western wanderings. Finally he took his steamboat plans to France, but revolution-torn Paris had no time for a shabby American inventor. He worked his passage back to Boston as a common seaman, arriving ill and disheartened. After failure to raise money in New York, he thought of his claims in Kentucky. He came west, and found his land occupied by squatters. He took a room in a boarding house in the inland settlement of Bardstown. There he built a model of a steamboat which ran successfully on the town creek, but still no one would provide money to build the boat that would make history on the Ohio. On a summer night in 1798 he swallowed a glass of poison and his long dream was ended. He had written in his journal: "I know nothing so vexatious to a man's feelings as a turbulent wife and steamboat building." He was buried in a weedy cemetery behind the Bardstown jail.

Robert Fulton had no more genius than poor John Fitch, but he had better fortune. Behind his invention were powerful backers—Benjamin West and James Watt of England, Robert Livingston and his brother Edward, who after resigning the mayor's office in New York had become an eminent lawyer and land-owner in Louisiana, DeWitt Clinton, future father of the Erie Canal, and Daniel D. Tompkins, four-times governor of New York. After its demonstration on the Hudson, "Fulton's folly" was the wonder of the age, and Fulton and Livingston secured their monopoly for steamboating in the west. In 1810, back from his honeymoon survey of the rivers, Nicholas Roosevelt opened an office in Pittsburgh and began building for Fulton and Livingston the first steamboat beyond the mountains.

The western trade was ready for a new carrier. While Roosevelt's boat was building on the river bank at Pittsburgh, readers of *Niles' Register* found this account of frontier commerce:

Louisville, Ken., May 31, 1811,—
The following is an estimate of the boats and their loading which passed the falls of the Ohio (Louisville) from Oct. 5, 1810 to May 5, 1811

Boats	*number*	743
Flour	*barrels*	129,483
Bacon	*pounds*	604,810
Whisky	*barrels*	9,477
Cider	*ditto*	2,513
Pork	*ditto*	13,562
Apples	*ditto*	2,513

Oats	bushels	4,020
Corn	ditto	47,795
Merchandise		$355,624
Cheese	barrels	5,141
Beans	ditto	606
Plank	feet	1,483,130
Butter	pounds	24,641
Live hogs	number	908
Cider-royal	barrels	1,350
Lard	pounds	465,412
Onions	barrels	218
Potatoes	bushels	1,811
Hemp	Cwt.	630,562
Dry Fruit	barrels	263
Yarn & Cordage	pounds	113,015
Fowls	number	1,207,338
Shoe thread	pounds	2,592
Country linen	yards	8,140
Horses	number	292
Beer	barrels	277
Tobacco	hhds	2,311

and a number of articles too tedious to be calculated.

A Mr. Bowman, a pilot at Jeffersonville, took 106 boats over the falls of the Ohio, during the aforesaid period, of whose cargoes no notice is taken in the above.

The foregoing is a return made by the *regular* pilots, who agree in stating that during the high water at least one-third as many more passed without their assistance. This estimate, therefore, gives the whole probable number of boats that passed the Falls at nearly 1200, wafting the rich produce of the western parts of Pennsylvania and Virginia with those of the state of Ohio and a part of Kentucky,

to the markets of the sea-board. WHAT A PROS-
PECT!

On May 26th there arrived at Cincinnati the barge
Cincinnati from New Orleans with sugar, hides, crates and
logwood. It was a big craft, one hundred-foot keel, sixteen-
foot beam, rigged sloop fashion, sixty-four tons burden; at
Louisville eighteen men heaved and grunted to warp it over
the Falls. It had *sailed* from New Orleans in March, coming
up against the spring current, the first rigged vessel ever to
arrive on the Ohio from below. Commerce couldn't wait.

The year 1811 was a time of wonders in the West. That
spring the snows went off the Alleghenies under a warm south
wind and high water poured down the great valley. All the
Ohio rivers overflowed their banks; squatters and settlers
scrambled out of the bottoms while muddy waters drowned
their fields and swept their cabins on toward the Mississippi.
That summer a "cold plague" chilled the Ohio country
and hailstones as big as walnuts pelted the stunted crops.
Armies of gray squirrels moved south, rushing like wind
through the forest, swimming the Ohio in massed gray acres
and hurrying on into Kentucky. Vast flights of passenger
pigeons shadowed the sky; at the roosting places great trees
broke under their weight. In September an eclipse darkened
the sun and the night sky showed a comet with its ghostly
tail of fire. At Cincinnati, Jared Mansfield, Surveyor-General
in the West, set up his transit to measure the comet's path.

It was a restive year, a time of stirrings and strivings,
of urgencies and portents as though the future were hurrying into the wild dark country. The year ended with war
cries at Tippecanoe and war fever spreading across the nation. Then came the shuddering of earthquakes; they began
in the western country a week before Christmas and continued for two months. At Zanesville on a sleety February
day a tremor shook the stone statehouse and the steeple
wavered against the sky. Law-makers rushed across the legis-

lative hall, threw up windows and jumped out; committee-
men scrambled down the heaving stairs. At Springfield, over
in western Ohio, houses rocked and chimneys fell. "Glory to
God!" cried Sister Gardiner. "My Savior is coming!" For
hundreds of miles through the frontier buildings were
shaken, chimneys cracked and tumbled. Out on the coast of
Missouri the huge Mississippi threw up geysers of red mud
and changed its ancient course.

In this year of wonders Zadok Cramer in his *Naviga-
tor* wrote about the greatest wonder of all. "There is now on
foot a new mode of navigating our western waters, particularly the Ohio and the Mississippi rivers. This is with boats
propelled by the power of steam. . . . It will be a novel
sight, and as pleasing as novel to see a huge boat working her
way up the windings of the Ohio, without the appearance of
sail, oar, pole, or any manual labor about her—moving
within the secrets of her own wonderful mechanism, and
propelled by power undiscoverable!—This plan, if it suc-
ceeds, must open to view flattering prospects to an immense
country, an interior of not less than two thousand miles of as
fine a soil and climate as the world can produce, and to a
people worthy of all the advantages that nature and art can
give them. . . . The immensity of country we have yet to
settle, the vast riches of the bowels of the earth, the unexampled advantage of our water courses, which wind without
interruption for thousands of miles, the numerous sources
of trade and wealth opening to the enterprising and industrious citizens, are reflections that must rouse the most dull
and stupid."

At Pittsburgh men shouted, ropes creaked and hammers clattered as the big *New Orleans* grew on the landing.
One hundred and thirty-eight feet long, with a twenty-six-
and-a-half-foot beam, and twelve feet of depth in her hull,
she would carry three hundred and fifty tons. There was a
long cargo deck, a spacious cabin surmounted by a wheelhouse, a lofty smokestack and big paddle wheels. Accounts
of this wonder spread and grew. *Niles' Register* reported her

at the wrong place, under the wrong name, with exaggerated capacity. "A ship of 450 tons has lately been launched in the Scioto River! The steamboat of *Ohio* to carry 450 tons!!"

After a trial run on the Monongahela the big craft, painted blue as the Ohio sky, made ready for the long voyage to New Orleans. When it was known that Lydia Roosevelt planned to accompany her husband, Captain Roosevelt was begged not to risk his wife's life by letting her make the journey. At the end of October, with a flag fluttering from the jackstaff and a trumpet sounding from her wheelhouse, the *New Orleans* cast off. Steam seethed in the boilers, smoke puffed up from the chimney, paddle wheels churned the river; a crowd watched her disappear down the hill-framed river. Aboard were Captain Roosevelt and his wife, an engineer, a pilot, six deck hands, two serving women, a man waiter, and a cook. There was also Mrs. Roosevelt's big black Newfoundland dog, Tiger.

Cincinnati had no accommodations for so big a craft, and the steamboat anchored in the stream. Thousands came down the steep streets to look at her, and hundreds pulled out on skiffs to climb aboard. Woodmen brought out fuel on loading barges. Along the landing keelboatmen shook their shaggy heads over the steamboat and doubted it would ever reach the Mississippi.

Eight days from Pittsburgh, the steamer arrived at Louisville on a moonlit night, paddle wheels splashing, ranked portholes agleam, steam hissing from its boilers. Among the crowd jamming the river bank some thought the comet had plunged into the river. The Roosevelts were escorted ashore to a lavish dinner; in return they entertained the Louisville officials with a steamboat dinner and took them on a short run up the river.

While they waited for high water to run the falls, a child was born to Lydia Roosevelt. At the end of November, after a heavy rain, the *New Orleans* got up steam, steered into the current and ran swiftly through the foaming chute. The falls were considered the chief hazard, but a greater was coming. In the Mississippi, near New Madrid, Missouri, the steamboat met the earthquake. The river banks heaved and trembled. The earth opened into fissures, erupting clouds of sand and water. Islands disappeared, the wind brought gaseous vapors, the sun hung dully in a hazed gray sky. But the steamboat kept on her way. Rolling through the heaving water she steamed on toward New Orleans.

For two years this pioneer steamboat ran passengers and cargo between New Orleans and Natchez. It made a profit of $25,000 on the first year's operation, and its entire cost had been earned before the summer of 1814 when it struck a snag and foundered in the lower Mississippi. At that time Fulton and Livingston had a second steamer building at Pittsburgh, under supervision of Benjamin H. Latrobe. Late in 1814 the *Vesuvius,* 340 tons, took over the Natchez-New Orleans trade. Other craft followed—the *Aetna* on a Natchez-Louisville schedule and the *Buffalo* running between Louisville and Pittsburgh.

The steamboat had come to stay, and soon the Fulton-Livingston monopoly was disputed by frontier enterprise. Or, rather, it was ignored. Western builders launched steamboats—the *Comet,* the *Enterprise,* the *Zebulon M. Pike,* the *Despatch,* the *G. Washington.* The *Enterprise,* under Captain Henry M. Shreve, steamed from Pittsburgh to New Orleans where it helped Andrew Jackson defeat the British. Then Captain Shreve headed his craft upstream against high water in the spring of 1815. Twenty-five days from New Orleans the *Enterprise* stood panting at the Louisville landing. The currents had been conquered.

Nicholas Roosevelt had retired, going to live in the serene town of Skaneateles, beside one of the Finger Lakes in western New York, but shipyards were busy in a dozen towns on the Ohio. Between 1817 and 1820 sixty steamboats were launched in the western rivers. By 1837 three hundred steamers kept the frontier commerce moving—pork, whisky, apples, cheese, flour going down the rivers; coffee, sugar, rice, molasses, cotton coming back. In plush cabins tourists

mixed with planters, merchants, army officers, land speculators. Below them, amid bags and bales of cargo, milled the
deck passengers—immigrants, movers, farmers, laborers and
flatboatmen coming back from Natchez and New Orleans.

Deck fare cost a fraction of cabin fare—one-fifth of it
in the early 1830s, when a man could travel on deck from
Louisville to New Orleans, thirteen hundred miles, for four
dollars. Down there at the water line swarmed the crude life
of the frontier—men, women and children in wadmal, buckskins, and homespun, sleeping on planks or boxes, cooking
at an open-mouthed stove, crowding the rails in fine weather
and huddling against the boiler bulkhead when the river fog
blew in. Anyone could travel in the western country.

Even the low deck fare was reduced for a man who
would work with the wood gang. "Wood-pile, wood-pile,
where are the wooders?" cried the mate at any hour of day
or night, and the wood gang scrambled ashore. A shrewd
Scotch traveler, James Logan, gave an account of his part-
time labor from St. Louis to Pittsburgh: "The most dis-
agreeable part of the business was carrying the wood from
the banks of the Mississippi. The first time I tried it was
after having lain down on the floor, with nothing between
me and the boards, as near to the stove as I could get, and
covered myself with a single blanket . . . when about midnight, having fallen into a sound sleep, I was roused by the
mate. I started with the rest, about twenty. A plank was
thrown out, resting on the shore, which presented a perpendicular bank nearly twenty feet high, up which we had to
go by candle-light. Following the example of my companions, I placed four or five pieces on my shoulder, and trudged
warily along the narrow plank. We took in about six cords,
and had no more wood to carry until next forenoon. This
second trial was worse than the first. The bank was higher,
and between it and the water was a space covered with mud
of about fifteen feet. We pitched the wood down upon this
place, which was so soft that many of the billets sank out of
sight and several others were trampled down in carrying the

rest. We were obliged to make a path by laying down blocks, which we replaced by others as they sunk. This was the worst wooding place on our whole route. We carried in about six cords, and were employed about an hour, whereas at the previous turn we had accomplished our task in half that time. The labor was excessive and caused profuse perspiration, but I continued at it until finished. On our reaching the Ohio, we found the task much easier, as there were generally large scows waiting, which were fastened to the steamer, which continued running whilst we were employed in throwing out the wood into the boat, where others piled it up. The labour increased at Louisville, on account of the diminished number of passengers. One night I was called up twice to wood, once at twelve, the other time at two o'clock."

On a thirteen-day trip this deck-passenger earned a reduction of one dollar in his fare by stumbling out to the woodyard at twenty-five places on the Ohio. It was a strenuous way to save a dollar, but the deckers were willing. Even immigrant women sometimes joined the wood gang. "German women, fresh from Europe," wrote an observer, "were only too glad 'to wood,' and we have seen them . . . clean out a wood yard in a short time."

The deckers had a more strenuous life than the cabin passengers, and they made a more hazardous journey. Close to the water and to the boilers, they were the inevitable victims of collision or explosion. When the *Helen McGregor* exploded near Memphis in 1830, the forty fatalities were all "on deck." In the explosion of the *Majestic* in 1835, sixty German immigrants were killed. When the *Moselle* and the *Orlando* blew up in 1838, two hundred deck passengers were lost.

Disasters were common in the early steamboat trade. In 1817 the pioneer *Zebulon M. Pike* churned up to St. Louis, the first steam vessel in the upper Mississippi. By 1840 the *Pike*, number eight, and the *Ben Franklin*, number seven, were calling at St. Louis; all their predecessors had been burned, wrecked or exploded. Boats did not grow old on the western rivers.

But the trade grew prodigiously, and the West grew with it. In the keelboat age goods were brought over the mountains and delivered in Cincinnati at a cost of eight dollars a hundred pounds. On steamers the same products came up the rivers from New Orleans at one dollar per hundredweight. The frontier produce had a cheap and ready market, and new waves of settlers streamed into the public lands. The population of Ohio doubled in the 1820s. Indiana's population trebled in the ten years following statehood in 1816. Immigrants and movers crowded the steamboat landings, hills of cargo rose on the levees. Pittsburgh began making iron products and sending them down the great valley. Wheeling shipped out flour, glass, pottery and paper. Cincinnati, the prodigy of the West, became "Porkopolis." In 1817 a talkative Cincinnati barber told a newcomer: "Now, sir, in dull times when money is scarce these hogs . . . are not weighed—they are not counted—they are *measured*, sir—not individually but aggregately; measured by the lot and sold by the acre. So much for a lot of five acres and so much for a lot of ten acres. The western people, sir, love to do business upon a great scale, and this selling hogs by the acre suits their mind." Some acres of live hogs were shipped by steamboat, but most were slaughtered and packed in "Porkopolis." The steamboat delivered barreled pork and lard and bagged hams and bacons a thousand miles away. The Ohio, river of the western wilderness, was becoming the highway of the nation.

In 1835 the steamboat *Alpha* left Rising Sun, Indiana, to load a cargo that signified the end of an era. The *Alpha* steamed up the Tennessee to Florence, Alabama, where two keelboats were lashed to its sides. Aboard filed 511 abject Creek Indians with blanketed bundles on their backs. They were being moved to Indian Territory, beyond the Mississippi. The *Alpha* tied up every night of the long journey;

the Indians went ashore, cooked their ration of corn and
beans and bacon, and made camp. Next morning they were
on the way again. On the 2nd of January, 1836, the *Alpha*
pushed into the Arkansas River. There one of the keelboats
struck a snag and foundered; two hundred frightened Indians crowded onto the steamer. At last they reached Fort
Smith in Indian Territory. While the exiles marked out a
village far from their ancestral lands, the *Alpha* took on
twenty-five barrels of pecans and headed home to Indiana,
the white man's country.

Ohio had two coasts—a hill-framed river and a sky-
lined lake. In 1818 the first Great Lakes steamer, *Walk-in-
the-Water,* plodded over empty Lake Erie, trailing its woodsmoke from Buffalo to Cleveland and Detroit. In the summer
of 1819 it made a voyage to far-off Michilimackinac with
a hundred passengers and $200,000 in cargo. That pioneer
steamer ran aground a few miles out of Buffalo on a stormy
autumn night in 1821. But already the *Superior* was building and soon, throbbing with the engine salvaged from the
wrecked *Walk-in-the-Water,* it took up the Lake Erie schedule. For years the *Superior* carried settlers to northern Ohio,
Michigan, Indiana and Illinois. When the Erie Canal was
opened in 1825 the Great Lakes were wedded to the ocean.
Immediately Lake Erie became a throughway to the West
and the lake trade was the fastest-growing business in America. Thousands of immigrants stepped out of canal barges
at Buffalo and looked westward over the wide waters. In
Buffalo harbor lake boats were unloading fish, furs, corn and
wheat. When they steamed back up the lake they carried the
founders of new settlements in the western woods and prairies.

In the spring of 1830 a Buffalo shipping company announced a line of six steamers that would maintain a daily
schedule between Buffalo, Cleveland and Detroit. The *Superior, William Penn, Niagara, William Peacock, Enterprise*
and *Henry Clay* plied the waters of Lake Erie with "strict
and unremitting attention to the accommodation of immi-

grants going west." In June of 1833 Daniel Webster, on a tour to the western states, stopped at Buffalo to christen a new ship named for him. Standing under an eagle-crowned flag and a rippling banner bearing the words *Liberty and union, now and forever, one and inseparable,* his long hair blowing in the lake wind, the massive statesman recalled an earlier picture of the West. "Eight years ago [when the Erie Canal was opened] I enjoyed a brief visit to this place. There was then but one steamboat on Lake Erie; it made its passage once in every ten or fifteen days. . . . There are now eighteen steamboats plying the lake, all finding full employment." He went on to describe the astonishing growth of commerce on the lakes—"a new source of national prosperity, and a new bond of national union."

That year three thousand barges were shuttling back and forth on the Erie Canal. They left Albany at every hour, day and night, loaded with plows and axes, chains and harness, or jammed with immigrants and their belongings. At Buffalo the immigrants thronged the waterfront. In the grain schooners they saw men knee-deep in golden wheat, scooping it up with shovels, spilling it in the water and scattering it on deck, as though there were untold quantities where it came from. The peasants from Norway and Scotland, from Germany and Holland, could hardly wait to get to the region of such rich harvests.

In the fall of 1833 the one-legged traveler Charles Fenno Hoffman limped onto the stage coaches and steamboats of the west, jostled settlers, speculators, traders and immigrants, kept his eyes and ears open. He was a frontier news correspondent, sending back to the *New York American* letters full of humor, color and vivid human interest. He rode a stage from Pittsburgh to Cleveland; after two hundred miles of forest-walled roads he looked over Lake Erie "like one who has come out of a pent-up chamber into the full and free air of heaven." Cleveland, with the inland commerce pouring out of the Ohio Canal, was a different place from the crude garrison town that William Henry Harrison had inspected in 1813, or the village where Irad Kelley had operated the Post Office in his store in 1820. "Building lots," reported the correspondent, "command now as many thousands as they did hundreds of dollars five years since. The town which can already boast of a public library, a fine church, two capital taverns, and many handsome private dwellings, is laid out with broad streets and a spacious square in the center. The business part is as yet beneath the bluff, where a single winding street runs along the bank of the river towards the lake; but the main street above is already the scene of much bustle, and bears about the same relation to that below as Broadway does to Southstreet in New-York city."

On his third evening in Cleveland, Hoffman limped out of the reading room of the Franklin Hotel and up to his own chamber. Just then a clangor of bells came up from the harbor. It was his ship, the *New York,* off-schedule in the stormy autumn season. After cramming clothes into his trunk he got downstairs in time to board the waiting carry-all. In the windy darkness they rattled down steep streets to the quay. It was a wild and gusty night, torches flaring, lanterns jerking along the jetty, shadows grappling over boxes and barrels on the landing. Above the rumble of wheels and the slap of water rose the voices of the western country—the cries of stevedores, the shouts of ship's officers and the clamor of immigrants "screaming to each other in half as many languages as were spoken at Babel."

With a last shout from the wheelhouse the wet lines came aboard, steam roared, the paddle wheels churned black water. Soon Cleveland was a smolder of stars in the darkness, with the jetty light fading over the windy lake.

That night Captain Fisher showed the newspaper man around the ship by lantern light, and gave Hoffman his best story: "Our course first led us through a group of emigrants collected around a stove, mid-ships, where an English mother nursing her infant, a child lying asleep upon a mastiff, and a long-bearded German smoking his meerschaum on the top of a pile of candle-boxes, were the only complete figures I could make out from an indefinite number of heads, arms, and legs lying about in the most whimsical confusion. Passing farther on, we came to two tolerable cabins on either side of the boat just forward of the wheels, both pretty well filled with emigrants, who were here more comfortably bestowed. We next passed the forward bar-room (there being another abaft for cabin-passengers), and finally came to the bow, of which a horse and several dogs had already been the occupants for so many days,—the New-York having been twice driven into port and delayed by stress of weather,—that it might have been mistaken for either stable or kennel. We next ascended a steep stairway to the upper deck of all, and I here spent some moments rather amusingly in surveying the furniture of the emigrants with which it was crowded. They differed according to the origin of their owner. The effects of the Yankee were generally limited to a Dearborn wagon, a feather-bed, a saddle and bridle, and some knick-knack in the way of a machine for shelling corn, hatchelling flax, or, for aught I know, manufacturing wooden nutmegs for family use. Those of the Englishman are far more numerous; for John Bull, when he wanders from home, would not only, like the roving Trojan, carry his household gods with him into strange lands, but even the fast-anchored isle itself, could he but cut it from its moorings. Whenever, therefore, you see an antique-fashioned looking-glass, a decrepit bureau, and some tenderly-preserved old china, you will probably, upon looking further, have the whole house-keeping array of an honest Briton exposed to your view.

"But still further do the Swiss and Germans carry their love of family relics. Mark that quaint-looking wagon which lumbers up a dozen square feet of the deck. It might be worth something in a museum, but it has cost five times its value in freight to transport it over the Atlantic. What an indignity it is to overwhelm the triumphal chariot with the beds and ploughs, shovels, saddles, and sideboards, chairs, clocks, and carpets that fill its interior, and to hang those rusty pots and kettles, bakepans, fryingpans, and sauce-pans, iron candlesticks, old horse-shoes, and broken tobacco-pipes, like trophies of conquest over Time, along its racked and wheezing sides. That short man yonder, with square shoulders and a crooked pipe in his mouth, is the owner; he, with the woollen cap, that is just raising his blue cotton frock to thrust hand into the fob of his sherrivalleys. That man had probably not the slightest idea of the kind of coun-try he was coming to. His eyes are but now just opening to his new condition; nor will he sacrifice a particle of his use-less and expensive trumpery until they are completely open. That man has not yet a thought in common with the people of his new abode around him. He looks, indeed, as if he came from another planet. Visit him on his thriving farm ten years hence, and, except in the single point of language, you will find him (unless he has settled among a nest of his countrymen) at home among his neighbours, and happily conforming to their usages; while that clean-looking Eng-lishman next to him will still be a stranger in the land."

At the far end of Lake Erie was the bustling town of Detroit, gateway to the new settlements in Michigan and hub of roads leading to northern Indiana and Illinois. Masts of sailing ships and stacks of steamers rose above its river front. Life swarmed up Woodward Avenue and Griswold Street—merchants, speculators, army men, horse and cattle traders, westward-moving Yankees and the polyglot tide of immigrants. In the month of May, 1833, ninety steamboats arrived at Detroit, each one bringing hundreds of eager set-tlers to the west. In a single day five thousand persons took passage out of Buffalo. During the navigation season of 1836, two hundred thousand land-seekers passed through De-troit. By wagon and ox-cart, on horseback and afoot they pushed on to the public lands.

By 1840 the urgent immigrant trade moved on past Detroit; it steered up the long seaway of Lake Huron, through the straits of Mackinac, and down Lake Michigan. It was a long way from Buffalo to Sheboygan, Manitowac, Milwaukee, Racine and Chicago, and a man had time, day after day watching the changing shores, to wonder about the land he would make his own. Old World peasants in homespun shawls and blouses counted their coins in secret and stared again at the wide new country with its endless tracts of public land. Public land! In the countries of Europe land was for the great families. But the New World held land for all with the will to possess it. Their minds repeated the promises. *A day's labor in this country will buy an acre of wild land. . . . A man can make four Norwegian dollars a day working on the canal. He can soon pay for a quarter-section of public land and begin farming for himself. . . . The land is level and the soil is deep. It yields richly from the first season.* Staring from the rail with their minds working, these people had many memories—a steep valley in Norway, a gray fishing town in Ireland, the dyke-walled fields of Holland, the moorsides of Scotland, a cobbled village street in Germany or Sweden. But they shared a common hope. Beyond the blue waters in a new country they would mark the corners of their land and bring the fields to harvest.

Some of them did not drive their corner stakes. On a windless summer night in 1841 the steamship *Erie,* bound from Buffalo to Chicago, exploded in the middle of Lake Erie. As smoke and flame swept through the passageways, two hundred immigrants struggled to reach the upper decks. Some suffocated in the heat and smoke, others leaped into the lurid water. Fourteen years later a salvage tug brought up the sunken hull. From it came thousands of foreign coins: sovereigns and francs, marks and kroner that had left the Old World to buy American land. There were many disasters—the *Phoenix* burning on a November night in Lake Michigan with two hundred fifty Hollanders aboard, the big new *Atlantic* with five hundred passengers rammed by the *Ogdensburg* on a foggy night in Lake Erie, the *G. P. Griffith* burning like a torch just before a June daybreak a few miles out of Cleveland.

But multitudes of new citizens claimed their future in the wilderness. Between 1830 and 1840 the population of Michigan grew from 31,000 to 212,000, and in the next decade Wisconsin grew from 30,000 to 300,000. On the lake shores and along the rivers grew the towns of Norway, Brussels, Germantown, Denmark, Holland, Vriesland, and Vreeland.

With the Ohio, the upper Mississippi and the Great Lakes, the Northwest was girdled by water. In the years of the great land rush the waterways brought the founders of new counties and new commonwealths. By 1840 it was common for Eastern travelers and European visitors to make a "grand tour" of the west, going by steamboat down the Ohio, up the Mississippi, and back by way of Mackinac, Detroit and Niagara. They saw the public lands filling up with private enterprise, men of many nations becoming a new nation as they cleared the forests and plowed the prairie sod.

CHAPTER SEVENTEEN

TOLLGATE AND TOWPATH

It is said that, many years since, some persons in Spain proposed to the government to cut a canal across a part of the country, for the purpose of rendering the transportation of goods more cheap and easy. The subject was referred to a council of monks, who, after solemn deliberation, declared it as their opinion that, if Heaven had designed that water should flow in the proposed route, a natural channel would have been provided for it. This was thought a sacred opinion . . . and the project was abandoned. But the people of this country take a different view of the matter.

—PETER PARLEY: *Tales About the United States of America*

Roads and canals are veins and arteries to the body politic that diffuse supplies, health, vigor, and animation to the whole system.

—ETHAN ALLEN BROWN

O N THE Fourth of July, 1825, the settlers came streaming in by every road, trace, trail and forest path. It was more than a band concert and a Congressman that emptied the clearings of Belmont and Licking Counties. Two celebrations enlivened that day in the Ohio country—one in a brushy field at the head of the Licking River, the other, seventy-five miles east, in the hillside village of St. Clairsville. Early on that summer morning the two crowds gathered—horses, mules, and ox-teams, wagons, carts, and carriages, old and young, men and women, children and dogs. After years of talking, arguing, figuring, surveying, and legislating, two historic projects were on the way. What brought

325

the crowds in buckskin, homespun and broadcloth was a man with a spade.

In front of the spired courthouse at St. Clairsville, while late-comers crowded the dusty street, a relay of Ohio Assemblymen filled the warm air with the magic phrase "internal improvements." The Cumberland Road, begun at Cumberland, Maryland, in 1811, had reached over the mountains to Wheeling on the Ohio by 1818. Now, seven impatient years later, after hotly argued surveys and federal acts providing revenue from the sale of public lands, the great highway was to cross the central counties of Ohio. Already, while only surveyors' stakes and blazes marked its way through the wilderness, the road was talked about in every tavern, blacksmith shop and trading post. People called it the Old Pike, the Great Western Road, Uncle Sam's Road, the National Road; it was the federal government's first highway project. Now, to the restless crowd at St. Clairsville, it was Ohio's Road. It would run west toward the setting sun, bringing life, trade and prosperity to the inland country, linking the western people to the seaboard.

With a final burst of oratory from the courthouse steps and a blast of band music from under the dusty maple trees, the first road-builder's spade was pressed into the Ohio earth. After a noisy picnic on the courthouse square the settlers rocked home, over stumps and roots and boulders. But they saw a straight broad highway, smooth as a barn floor, leading over the Ohio hills. The sale of the public domain would pay for the labor of thousands of teamsters, diggers, graders, and in every township that it touched the Road would magically multiply the value of land.

On that same day the settlers of Licking County followed a marching company of militiamen, a mounted troop of cavalry and a file of mud-splashed carriages to a field three miles southwest of the county seat of Newark. There the troops stood at parade while Governor DeWitt Clinton of New York, "father of the Erie Canal," stepped out beside Governor Jeremiah Morrow of Ohio. Tall and powerful, with a broad, determined face that generations later would scowl from every package of American cigarettes, Governor Clinton sank a gleaming spade into the muddy ground. Licking County was soggy from a three-day rain. He raised a dark chunk of earth and dropped it into a canal wheelbarrow. Governor Morrow added a second spadeful. Captain Ned King, of Chillicothe, sweating in his militia woolens, lifted the third bite of earth, and then the spade was passed among the frock-coated men in Governor Clinton's party. While thousands cheered, Captain King, still buttoned up to the chin, wheeled the load away. Tom Ewing of Lancaster—he would be President Harrison's Secretary of the Treasury fifteen years later—mounted a plank stand and began an oration on the future of the West. To protect the speaker from the crowd a square of horse troops surrounded the platform. All the horse flies of Licking County were on hand, and Tom Ewing's speech was lost in the stamp and swish of the horses. That evening in a Newark tavern, reviewing the activities of the great day, Caleb Atwater commented: "I suppose it was all right to have the horses in front of the speaker's stand, for they cannot read and we can."

Anyone who could read soon knew that construction had begun on the "Roaring Canal," the great Ohio waterway which would link the Ohio River with Lake Erie. It would provide, by way of the Erie Canal just opened across New York state, a route for western produce to the eastern markets. From the river landing at Portsmouth to the harbor of Cleveland, it would bring the jangle of trace chains on the towpath, the call of barge horns at the locks, and to all the inland counties a living flow of trade.

Straight as a wagon tongue toward the west, over streams and river valleys, through woods and across the scattered prairies, ran the National Road. Westward went the clamor of ax and shovel, the creak of harness and the knock of wagon wheels, the clink of log chain and the clatter of scoop-buckets. From Bridgeport on the Ohio the road was completed through St. Clairsville to Cambridge in 1827. It was open to Zanesville in 1830, to Columbus in 1833, to Springfield in 1838. It crossed the Indiana boundary in 1840. At last it spanned the Wabash at Terre Haute, and entered Illinois—a dusty track through a magnificence of waving grass. In 1850 it reached its western terminus, the old Illinois capitol of Vandalia.

Behind the noise of construction came the noise of commerce—hoofbeats on the macadam road, drovers shouting at sheep, hogs and cattle, stage horns blaring, bells shaking from the hames of six-horse teams ahead of the rumbling Conestogas. In 1832 the Zanesville tollkeeper tallied the new traffic: 35,310 men on horseback, 16,750 horses and mules driven, 24,410 sheep driven, 52,845 hogs driven, 96,323 cattle driven, 14,907 one-horse carriages, 11,613 two-horse carriages and wagons, 2,357 wagons with more than two horses. Tollgates barred the road every ten miles, with a tollman's cottage beside each barrier. The tolls ranged from thirty cents for a Pennsylvania wagon with ten thousand pounds of freight lashed under its canopy to one cent for a driven cow. Hog drivers paid a cent for every five hogs in their swarming, grunting drove. By 1838 tollgates in Ohio were collecting two hundred dollars a day.

The freight was carried in big canvas-covered wagons. With red wheels, blue side-boards, and white canopy, they were as patriotic as a national banner. Past them rattled the light express carts and the fast stage coaches, with passengers watching the flying landscape from side windows and the driver swaying on his lofty box.

Western stages, carrying six to ten passengers, were fitted with sand boxes, mud skirts, fluid lamps, boot and bag footboards. Their door panels showed scenes of forest and mountain, a sunburst, a national emblem, or a portrait of Andrew Jackson, Henry Clay or William Henry Harrison. They were named like steamboats—*Keystone State, Buckeye*

State, Empire State, Granite State, New Orleans, Natchez, Queen City, Cumberland, Potomac, General Lafayette, Colonel Benton, General Harrison, Ivanhoe, Rob Roy, Lochinvar. The driver, arrogant as any steamboat captain, wore a red vest, peaked cap and yellow buckskin gloves; in winter he wrapped himself in buffalo robes and a bearskin cap.

By 1840 half a dozen stage lines ran rival schedules across Ohio—the Ohio State Company, the People's Line, the Citizens' Line, the Pioneer Line, the Defiance Line, and the Good Intent Line which advertised teetotaling drivers and urged its travelers to abstain from alcoholic drink. For one season, in 1836-37, a pony express, with mail stuffed in the saddlebags, dashed past the drovers, peddlers, freighters and coachmen.

Beyond Richmond, Indiana, the road was rough and strenuous, but the traffic kept coming. Straight through Indianapolis, past the new Hoosier statehouse, came powerful Pennsylvania teams and freight wagons, wiry Maryland ponies with "shake guts" carts, bony southern horses drawing Carolina traps and buckboards, occasionally a roofed shanty on wheels with children peering through a window and supper smoke sifting from the chimney. The town joker, watching one of these house-wagons pass, looked down the road to see if the barns and outhouses would fetch up the rear.

For hundreds of miles along the Main Street of the West, farmers hung out signs—MOVERS ACCOMMODATED ... TRAVELERS' REST ... MOVERS TAKEN IN HERE. At first any shelter on the long road was a "tavern," but soon the stage coaches pulled up at travelers' inns where food and fire were waiting. Wagon houses accommodated the freight teamsters with a long dining table, a big fireplace and a common sleeping room under the roof; outside was a gashed and trampled wagon yard and in back a stable for the teams. In inns, depots, taverns and stables placards announced land for sale and described the attractions of townsites (some of them still unpeopled) along the pike. Uncle Sam's Road poured life into the new country.

Each year the freight commerce increased—farmers hauling corn, wheat, tobacco; droves of hogs, sheep and cattle filling the eighty-foot roadway; the big Conestogas bringing muslin and calico, hoes and hinges, buckets and kettles, earthware and ironware. The covered wagons came with music. Each horse carried a set of bells, treble for the lead horse, a mellow bass for the wheel horses, mounted on an arched frame over the harness collar. "I'll be there with bells on!" was a wagoner's cheerful cry as he mounted his box and gathered up the reins. While the country rolled past, field and forest, hill and valley, swamp and meadow, he sang to the chiming bells and the rumbling wheels.

> *When first I went a-waggoning,*
> *A-waggoning did go—*

At night in the wagon house he devoured a big supper, downed a mug of Old Monongahela, and stretched himself by the fire. With other drivers he discussed political questions, traded news of the road, and damned all canal boats and their crews.

Famous men traveled the stage lines on the Great Western Road—Henry Clay, Tom Corwin, Tom Ewing, Governor Cass, General Harrison. But the pike's prophetic commerce was the great tide of immigrants. In 1840 Ohio, with a million and a half people, was the third state in the Union; Indiana had nearly seven hundred thousand, Illinois almost half a million. In Ohio one tenth of the public land was still for sale, in Indiana one fifth, in Illinois one half. To those tracts of wilderness came thousands of one-horse wagons with family goods jammed between the sideboards. On the driver's seat a woman held a child in her lap. The man walked at the horse's head, the children trailed behind. Somewhere in the western country they would stop at a district land office. On the wall they would see the public lands marked out in timbered sections, prairie sections, grass-and-wooded sections, rolling lands and flat lands, ridges and river bottoms. They would make their choice, count out their money, and find their corners. A few seasons later their corn and wheat would rumble over the Road that had brought them there.

The National Road was the road of capitals. It began at Washington and Baltimore; it led through Columbus, Indianapolis and Vandalia, pouring its commerce past the porticoes of three western statehouses. The road was laid out, though unimproved, to Vandalia in 1839 when the Illinois government was moved to Springfield. Then Vandalia was left drowsing in the summer sun, and the great road lost its traffic to the new smoke-puffing locomotive. Still families of movers creaked in to Vandalia, and an occasional caravan rocked on over sixty rough miles to St. Louis. But the road was no longer Uncle Sam's broad highway; federal appropriations had ended in 1838. Vainly Indiana and Illinois petitioned Congress. Senator Tom Corwin of Ohio called for extension of the road to the Mississippi, but the expanding West was already draining off the trade and population of the southern states. Southern Congressmen, arguing States' Rights, insisted that internal improvements were a local issue. So the National Road was relinquished to the states, and there was no money in the state treasuries to maintain and extend it. By 1850 its great years had ended, and railroad trains were rumbling past the old wagon stations.

But at the end of the road, in the dreaming old statehouse grounds where young Abe Lincoln had stretched his long legs under a Congressman's bench, the memory remained. The motor age of the twentieth century brought the road to new life as U.S. 40, with a race of travel that dwarfed the commerce of the old pike. But the ghosts were there. Around the old Vandalia statehouse hung echoes of teamsters' cries, the clatter of hoofs and the rumble of iron-tired wheels, and the creaking of movers' wagons rolling toward the West. There in 1928 was erected the Madonna of the Trail, a woman in pioneer dress with a child in her arms and another at her side. She looks at the race of trucks and motor cars, but what she sees is a wild and empty country with its future yet to come.

In 1797 Moses Warren, surveyor for the Connecticut Land Company, measured the old portage path at the present site of Akron. He found the Cuyahoga and Tuscarawas rivers 644.55 chains apart—just eighty-eight paces over eight miles. A few years later at the headwaters of the Licking, surveyors measured the shorter portage to the Scioto. Over these two heights of land and along the winding rivers the Ohio Canal was projected, and after years of controversy and debate the first ceremonious earth was dug at Licking Summit in 1825. When it was completed, in 1833, the Ohio River was joined to Lake Erie. It was an ancient route of commerce, used by the Indians before there was a land warrant or a land office in all that country.

By 1825 one-sixth of Ohio was under cultivation. The settled areas lay along the southern rivers, the Muskingum, Scioto and Miami. Development of the inland country waited upon internal improvements. Roads and canals would transform the wilderness. When the National Road was projected across central Ohio and the Ohio Canal promised prosperity to the eastern counties, a second canal was projected in the west, to link Cincinnati and Toledo by way of the Miami and Maumee river valleys. This, too, was an old canoe route of the Indians and traders.

On his Ohio visit in 1825 DeWitt Clinton pressed a second spade into the ground. Two weeks after the gala Fourth of July at Licking Summit, the New York governor was welcomed at Middletown on the Miami and escorted to a field a mile south of the village. On a flag-draped platform, above blaring bands, uniformed militiamen and a crowd of Miami Valley settlers, he took his place with Governor Morrow and General William Henry Harrison. After the speech-making the dignitaries stepped down and each of them "raised a sod" where the Miami Canal would soon carry the region's commerce. Butler County settlers scrambled for that symbolic earth. They clutched it in their hands and crammed it in their pockets. Home to their clearings they carried fistfuls of that first excavation. They had a fruitful land around them, but the canal would make it ten times richer.

Soon the Miami Valley newspapers were printing bold advertisements: *Valuable land for sale . . . fronting on the canal. For sale lots . . . on Canal Street and the Basin . . . valuable. Building lots in the town of Dayton advantageously situated for business . . . on the Basin connected with the Miami Canal. Businessmen who wish to make profitable speculation, take notice.* Outside of town and away from the canal banks it was the same story. Farmland worth five dollars an acre in the early 1820s sold for twenty dollars when the canal came through.

The western settlers had a rich country—"Tickle the earth with a hoe and it laughs into harvest"—but a remote one. It could produce boundless crops of corn, wheat, tobacco, pork and wool, but its one natural highway, the Ohio, flowed west, away from the American market. The Ohio and the Mississippi carried the western harvest to New Orleans, where some of it was consumed and the rest was loaded into ships for the long voyage to Baltimore, Philadelphia and New York. In the summer of 1812 James McBride of Hamilton on the Miami River formed a partnership with Joseph Hough to take a cargo of flour, whisky and apples to New Orleans. After weeks of whittling pegs, hauling planks and putting them together, they had a flatboat ready. It was a floating box, eighteen by eighty feet, deep enough to hold six tiers of barrels down the center under the peaked roof, five tiers elsewhere. Six feet of low-roofed deck on their stern made up their cabin, which soon reeked of apples, potatoes, frying pork and drying clothes. With their load aboard, McBride and Hough pushed off from the Hamilton landing. Poled, paddled and "cooned" along by hand-power, their clumsy craft crept past the shoals, bends and bars of

the Miami. It moved between big cooper shops and packing
sheds in Cincinnati and swung into the Ohio's current. Weeks
later they peddled cargo, a few barrels at a time, at landings on the Mississippi, and sold the rest at New Orleans. It
was a long trip to market and they had a long trip home,
riding horseback through the gloomy Natchez Trace and over
the hills of Kentucky. Next year, if the autumn rains were
enough, they would float another flatboat on the Miami and
load another cargo of whisky, pork and apples. Prosperity in
the West rose and fell with the rivers.

In those years wheat sold in Indiana for twenty-five
cents a bushel, while it brought a dollar and a quarter in New
York and Philadelphia. Corn was a dollar a bushel on the Atlantic seaboard, fifteen cents on the Ohio. In the interior
western districts a load of grain might bring nothing at all.
Before the canal came through, a Wayne County farmer tried
to find someone to buy his wagonload of wheat. At last,
lurching past the land office in Wooster, he met an interested
storekeeper. "What will you pay?" asked the farmer. "Two
bits a bushel," said the storekeeper, "for enough to fill that
mudhole in the street."

In Cleveland in 1816 Mayor Alfred Kelley watched
four- and six-horse teams, laboring over wretched roads,
bring pork, wheat and flour to the river mouth where it
was loaded into schooners for the voyage to Buffalo. Occasionally a "bell-team wagon," its canvas swaying, would pull
up to the Kelley Brothers' store to unload Pennsylvania merchandise. Cleveland was a remote village, with a huddle of
houses and wharves under the steep river bank and a tiny
cluster of settlement on high ground around the public
square, where an iron wagon tire was struck with a hammer
at nine P.M. to tell the Clevelanders another day was ended.
Over on the west bank of the Cuyahoga near the lake five
Irish families squatted in the rushes, trapping muskrats
and catching fish, living like the vanished Indians. Young
Alfred Kelley was already a member of the State Assembly.
In Columbus he did not forget the wagons lurching over the

rugged road beside the smooth water of the Cuyahoga. He became the "father of the Ohio canal system." As Assemblyman he pushed bills through the legislature, and as Canal Commissioner he studied surveys, signed contracts, kept accounts and records. While work gangs hacked, scooped, shoveled, dragged and graded, Alfred Kelley was lawyering and lobbying, building up the canal fund, keeping a sharp eye on the canal contractors. Where the ditch was dug he tramped along the canalbank, poking an iron rod at soft places in the towpath or the fill.

On July Fourth, 1827, after two years of construction, the first segment of the canal was open and a fleet of festive barges passed from Cleveland to Akron. Alfred Kelley rode in the *State of Ohio,* decked with flags and bunting, with Captain Job Harrington's black horses arching their necks on the towpath. Already Cleveland was a different place from the village that had made Alfred Kelley its first mayor. Crowds lined the river bank and followed the guests up the bluff and along Superior Street to an arbor on the public square where the opening of the canal was celebrated with patriotic fervor. That night visitors and townsmen sat down to a sumptuous Canal Banquet. After a toast to "Canals and Roads—the favorite policy of Ohio—May their construction progress, until boats may glide and wheels roll, unobstructed to every part of the Continent," Alfred Kelley proposed a toast to "The PEOPLE of the State of Ohio for their accomplishments despite their youth, poverty, diversity, and sectional jealousies."

In that first season, from July 4th to December 17th when the canal froze tight, ten thousand barrels of flour, whisky, pork, butter, cheese, and wool passed through Cleveland. Alfred Kelley's village was booming.

To the silent counties the canal brought a commotion. Construction towns went up and work crews hacked through the forest and dug through the swamps. Now the Irish squatters at Cleveland had a job at eight dollars a month, plus bed, board and whisky. In settled districts Ohio farmers took contracts for the digging through their townships. Abram Garfield of Stark County extended the canal for half a mile through his farm, glad to have cash wages for his neighbors and himself. Fifty years later in the White House at Washington his son recalled a boyhood beside the canal and some seasons as mule-driver on the towpath that his father had built. Farmers and woodsmen, Irish crews from the Erie Canal and German laborers fresh from the Rhine hillsides kept the big ditch growing. It was finished in 1833, a waterway stretching three hundred and nine miles from the Ohio to Lake Erie. Then passengers on the canal packets could cross the state in eighty hours. From the cabin roof they watched the land drift by—fields and forest, farms and settlements, villages growing at the locks, and lines of farm wagons bringing the harvest of the inland country.

When the first spade was dug into Licking Summit, wheat in interior Ohio brought fifteen cents a bushel in barter. Now it brought a dollar in cash. Eastern merchants thronged the canal towns, buying wheat, corn, pork, lard for shipment to Cleveland, Buffalo and the East. Potatoes, formerly left to rot in the fields, had a lively market at sixty cents a bushel. On the towpath the mules leaned into their collars and the towrope tightened. In a year they moved two million bushels of wheat, six hundred thousand barrels of pork, three hundred thousand bushels of corn, a hundred thousand barrels of salt, twelve thousand barrels of whisky. In Cuyahoga County Horace Perry had cursed the canal builders for ruining his farm on the Newburgh road; the big ditch separated his meadow from the upland. Then his wife lost her hat in the canal when the first barge went through. "There!" he cried, "I knew the ——— canal would be the ruin of me. There goes my wife's new bonnet!" A year later his farm was worth ten times what he had paid for it. In all the canal counties land prices climbed like corn in the bottom fields.

In August, 1827, the first boat on the Miami Canal carried a gala party from Middletown to Hamilton. By November of 1828 the canal was completed to Cincinnati, a distance of forty-two miles. On the crisp day of November 28th three boatloads of passengers made a pleasure trip, with crowds cheering at every lock, from Cincinnati to Middletown and return. By 1832 a thousand people a week traveled in the packets *General Marion, Governor Brown, General Pike, General Harrison,* and scores of others. Then came the real business of the canal—ale, anvils, ashes, bacon, barley, bark, beans, beef, beer, blood, bran, bristles, brooms . . . machinery, manure, marble, millstones, molasses . . . salt, saleratus, saddle-trees, sand, seeds, soap, spikes . . . starch, staves, stone, straw . . . tar, tallow, timber, tobacco, tombstones. The published list of canal trade in the 1840s goes on for a solid, close-printed page. Industries developed along the towpath—gristmills, forges, paper mills, tombstone shops, lumberyards, packing plants, malt works, breweries. Canal land climbed from fifteen to two hundred dollars an acre.

The storekeepers McBride and Hough, who had loaded a flatboat with Miami Valley pork and whisky for far-off New Orleans, saw canal boats carrying mountains of produce. In the year 1850 out of Hamilton went a hundred thousand bushels of corn, twenty thousand barrels of flour, a million pounds of bacon, a million pounds of lard, ten thousand barrels of pork, and whisky enough to float a fleet of flatboats.

At that time young William Dean Howells was growing up in Hamilton. He had no mind for statistics of the canal, but he knew it was good for swimming, fishing and skating. Years later, in *A Boy's Town,* he wrote about that bit of paradise, the Hamilton basin: "It was bordered on either side near the end by pork houses, where the pork was cut up and packed, and then lay in long rows of barrels on the banks, with other long rows of whisky barrels; cooper shops, where the barrels were made, alternated with the pork houses. The boats brought the salt and carried away the pork and whisky, but the boy's practical knowledge of them was that they lay there for boys to dive off of when they went

in swimming, and to fish under. . . . In summer we led a
kind of amphibious life, as boys stayed in water as much as
on land. During winter ice skating took over and the basin
resembled a Dutch canal." It was common to skate from Hamilton to Middletown and back on a brisk January day.

Canal fever raged in all the construction camps,
where clouds of mosquitoes tormented the crews. A more
fervid fever swept Indiana in the years of internal development. In 1832 work began on the Wabash and Erie Canal,
to link the interior counties with Lake Erie and the Ohio. In
that year the National Road was reaching westward and
public land sales were climbing throughout the state.
"Wherever the surveyor took the magic chain and compass,"
wrote a later Hoosier, "no matter how remote from population, there it became certain that a mighty city would at no
distant day arise." In the fall of 1835 land auctions at La
Porte went on for four weeks, with crowds streaming in
from all directions. When the sale was over, three hundred
thousand dollars had been counted out in the district land
office. The next year land sales in Indiana exceeded three
million acres.

Indiana's fields and pastures were spreading. "And
where are our markets?" asked a writer in the *Indiana Journal*. "For horses in the states of Alabama, Carolina, and Virginia; for cattle, Philadelphia and Lancaster, for hogs at
Cincinnati and Madison, or the states of Virginia and Carolina, and for corn and flour at New Orleans. . . . Most of
the markets are halfway across the continent." Pointing to
the roads and canals of New York, Pennsylvania and Ohio,
Governor Noble called for a general system of internal improvements that would carry Indiana produce to profitable markets. In January, 1836, he signed an act instituting a
"Mammoth Internal Improvement Program" of canals, rail-
ways and turnpikes. It would provide for the Whitewater
Canal extending from the National Road through the populous southeastern corner of Indiana to the Ohio River, for a
Central Canal linking Indianapolis with the upper Wabash

and the Ohio, for an extension of the Wabash and Erie Canal from the mouth of the Tippecanoe River down the valley of the Wabash to Terre Haute and connecting with the Central Canal; also for a macadamized turnpike from New Albany on the Ohio to Vincennes on the Wabash; and a railroad or canal from Fort Wayne to Lake Michigan. Altogether the program promised Indiana nearly thirteen hundred miles of new transportation.

It was a heady time for the West. While this network of improvements was envisioned in Indiana, the Illinois assembly granted fifteen railroad charters and passed an act calling for a canal to link Lake Michigan with the Illinois River; in the summer of 1836 canal lots boomed in Chicago and people talked about a steamboat trade between Lake Michigan and the Mississippi. In Michigan twenty-five-year-old Governor Stevens T. Mason proposed to his Assembly an internal improvement program including three railroads and two canals across lower Michigan, to link Lakes Huron and Michigan, a web of plank roads radiating from Detroit, and a canal around the rapids of the St. Mary's River at the foot of Lake Superior.

In Indiana the act of 1836 set off great celebration and a frenzy of land speculation. Indianapolis people decorated their houses at news of the legislation, and bonfires blazed in the streets. Land prices spiraled in all sections of the state. New townsites were plotted at section corners and half-cleared farms sold at fantastic prices. There was a year of reckless speculation and thinly stretched credit. Then, in the spring of 1837, financial panic broke across the country. Banks closed their doors, docks and landings grew silent. The land offices were almost empty; sale of the public lands fell from twenty million acres in 1836 to five and a half million in 1837. Instead of a golden flow of goods to distant markets, Hoosier farmers sold oats at six cents a bushel, eggs three cents a dozen, chickens half a dollar a dozen. Cattle and hogs at the great Cincinnati market brought two and a half cents a pound. In Indiana land sales dropped in 1837 to a third of sales for the previous year, and in 1838 to a third of that. By 1840 just two hundred eighty-one miles of the Mammoth Improvement Project had been completed. The Whitewater Canal, the Madison and Indianapolis Railroad, the New Albany-Vincennes turnpike were turned over to private companies for completion and operation.

The Whitewater Canal was opened in 1839. From the front stoop of his "log cabin" at North Bend old General Harrison, whose name was painted on packets, barges and line boats on all the western canals, watched the horses plodding on the towpath and the slow barges passing with the harvest of the West. Perhaps he recalled the pack-horse trains bringing corn and bacon to the lonely settlement of North Bend in the vanished wilderness.

The Wabash and Erie Canal remained a project and a property of the Hoosier state. It was completed to Peru in 1837, to Logansport in 1838, to the Tippecanoe River in 1841; on July Fourth, 1843, it was formally opened at Fort Wayne. On that day Lewis Cass, formerly Territorial governor of Michigan, stood above the lock gates and addressed a crowd anxious to forget the hard times since 1837. Governor Cass, friend of Harman Blennerhassett, comrade of General Harrison, discoverer of the source of the Mississippi, had traveled the Wabash in a bark canoe and had followed the portage path now cut by the canal. He had seen Indiana a savage country, now he saw it changed past recognition. "The war drum is silent and the Indian has departed. . . . The forest is fading and falling and towns and villages are rising and flourishing." It was true, especially along the canal route. In Fort Wayne, Huntington, Wabash, Peru, Logansport, Delphi, Lafayette, Covington, Attica, long lines of wagons brought the Hoosier harvest, and canal boats, with horns blowing for the locks, carried it away.

CHAPTER EIGHTEEN

COONS, CABINS, AND

TIPPECANOE

W HEN WILLIAM DEAN HOWELLS sat in his Boston study in the spring of 1890, looking out at the new-leafed trees on Commonwealth Avenue, he saw the dusty streets and the curving river of his Ohio boyhood. He was fifty-five years old, with memories of the canals of Venice, the boulevards of Paris, the squares of London and the fountains of Rome. But in that spring a deeper past came back. He began to write about the town of his boyhood.

"It had a river, the great Miami River, which was as blue as the sky when it was not as yellow as gold; and it had another river, called the Old River, which was the Miami's former channel, and which held an island in its sluggish

341

loop; the boys called it The Island; and it must have been
about the size of Australia; perhaps it was not so large.
Then this town had a Canal, and a Canal-Basin, and a First
Lock and a Second Lock; you could walk out to the First
Lock, but the Second Lock was at the edge of the known
world, and, when my boy was very little, the biggest boy
had never been beyond it. Then it had a Hydraulic, which
brought the waters of the Old River for mill power through
the heart of the town, from a Big Reservoir and a Little
Reservoir; the Big Reservoir was as far off as the Second
Lock, and the Hydraulic ran under mysterious culverts at every street-crossing. All these streams and courses had fish in
them at all seasons, and all summer long they had boys in
them, and now and then a boy in winter, when the thin ice
of the mild Southern Ohio winter let him through with his
skates. Then there were the Commons; a wide expanse of
open fields, where the cows were pastured, and the boys flew
their kites, and ran races, and practiced for their circuses."

All that boyhood world was exciting, the canal boats
and the land auctions, the stagecoach horns and the cries
of the hog drovers, the bonfires and torchlight parades on
election nights. There were memories enough to fill the
pages of a glimmering and nostalgic book.

Every town in the West knew the excitement of politics. The roads to Ohio had brought men of many views:
federalism and republicanism, abolition and state's rights,
high tariff and no tariff, pro-Irish and anti-Irish, paper cur-
rency and hard money, high taxes and low taxes and no
taxes at all. All kinds of voices sounded in the town halls
and taverns and in the close-printed columns of western papers. Election time was a season of monster meetings, shrill
parades, fist-fights and barbecues and shouting in the shade
of the courthouse square.

When Howells remembered his boyhood he recalled a
Whig town. Even the boys in Hamilton had Henry Clay Clubs,
Buckeye Clubs, Tippecanoe Clubs. "The business of a Whig
Club among the boys was to raise ash flag-poles, in honor of

Henry Clay's home at Ashland, and to learn the Whig songs and go about singing them. You had to have a wagon, too, and some of the club pulled while the others rode; it could be such a wagon as you went walnutting with; and you had to wear strands of buckeyes round your neck. Then you were a real Whig boy, and you had a right to throw fire-balls and roll tar-barrels for the bonfires on election nights.

"I do not know why there should have been so many empty tar-barrels in the Boy's Town, or what they used so much tar for; but there were barrels enough to celebrate all the Whig victories that the boys ever heard of, and more, too; the boys did not always wait for the victories, but celebrated every election with bonfires, in the faith that it would turn out right. . . . The way they used to build their bonfires was to set one tar-barrel on top of another, as high as the biggest boy could reach, and then drop a match into them; in a moment a dusky, smoky flame would burst from the top, and fly there like a crimson flag, while all the boys leaped and danced around it, and hurrahed for the Whig candidates. Sometimes they would tumble the blazing barrels over, and roll them up and down the street.

"The reason why they wore buckeyes was that the buckeye was the emblem of Ohio, and Ohio, they knew, was a Whig state. I doubt if they knew that the local elections always went heavily against the Whigs; but perhaps they would not have cared. What they felt was a high public spirit, which had to express itself in some way. . . .

"There were always fights on election-day between well-known Whig and Democratic champions, which the boys somehow felt were as entirely for their entertainment as the circuses. . . . The fighting must have come from the drinking, which began as soon as the polls were opened, and went on all day and night with a devotion to principle which is now rarely seen. In fact, the politics of the Boy's Town seem to have been transacted with an eye single to the diversion of the boys; or if not that quite, they were marked by traits of a primitive civilization among the men.

The traditions of a rude hospitality in the pioneer times still lingered, and once there was a Whig barbecue, which had all the profusion of a civic feast in mediaeval Italy. Every Whig family contributed loaves of bread and boiled hams; the Whig farmers brought in barrels of cider and wagon-loads of apples; there were heaps of pies and cakes; sheep were roasted whole, and young roast pigs, with oranges in their mouths, stood in the act of chasing one another over the long tables which were spread in one of the largest pork-houses, where every comer was freely welcome."

The son of an itinerant anti-slavery editor, young Howells knew the excitement and the hard times of frontier journalism. As villages grew at the crossroads, newspapers spread through the western country. By 1810 Ohio had sixteen weeklies, printed on crude hand presses on paper made by hand in the pioneer mills. Some early editors set the type, printed the weekly edition, then rode horseback with bulging saddlebags to deliver the sheet to their subscribers. The editor of the *Cleveland Herald,* who distributed three hundred copies throughout Cuyahoga and Lake counties, recalled: "I frequently carried a tin horn to notify the yeomanry of the latest news, which was usually forty days from Europe and ten days from New York. This service was performed throughout the year, through rain, snow, and mud, with only one additional charge of fifty cents a year on the subscription price; and as the number of papers carried averaged about sixty, the profits may be readily calculated." Editors often took pork, potatoes, cheese and whisky in payment for subscriptions. The publishing motive was not to make a profit but to make an impression, to raise a voice in public matters.

The shrillest voice in the 1830s was that of James G. Birney who filled the columns of *The Philanthropist* with his ardent abolitionism. Son of an Irish ex-patriate who held extensive lands in Kentucky, Birney became a planter and politician in Alabama. When gambling and neglect of his plantation left him penniless, he sold his land and slaves, recouped his fortune as a lawyer (one of his clients was the Cherokee nation), and began crusading for the repatriation of slaves to a colony in Africa. In 1836, the year when the Anti-Slavery Society met in A. A. Bancroft's "Hall of Freedom" barn near Granville, Ohio, Birney issued at Cincinnati the first number of *The Philanthropist,* urging the abolitionists to action. This stormy issue aroused hot feeling in the border city. On the warm night of July 30th, 1836, a mob attacked the print shop, on Pike Street just off Broadway. They smashed the type fonts, tore the press from its foundations, and dragged it to the foot of Main Street and over the cobblestoned levee. With a final roar of triumph they heaved it into the Ohio. Birney was away from Cincinnati and out of reach, but all night long the mob roamed through the dark streets of the Negro district. The next day young Henry Ward Beecher denounced the rioters in his Cincinnati *Journal,* and while his paper was being distributed the twenty-three-year-old editor, with a pistol in his belt, joined the corps of deputies for the protection of Cincinnati Negroes.

Birney found another printer and continued to issue *The Philanthropist,* and following his own doctrine he harbored under his roof a runaway mulatto girl. When this case was brought to court, he was defended by Salmon P. Chase. Though acquitted, Birney left Cincinnati, moving first to Indiana and then to Michigan, where he continued to be the spokesman for the Anti-Slavery Society. In the Whig convention of 1840, when Harrison's views proved too mild for them, the Abolitionists nominated James G. Birney for the Presidency. Again he was threatened with violence, but it was a fall from a horse, in 1845, that ended his public career.

Sitting in his Boston study half a century later, Howells recalled how the West had sent its hero to the White House. "The Whigs," he remembered, "always had the best processions, and one of the most signal days of my boy's life was the day he spent in following round a Henry Clay procession, where the different trades and industries were represented in the wagons. There were coopers, hatters, shoe-

makers, blacksmiths, bakers, tinners, and others, all hard at
work; and from time to time they threw out to the crowd
something they had made. My boy caught a tin cup, and if
it had been of solid silver he could not have felt it a greater
prize. He ran home to show it and leave it in safe-keeping,
and then hurried back, so as to walk with the other boys
abreast of a great platform on wheels, where an old woman
sat spinning inside of a log-cabin, and a pioneer in a hunting shirt stood at the door, with his long rifle in his hand. In
the window sat a raccoon, which was the Whig emblem, and
which, on all their banners, was painted with the legend,
"That same old Coon!" to show that they had not changed at
all since the great days when they elected the pioneer, General Harrison, president of the United States."

The election of Old Tippecanoe was the great event
in frontier political history. For five years, while Harrison
was defeated in 1836 and the movement gathered for his triumph in 1840, it filled the West with furor. Its echoes still
linger in the folklore of American politics.

In 1833 Michel Chevalier, a French engineer who
came to America to study river transportation, paid a visit
to Cincinnati and made a note about a man he saw in the
Main Street Hotel. "I met with an incident in Cincinnati
which I shall long remember. I had observed at the hotel
table a man of about medium height, stout and muscular,
and of about the age of sixty years yet with the active step
and lively air of youth. I had been struck with his open and
cheerful expression, the amenity of his manners, and a certain air of command which appeared through his plain
dress. 'That,' said my friend, 'is General Harrison, clerk of
the Cincinnati court of common pleas. . . . He is now poor,
with a numerous family, neglected by the federal government, although yet vigorous, because he has the independence to think for himself.' "

Not everyone saw in William Henry Harrison the
cheer and vigor that M. Chevalier described. He had been a

Territorial Governor, army General, United States Congressman and Senator, and Minister to Colombia, but now his career seemed past. He was an old, tired man, his long face sallow with recurrent attacks of ague and furrowed with domestic worry. Some of the lines had been put there by his sons. The oldest, Symmes Harrison, had left a reputation for loose financial dealing as Land Agent at Vincennes; when he died in 1830 his widow, the daughter of General Zebulon Pike, brought her five children to Harrison's "log cabin" at North Bend. William Henry, Junior, had abandoned a law practice for indifferent farming and persistent drinking; when he died his family also moved under the General's roof. The fourth son, Benjamin, was given a medical education which he never put to use. To break him of drinking whisky his father sent him in 1833 on a trapping expedition to Wyoming, along with William Sublette and Jim Bridger. He came back penniless and still drinking, and the General sent him off to Texas, hoping he could make a living there. A few years later news of his death caused the General to cancel a campaign speech to ten thousand people gathered in a field outside of Springfield, Ohio. For ten years he struggled to pay off his sons' debts.

With the old General in the Main Street Hotel was his favorite son, Carter Bassett Harrison. He had been born at Vincennes in the historic autumn of 1811 while his father was on his way up the Wabash to the battle of Tippecanoe. He was with the General in the embassy at Bogotá, in the high Andes, during the year 1829. Now, in 1833, he had just come from Miami University to read law in Robert Schenck's Cincinnati office and to help his father in the common pleas court. He was the youngest, the sunniest, the most promising. But he did not live to find the measure of his talents. He died in 1839, after beginning the practice of law in Hamilton.

Perhaps the "Harrison for President" movement began when the General was summarily recalled from his mission in Colombia by President Jackson. In Cincinnati he was given a four-hour banquet in Mrs. Trollope's fantastic hall on the site of old Fort Washington where young Captain Harrison had brought his bride thirty-five years before. One of the toasts at that "Union Dinner," with Jackson men and Whigs sitting down together, was "The Site of Fort Washington—a fit place to do honor to them in their old age, who in early life, were its defenders." The whole program recalled the frontier past and Harrison's strenuous part in the winning of the West. A groundswell was beginning.

In the early 1830s, while he worked his North Bend farm and sold his Indiana lands to meet his sons' increasing debts, General Harrison seemed forgotten except for criticism of his military timidity and political self-seeking in years past. But that criticism kept his name in print, a name that reverberated with the struggles and victories of the frontier West. When Harrison wrote a letter defending his record at the Battle of the Thames, *Niles' Register* gave it wide circulation along with a warmly sympathetic editorial comment by Hezekiah Niles. It was not long before western newspapers began suggesting a homespun Harrison as the man to run against the effete Van Buren. In western hotel registers men recorded their political choice—"Hurrah for Harrison" . . . "Whole Hog for Harrison" . . . "Harrison up to the Shoulders." Tippecanoe Clubs sprang up wherever old soldiers remembered the western campaigns, and from his "log cabin" on the North Bend farm Harrison wrote to an influential Whig friend in New York:—"Some folks are silly enough to have formed a plan to make a President of the United States out of this *Clerk* and Clod-hopper!"

In the second week of December, 1835, a stormy Whig convention nominated Harrison. On February 22nd a great rally crowded the statehouse grounds at Columbus. A thousand delegates devoured a huge barbecued ox, while other thousands paraded through the streets. It was the beginning of a hectic campaign in which Harrison toured from the Wabash to the Potomac and the Hudson. Everywhere he went the gray-haired farmer and General called people's memories back to heroic and strenuous years. Though he lost the election in November, that contest showed the West its political power; Ohio alone cast eighty-two thousand more votes than all the states of New England. The time would soon come when the West would have its way.

Four years later Harrison, older now and wiser in the ways of politics, was again nominated in the great convention at Harrisburg. When the Democrats convened in Baltimore in the first week of May, 1840, the Whigs were arrogant. Outside the convention hall they assembled a clamorous procession, with log cabins, huge cider barrels and live coons in the crotches of trees. At the head of the parade a lofty banner told every Democrat in Baltimore that

> *The people are coming from plain and from mountain*
> *To join the brave band of the honest and free.*
> *No strength can restrain it, no force can retain it,*
> *Whate'er may resist, it breaks gallantly through.*
> *And borne by its motion, as a ship on the ocean,*
> *Speeds on his glory Old Tippecanoe.*

So the Whigs marched and sang, and in the convention hall the Democrats could hardly hear their own nominating speeches.

Two hours in the past of William Henry Harrison had cast long shadows over his life and over the nation. On the day before Christmas, 1799, in Congress Hall in Philadelphia the spare young delegate from the Northwest Territory first argued for a new land law. Ever afterward grateful frontiersmen remembered him as the farmer's friend. At daybreak on November 11, 1811, at Tippecanoe Creek, quavering Indians rushed his surprised, untested troops. General Harrison rallied his men, kept their lines intact, drove the warriors back to Prophet's Town. It was a small battle, soon ended, but it launched the war that freed the western border and it made Harrison the hero of the West. For years the name Tippecanoe hung like an echo over the frontier country.

In the campaign of 1840 the tidal wave for Old

Tippecanoe first showed itself in a massive rally on the Tippecanoe battlefield. The great day was May 29th, but the demonstration began weeks earlier. On the 18th of April a Whig paper in Indianapolis called for a rally of the Boys of Indiana: "Every man with his wagon, and horses or ox team, horseback or with his knapsack, with his week's provisions, be up and ready to march to Tippecanoe . . . to engage in political conflict for the brave Old Hero who never lost a battle, and who stayed the Indian's tomahawk upon the ground where so many of his friends will once more enlist under the banner of him who is beloved by his old soldiers and despised by the blood-suckers of the country, because he is literally one of us—one of the People—one who tills his own land . . . —one who when about parting with the brave little band who fought with him on the ground of Tippecanoe, told them that notwithstanding he wore the dignified title of 'General' and also 'Governor,' that he lived like themselves in an humble log cabin, and says he, while the heartfelt tears rolled down his cheeks, 'if you ever come to Vincennes, you will always find a knife and fork at my table and never find the door shut and the string of the latch pulled in.' Such is the man and such the day and occasion for which we meet together on the Tippecanoe Battle Field. Who will stay at home on that day?"

Not many stayed home. Through days and weeks of rainy weather, over muddy roads, came caravans from every corner of Indiana, and from Ohio, Michigan, Illinois, even from Kentucky and Tennessee. A motley delegation from the southern counties of Indiana gathered at Indianapolis and marched the sixty-five miles to Tippecanoe, singing in the rain and sleeping in barns through Boone and Clinton counties. On the battlefield along the swollen creek they set up tents and kept cooking fires smoldering. Old soldiers fought the battle over again, pointing out to their sons the fringe of woods where the Indians had crept up in the before-daybreak rain, the prairie where the troops had pushed them back, the wet lowlands where the savages had fled.

For a week the vast crowd gathered, bringing bands, banners, wagonloads of pork, cider and corn meal, herding beef cattle into a slaughter pen. At night campfires twinkled over miles of field and prairie. With a clatter of hammers a huge log cabin went up in the grove; beyond it rose a speakers' platform, and long tables stretched under the trees. Oxen, sheep, and pigs roasted over trench fires. There were feasting and speaking and cheering, and at all hours from dawn to midnight the voice of thousands singing:

The iron-armed soldier, the true-hearted soldier,
The gallant old soldier of Tippecanoe.

On the big day the sun shone and a grand procession rolled through the streets of Lafayette and over the Tippecanoe prairie. Behind the brig *Constitution,* drawn by six white horses, came log forts, log cabins, war canoes, prodigious eagles, mammoth cider barrels and trees full of coons— all to the music of marching bands from Evansville, Vincennes, Terre Haute, Crawfordsville and Richmond. *Niles' Register,* quoting the Lafayette *Free Press,* gave it a four-column story: "—The fires of enthusiasm fanned to a flame at the altar of liberty on that Bunker Hill of the West will spread abroad in the whole length and breadth of this glorious land. . . . But who shall describe the tremendous outpouring of the people? To be known it must have been seen."

The reporter described it, just the same, breathlessly picturing the thousands streaming through Lafayette with shouts of welcome at every turn, and other thousands pouring from steamboats at the Lafayette landing amid the bang of muskets and the boon of cannon. In the crowd were old soldiers, old settlers and old Indian chiefs, young men from farms, villages and canal towns, horse-traders, mule-traders, Congressmen, schoolmasters, frontier preachers, Yankee storekeepers, Pennsylvania blacksmiths, Southern cotton farmers, Irish and German immigrants. The reporter counted badges from every country in Indiana and most counties in Ohio, and from Kentucky, Tennessee, Michigan, Massachusetts, Il-

linois, Missouri and the Territory of Iowa. "Every avenue
leading toward the battleground was filled with wagons,
loaded with delegates, horsemen, and foot passengers, wend-
ing their way to this proud spot for our American arms—and
when all were assembled, such a multitude has never been
beheld in the interior of the United States; the number cannot, with any approximation to certainty, be ascertained—it
is variously guessed at from forty thousand to fifty thousand,
all agree that there were fifteen acres of men besides from
three thousand to six thousand females, and the encampment
might not inappropriately be compared to Darius' vast encampment preparatory to his descent upon Greece; and this
vast concourse of citizens spontaneously assembled at a season of the year when the agriculturalist has much to do at
home, when all classes are ground down as it were to powder, by an iron administration. But such a universal enthusiasm pervades this section of country in favor of General
Harrison, that nothing could restrain the people fron seizing
the occasion to do him honor."

All day the grove rang with music, speeches, shouting
and singing. At sunset, after a huge supper at the long tables,
came a last oration from the speakers' stand and a burst of
fireworks over the dark prairie. For good omen, after the last
rocket had arched over Tippecanoe Creek and the last cannon had sounded, a stream of ghostly banners lit the northern sky. It was an unseasonable and splendid aurora, which
the crowd hailed "as a sign hung out in the clouds to
cheer them on in their glorious work of reform."

Other monster rallies dwarfed the old camp meetings
in the western country. The campaign in Ohio had begun on
February 21st, when twenty-five thousand came to Columbus through a pouring rain to ratify Harrison's nomination.
Ross, Pike, Jackson and Scioto counties sent thousands by canal boat. The National Road streamed with delegations from
Licking, Muskingum, Guernsey, Stark and Montgomery
counties. The Mad River Trappers arrived with a log cabin
on wheels and coonskins on the wall. In a steady rain crowds

milled over the statehouse grounds while a procession moved
up High Street—a full-sized brig on wheels, rigged and
manned, with a portrait of "The Farmer of North Bend" at
the masthead, a model of Fort Meigs mounted with real cannon, a replica of the blockhouse at Fort Washington, an open-
sided land office where a settler could buy his farm under the
historic Harrison Land Law.

All summer long, while the roads dried out and corn
tasseled in the fields, Tippecanoe fever raged in the West. On
a June day at Fort Meigs twenty thousand cheering people
pressed toward a platform where General Harrison recalled
the old frontier. A few days later all the people of the Sangamon River counties in Illinois poured into Springfield where tall Abe Lincoln spoke from a wagon bed. On the
Fourth of July every town had its parade, with live eagles in
crates and live coons on the roofs of cabins and men carrying banners showing scenes in the life of Old Tippecanoe.

At the end of July a great celebration in Darke
County drew "an immense concourse" from Ohio and Indiana to the historic Greene Ville Treaty Grounds. By noon the
Mud Creek prairie was a sea of wagons, carts, carriages.
Delegates carried banners, streamers, pennons to a log platform on the site of the vanished blockhouse across the creek
from Tecumseh's Point. William Bebb, the ex-schoolteacher
of Paddy's Run, introduced General Harrison, who spoke for
two hours, recalling the men who had marched up the wild
Miami with Anthony Wayne and the great congress of the defeated tribes. Supper was laid on miles of plank tables and
bands played while the sun set over corn and wheat fields
where the Indians had camped. Torches flared under the
stars and speakers took the stand again. The crowd could
not hear enough of Old Tippecanoe and the new America.
"Go on! Go on!" they cried, until the last torches burned out
at midnight.

At the end of the summer came a huge meeting at Detroit and a record-breaking rally at Dayton where Harrison
spoke for an hour to a hundred thousand Miami Valley peo-

ple. In every town of the West log cabins rose in the middle
of Main Street or on the courthouse square. Log-cabin pictures bloomed in taverns, lobbies, offices and parlors. Log-
cabin magazines and songbooks flooded the country. Children ate log cabin candies and played with log-cabin toys.
Along the National Road farmers sold strings of buckeyes
and brooms of buckeye branches to sweep corruption out of
the government.

At North Bend above the river William Henry Harrison lived in a fourteen-room house, enlarged from the
original log cabin, surrounded by gardens, orchards, and
fruitful fields. But a hostile Baltimore editor had handed the
Whigs a slogan. "Give [Harrison] a barrel of hard cider and
a pension of two thousand a year . . . he will sit the remainder of his days in a log cabin . . . and study moral philosophy." That jibe the Whigs turned into a crusade. The West
was proud of its rugged past. What candidate had better
qualifications than a humble beginning and a life of accom-
plishment on the land? So William Henry Harrison, of
Berkeley on the James, of Grouseland on the Wabash, of
North Bend on the Ohio, became the log-cabin candidate.
The West was asserting itself, its memories, hopes and con-
victions, in the half-mythical person of Old Tippecanoe.
The campaign was a gathering of history and folklore, an assertion of the West's new-found identity and power.

By 1840 the frontier was another West, far beyond the
busy cities of the Ohio Valley. In 1832 George Catlin, on his
way to Indian country beyond the Missouri, stopped in Cincinnati. "Our town," a Queen City man told him, "has
passed the days of its most rapid growth. It is not far enough
west." All the way to St. Louis Catlin found men talking about the wild new territories, the hides, furs, silver of
the West, the trade with Santa Fé, the riches coming from
the far-off Yellowstone. In 1837 a restless schoolmaster in the
Miami Valley wrote to a friend in Pennsylvania: "The great
rage even here is to sell out and go West!" Lyman Beecher,

arriving in Cincinnati from Connecticut, found a phenomenal country—"a young empire of mind, and power, and wealth, and free institutions, rushing up to giant manhood with a rapidity and power never before witnessed below the sun."

But before the Ohio country settled into maturity, it put on the garb and re-enacted the lore of its frontier past. In that summer of 1840 it was brash, boisterous and yeasty, with the future all before it.

> *What has caused this great commotion*
> *All the country through?*
> *It is the ball a-rolling on*
> *For Tippecanoe and Tyler too.*

The hero was a settler, a soldier, and the farmer's friend. "The history of the West is his history." His enemies could label hin a coward, a land-grabber, a feeder at the trough of public office; they could concoct a story about a Winnebago squaw and two half-breed Harrison sons. They could call him General Mum the candidate who had no voice on any issue, or Old Granny, senile, doddering, and infirm. They could taunt him for living in a log cabin, or for owning a mansion on an Ohio estate. But the whole West was singing, and what the nation heard was "Tippecanoe and Tyler too!" When the votes were counted in November it was a landslide for the tired old General who now resigned his clerkship in the Cincinnati court.

Late in January, 1841, the presidential party left the Henrie House in Cincinnati, passed through shouting crowds down the steep street and boarded the flag-decked steamboat *Ben Franklin*. From the railed forward deck, while his Negro manservant stood by with an armload of buckeye canes and other parting gifts, the General made a short speech. "Fellow-citizens," he concluded, "perhaps this may be the last time I may have the pleasure of speaking to you on earth or seeing you. I bid you farewell, if forever, fare thee well." While the levee rang with the shouts of his people, steam hissed from the boilers and paddle wheels began to turn. Cannon boomed from both shores of the river. The crowd stood singing

>   —*borne by its motion, as a ship on the ocean*
>   *Speeds in his glory Old Tippecanoe,*

till the *Ben Franklin* rounded the upper bend.

At every town up the river—Maysville, Portsmouth, Gallipolis, Parkersburg, Marietta, Wheeling—bands played while the Presidential steamboat passed. At every landing farmers fired rifles and whooped across the water; all night bonfires twinkled on the hills. Near Pittsburgh the steamer ran aground, but a huge crowd waited through a chilly day on the Pittsburgh river front. Sunday the party spent at Pittsburgh, where the General attended church. Next day a steamboat took them up the Monongahela to Brownsville. A spanking new stage coach waited there, decorated with scenes from Harrison's life—the blockhouse of Fort Washington, the woods of Fallen Timbers, the battlefield of Tippecanoe, the farmhouse at North Bend. The journey over the mountains was spaced with receptions and celebrations. At Hagerstown, Maryland, a 112-pound cake appeared, iced with "The Hero of Tippecanoe." At Frederick the party passed through cheering streets to the train for Baltimore and Washington. The General entered Washington on February 9th, his sixty-eighth birthday. It was snowing, but he walked bare-headed through cheering thousands to the City Hall.

On Inaugural Day, March 4th, the President-elect admired a fine new coach presented by the Whigs of Baltimore and then climbed into the saddle of his favorite horse, Old Whitey. He rode down Pennsylvania Avenue escorted by his former aides at Tippecanoe and the Thames. Behind him followed a two-mile procession. As he reached the Capitol, twenty-six guns boomed from the Mall, one for each state in the Union. For an hour and forty minutes the President spoke bare-headed, without gloves or overcoat. At the end the artillery roared again and Harrison went to the White House for a half-hour's rest before a state reception.

The next days were crowded. Between hordes of office-seekers, department heads, spoilsmen, committee chiefs, he met old friends and comrades and led delegations from Indian tribes around the White House grounds. At the end of March he fell ill with pneumonia. After a few days he rallied, but only briefly. Half an hour after midnight on April 4th, just a month after taking office, President Harrison died.

Three days later a slow procession filed down Pennsylvania Avenue, with Old Whitey saddled and riderless clopping on the stones. The casket was brought to the East Room of the White House and the rector of St. John's Church read the funeral service. That summer the body of William Henry Harrison went back to the western country and was buried above the Ohio at North Bend. For years afterward steamboat captains saluted Old Tip with a long soft blast of the whistle as they passed.

William Henry Harrison was buried in a tamed and settled land, with schools and churches, courthouses and colleges where the Indian trails had crossed. What had happened there was now occurring in newer regions: surveyor, squatter, settler advancing into wild land, farmer clashing with speculator, barbarism contesting with culture. Across the continent went the philosophy strenuously shaped in the Ohio Valley, the principle that the public land was the people's land. The Harrison law of 1800 led ultimately to the law of 1862 when Abraham Lincoln, whose father had moved onto government land across the Ohio River, signed the Homestead Act in the conviction that the American destiny called for "settling the wild lands into small parcels so that every poor man may have a home."

In 1840, when the log cabin was not a dwelling but a political symbol, the Ohio country had become a bridge for American civilization to reach new frontiers. The Ohio fever was ended, but the same ardor and excitement was sending settlement to the Upper Mississippi valley, to the huge domain of Texas and the rich valleys of Oregon. It would send men to the final land rush in the Cherokee Strip of Oklahoma in 1893, four hundred years after the discovery of America, when the last frontier was crossed. In every new region the experience of the first frontier was repeated—the hope, the delusion, the hardship, the struggle, the inrush of many people and the raising of new communities upon wild land.

ABRIDGED BIBLIOGRAPHY

ALVORD, Clarence W., *Centennial History of Illinois*. Springfield, 1920

BALD, F. Clever, *Michigan in Four Centuries*. New York, 1954

BARNHART, John D., *Valley of Democracy*. Bloomington, Ind., 1953

BOND, Beverley W., *The Civilization of the Old Northwest*. New York, 1934

———, (ed.), *The Correspondence of John Cleves Symmes*. New York, 1926

———, *The Foundations of Ohio*. Columbus, 1941

BELOTE, Theodore T., *The Scioto Speculation and the French Settlement at Gallipolis*. Cincinnati, 1907

BERNHARD [Karl], Duke of Saxe-Weimar Eisenach, *Travels Through North America During the Years 1825 and 1826*. (2 vols.) Philadelphia, 1828

BIRKBECK, Morris, *Letters from Illinois*. London, 1818

———, *Notes on a Journey in America*. London, 1818

BRACKENRIDGE, H. M., *Recollections of Persons and Places in the West*. Philadelphia, 1834

BUCK, Solon J., *Illinois in 1818*. Springfield, 1917

BULEY, R. Carlyle, *The Old Northwest*. (2 vols.) Indianapolis, 1950

BURNET, Jacob, *Notes on the Early Settlement of the Northwest Territory*. Cincinnati, 1847

CHEVALIER, Michael, *Society, Manners, and Politics in the United States*. Boston, 1839

CLEAVES, Freeman, *Old Tippecanoe*. New York, 1939

CUMING, Fortescue, *Sketches of a Tour to the Western Country*. Pittsburgh, 1810. Thwaites *Early Western Travels*, viii.

DOWNES, Randolph C., *Council Fires on the Upper Ohio*. Pittsburgh, 1940

———, *Frontier Ohio, 1788–1803*. Columbus, 1935

ESARY, Logan, *History of Indiana*. Indianapolis, 1915

———, *The Indiana Home*. Crawfordsville, Ind., 1943

EYRE, John, *The Christian Spectator*. Albany, 1838

FAUX, William, *Memorable Days in America.* London, 1823. Thwaites *Early Western Travels,* xi-xii.

FEARON, Henry B., *Sketches of America.* London, 1818

FINLEY, James B., *Sketches of Western Methodism.* Cincinnati, 1854

FLINT, James, *Letters from America.* Edinburgh, 1822. Thwaites *Early Western Travels,* ix.

FLOWER, Richard, *Letters from the Illinois.* London, 1822. Thwaites *Early Western Travels,* x.

HALSTED, Murat, *Paddy's Run Papers.* Unpublished manuscript.

HANNA, Charles A., *The Wilderness Trail.* (2 vols.) New York, 1911

HAWLEY, Zerah, *Journal of a Tour.* New Haven, 1822

HIBBARD, Benjamin H., *A History of the Public Land Policies.* New York, 1924

HILDRETH, Samuel P., *Pioneer History of the Ohio Valley.* Cincinnati, 1848

HOFFMAN, Charles F., *A Winter in the West.* New York, 1835

HOWE, Henry, *Historical Collections of Ohio.* (2 vols.) Cincinnati, 1902

HOWELLS, William Cooper, *Recollections of Life in Ohio.* Cincinnati, 1895

HOWELLS, William D. *A Boy's Town.* New York, 1890

HULBERT, Archer B., *Ohio in the Time of the Confederation.* Marietta, 1918

———, (ed.), *Records of the Ohio Company.* Marietta, 1917

HUNTER, Louis C., *Steamboats on the Western Rivers.* Cambridge, 1949

JORDAN, Philip D., *The National Road.* Indianapolis, 1948

KINCAID, Robert L., *The Wilderness Road.* Indianapolis, 1947

MARRYATT, Frederick, *A Diary in America.* Philadeplhia, 1839

MARTINEAU, Harriet, *Society in America.* London, 1837

McBRIDE, James, *Pioneer Biography.* Cincinnati, 1869–71

McCARTY, Dwight G., *The Territorial Governors of the Old Northwest.* Iowa City, 1910

McDONALD, John, *Biographical Sketches.* Cincinnati, 1838

OGG, F. A., *The Old Northwest.* New Haven, 1921

———, (ed.) *Fordham's Personal Narrative.* Cleveland, 1906

OWEN, Robert D., *Threading My Way.* New York, 1874

PETERS, William E., *Ohio Lands and Their Subdivisions.* Athens, O., 1918

PRICE, Robert, *Johnny Appleseed: Man and Myth.* Bloomington, Ind., 1954

RAYMOND, Ethel, *Tecumseh.* Toronto, 1915

ROBBINS, Roy M., *Our Landed Heritage: The Public Domain 1776–1936.* Princeton, 1942

RODABAUGH, James H., *Robert Hamilton Bishop.* Columbus, 1935

ROOSEVELT, Theodore, *The Winning of the West.* (4 vols.) New York, 1900

ROYALL, Anne, *Sketches of History, Life, and Manners in the United States.* New Haven, 1826

SAKOLSKI, Aaron M., *The Great American Land Bubble.* New York, 1932

SCHNEIDER, Norris F., *Blennerhassett Island and the Burr Conspiracy.* Columbus, 1945

SMITH, Dwight L., *Wayne's Peace with the Indians of the Old Northwest.* Ohio State Archaeological and Historical Quarterly, LIX.

SWEET, William W., *The Rise of Methodism in the West.* New York, 1920

THWAITES, Reuben G., *Early Western Travels 1748–1846.* A series of annotated reprints. (32 vols.) Cleveland, 1904–7

TREAT, Payson J., *The National Land System 1785–1820.* New York, 1910

TROLLOPE, Mrs. [Frances], *Domestic Manners of the Americans.* London, 1832.

TURNER, Frederick J., *The Frontier in American History.* New York, 1920

UTTER, William T., *The Frontier State, 1803–25.* Columbus, 1942

VANCE, John L., *The French Settlement and Settlers at Gallipolis.* Ohio State Archaeological and Historical Quarterly, iii.

WELBY, Adlard, *Visit to North America.* London, 1821. Thwaites *Early Western Travels,* xii.

WHITTLESEY, Charles, *Early History of Cleveland.* Cleveland, 1867

WILLIAMS, Stephen R., *The Saga of Paddy's Run.* Oxford, O., 1945

WILSON, Frazer E., *Around the Council Fire.* Greenville, O., 1945

————, *Arthur St. Clair.* Richmond, O., 1944.

WINSOR, Justin, *The Westward Movement.* Boston, 1897

WITTKE, Karl, *We Who Built America.* New York, 1939

WRIGHT, Louis B., *Culture on the Moving Frontier.* Bloomington, Ind., 1955

YOUNG, Calvin M., *Little Turtle.* Indianapolis, 1917

INDEX

363

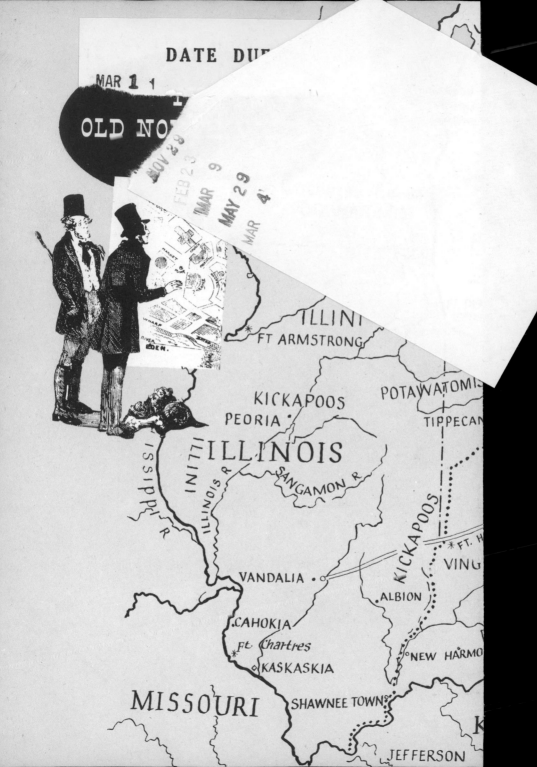